administration and development
in the Arab world

public affairs and administration
(editor: James S. Bowman)
vol. 14

Garland reference library
of social science
vol. 330

the public affairs and administration
series: James S. Bowman, editor

1. career planning, development,
   and management
   an annotated bibliography
      Jonathan P. West
2. professional dissent
   an annotated bibliography
   and resource guide
      James S. Bowman
      Frederick A. Elliston
      Paula Lockhart
3. American public administration
   a bibliographical guide
   to the literature
      Gerald E. Caiden
      Richard A. Loverd
      Thomas J. Pavlek
      Lynn F. Sipe
      Molly M. Wong
4. public administration in rural areas
   and small jurisdictions
   a guide to the literature
      Beth Walter Honadle
5. comparative public administration
   an annotated bibliography
      Mark W. Huddleston
6. the bureaucratic state
   an annotated bibliography
      Robert D. Miewald
7. labor management relations in
   the public sector
   an annotated bibliography
      N. Joseph Cayer
      Sherry S. Dickerson
8. public choice theory in
   public administration
   an annotated bibliography
      Nicholas F. Lovrich
      Max Neiman
9. public policy analysis
   an annotated bibliography
      John S. Robey
10. public personnel administration
    an annotated bibliography
       Sarah Y. Bowman
       Jay M. Shafritz
11. news media and public policy
    an annotated bibliography
       Joseph P. McKerns
12. equal employment opportunity
    and affirmative action
    a sourcebook
       Floyd D. Weatherspoon
13. voluntary associations
    an annotated bibliography
       Donato J. Pugliese
14. administration and development in the
    Arab world
    an annotated bibliography
       Jamil E. Jreisat
       Zaki R. Ghosheh

administration and development in the Arab world an annotated bibliography

Jamil E. Jreisat
Zaki R. Ghosheh

Garland Publishing, Inc. • New York & London
1986

© 1986 Jamil E. Jreisat and Zaki R. Ghosheh
All rights reserved

Library of Congress Cataloging-in-Publication Data

Jreisat, Jamil E.
  Administration and development in the Arab world.

  (Public affairs and administration ; vol. 14)
  (Garland reference library of social science ; vol. 330)
  Includes indexes.
  1. Arab countries—Economic policy—Bibliography.
  2. Arab countries—Social policy—Bibliography.
  3. Arab countries—Politics and government—1945–
  —Bibliography. I. Ghūshah, Zakī Rātīb. II. Title.
  III. Series: Public affairs and administration ; v. 14.
  IV. Series; Garland reference library of social
  science ; v. 330.
  Z7165.A67J73 1986   016.3389′00917′4927   85-32546
  [HC498]
  ISBN 0-8240-8593-0 (alk. paper)

Cover design by Alison Lew

Printed on acid-free, 250-year-life paper
Manufactured in the United States of America

contents

Series Foreword	vii
Foreword by Sami G. Hajjar	ix
Acknowledgments	xi
Introduction by Jamil E. Jreisat	xiii
1. Administration	3
2. Human Resources	25
3. Development: Socio-Political Factors	47
4. Development: Economics and Planning	89
5. Doctoral Dissertations	
A. Administration	133
B. Human Resources	166
C. Development	194
Author Index	247
Country Index	257

series foreword

The twentieth century has seen public administration come of age as a field of study and practice. This decade, in fact, marks the one hundredth anniversary of the profession. As a result of the dramatic growth in government, and the accompanying information explosion, many individuals—managers, academicians and their students, researchers—in organizations feel that they do not have ready access to important information. In an increasingly complex world, more and more people need published material to help solve problems.

The scope of the field and the lack of a comprehensive information system has frustrated users, disseminators, and generators of knowledge in public administration. While there have been some initiatives in recent years, the documentation and control of the literature have been generally neglected. Indeed, major gaps in the development of the literature, the bibliographic structure of the discipline, have evolved.

Garland Publishing, Inc., has inaugurated the present series as an authoritative guide to information sources in public administration. It seeks to consolidate the gains made in the growth and maturation of the profession.

The Series consists of three tiers:
1. core volumes keyed to the major subfields in public administration such as personnel management, public budgeting, and intergovernmental relations;
2. bibliographies focusing on substantive areas of administration such as community health; and
3. titles on topical issues in the profession.

Each book will be compiled by one or more specialists in the area. The authors—practitioners and scholars—are selected in open competition from across the country. They design their work to include an introductory essay, a wide variety of bibliographic materials, and, where appropriate, an information resource section. Thus each contribution in the collection provides a systematic basis for managers and researchers to make informed judgments in the course of their work.

Since no single volume can adequately encompass such a broad, interdisciplinary subject, the Series is intended as a continuous project that will incorporate new bodies of literature as needed. Its titles represent the initial building blocks in an operating information system for public affairs and administration. As an open-ended endeavor, it is hoped that not only will the Series serve to summarize knowledge in the field but also will contribute to its advancement.

This collection of book-length bibliographies is the product of considerable collaboration on the part of many people. Special appreciation is extended to the editors and staff of Garland Publishing, Inc., to the individual contributors in the Public Affairs and Administration Series, and to the anonymous reviewers of each of the volumes. Inquiries should be made to the Series Editor.

James S. Bowman
Tallahassee

foreword

Over the past thirty years, the Arab world, like the rest of the Middle East, has experienced an unprecedented transformation in virtually all aspects of physical and cultural life. Billions of dollars have been invested in development projects in Arab countries, the bulk of which were conceived and managed by public bureaucracies.

The process of transformation and development has not been, however, consistent; the record is one of success and failure in the formulation and implementation stages of policy. This volume traces these policies by focusing on the relevant literature. It references, in an easy-to-follow classification system, English-language materials, and compiles what is a thorough inventory of books and articles in the fields of administration, human resources, and socio-political and economic development about the Arab world. Additionally, it catalogues dissertations written on these subjects.

As a reference book, its merit and usefulness to students and scholars are intrinsic. There are, however, some unique features that should be briefly alluded to.

First, because the Arab world is not a monolithic system, consisting instead of many countries with different levels of development, the book provides a country index. Indeed, an appreciation of these differences is an essential prerequisite to the formulation of meaningful generalizations.

Second, it can generally be observed that Western knowledge regarding Third World countries and the Arab world in particular is deficient. This observation is especially true in the area of the internal processes of change and administration where aspects of culture, religion, history, economics, and politics appear to be meshed together in the eyes of the non-specialist. This book provides for the efficient use of information focused on these critical, but generally deemphasized, dimensions of Arab societies.

Third, the book's Introduction offers the reader a unique perspective and a guide for approaching development and administration in the Arab world by authors who are both intimately knowledgeable about that world and of Western, especially American, social science scholarship. Finally, Professors Jreisat's and Ghosheh's Arab backgrounds and American educational experiences lend greater credibility to the inevitable subjectivity associated with the choice of materials to be included and the manner by which to classify the various entries.

The compilation of a reference work is a laborious and an intellectually challenging task. Often, such works are of enduring value to readers. Given the scope and subject matter of this book, Jreisat and Ghosheh have exerted extensive effort in the United States and the Arab world to assemble and annotate these materials. This book will undoubtedly be frequently used by scholars and students of administration and development for years to come.

Sami G. Hajjar
University of Wyoming

acknowledgments

Several people contributed to the effort of producing this volume. Dr. James S. Bowman, series editor, commented on several drafts of the Introduction and provided cogent advice throughout the project's development. Appreciation is also expressed to the anonymous reviewer of the manuscript. Managing Editor Pamela Chergotis—and her precedessor at Garland Publishing, Inc., Julia Johnson—offered courteous and sympathetic guidance.

The University of South Florida's Public Administration Program provided some travel costs, as well as the time of two graduate assistants, John Lee and Jennifer Hagadorn-Freathy.

Dr. Zaki R. Ghosheh, my co-author, made valuable contributions from his position at the University of Jordan in Amman. Andrea Brunais, my wife, worked on the project from its inception, contributing research, writing, editing, and organization of data. To all I am grateful. None, however, bears responsibility for shortcomings or failures.

J.E.J.

introduction

This book examines the literature on administration, human resources, and development in the Arab world. It emphasizes contemporary societies and their internal dynamics, the least known and most critical aspects of Arab studies. The explosion of information about these societies makes its collection, classification, access, and ease of use imperative. Literature is drawn from 1970—1985, a period that supplied ample materials. This introduction underlines trends and characteristics of the relevant literature, explains the organization and classification system, and offers guidelines for use of this volume.

Accumulating and annotating articles, dissertations, and books on a specialized subject for 21 countries proved to be a large undertaking, one that initially appeared deceptively simple. One difficulty resulted from a paradoxical aspect of the subject itself. Administration, human resources, and development are broad areas with an interdisciplinary bent, attracting experts from various fields such as management, politics, economics, and sociology. At the same time, scholarship on the topic is fairly specialized and differentiated. Compared with Mark W. Huddleston's volume in this series, *Comparative Public Administration* (New York: Garland Publishing, Inc., 1984), for example, this work is more inclusive, dealing with development as well as administration, and yet more exclusive, as it concentrates on a specific region. Our search, therefore, was at once necessarily broad and comprehensive as well as specific and focused.

The Arab world consists of member countries of the Arab League.[1] To identify who is an Arab, however, is to evoke historical, sociological, geographical, or political interpretations. Maxime Rodinson (item 252) defines the Arab people as those who: speak a variant of Arabic and regard it as their natural language; consider as their patrimony the history and cultural traits of the people that has called itself and that others have called Arab; and claim Arab identity and possess an awareness of being Arab. Hence, the most recognized elements of Arabism are common language, culture, religion, history, and consciousness of common identity.

Divergencies among the Arab countries also are profound. Representing an aggregation of 21 national economies and different levels of economic and social development (Hashim, item 351), the Arab world's diversity includes dissimilar political structures and public policies, and varying levels of administrative capacity, organizational complexity, and citizen involvement in governance. Further, wide variations exist in per capita income level, literacy rate, size, level of urbanization, and ratio of foreign debt to gross national product. Therefore, readers must recognize the specific conditions of each society before making inferences or generalizations based on the literature. Mention of the "Arab world" may evoke conflicting images and notions in the Western mind. Hollywood and other Western views frequently reduce "the Arabs" to a category of exoticism onto which violations of social norms may be projected. Therefore, as French scholar Jacques Berque (item 168) notes, the Arabs feel "strongly that they [are] being studied not to be understood but to be reduced."

Nevertheless, Americans remain highly interested in the Arab world, attuned to its events, perplexed by its culture, conflicts, religious heritage, and wealth. Westerners recognize the region's strategic position in international spheres of economics and geo-politics. A major supplier of oil to the industrialized world, Arab countries constitute a significant, growing market for manufactured products and a source of increasing influence in the world financial system. Because of this continuous Western-Arab interaction, the need for current knowledge of the Arab world is essential not only to students and scholars, but also to diplomats, consultants, business people, and specialists in management and development.

The importance of this work is particularly compelling when we recognize that neither the contribution of the political perspective, most concerned with issues of foreign policy and

introduction

actions of political leaders, nor the legacy of Orientalism[2] and its preoccupation with past Arab systems and images provides a sufficient realistic focus on modern Arab societies.

Consequently, this reference work uniquely brings together results of 746 studies on current Arab affairs. From the start, it was easier to exclude topics from this reference than to include them; immediately excluded were areas of foreign policy, international relations, ancient history, linguistics, the Arab-Israeli conflict, and similar topics. For present purposes, "administration" and "development" comprise national planning; social, economic, and political development; and all of public administration's subfields (budgeting, personnel, organizational management, regulation, training, and so forth).

The method of selection of materials varied. Categories in periodical indexes were searched by subject matter and by country. Journals were inspected issue by issue. Card catalogues of two university libraries in the United States and two in the Arab world—in addition to the specialized library of the Arab Organization of Administrative Sciences—were systematically studied. References in journal articles were scanned and book reviews examined. All titles and annotations were classified by designated category. When references fit into more than one category, decisions were made on the basis of predominant characteristics, with cross listing limited to the most obvious overlapping. Finally, dissertations were compiled through a laborious perusal of *Dissertation Abstracts International*[3] and the *American Doctoral Dissertations on the Arab World*.[4]

References in Arabic are not cited because of the language barrier to Western scholars, and because of practical considerations of size and printing. Arabic publications are listed at the end of this essay and they are circulated regularly by the Arab Organization of Administrative Sciences and thus are accessible to those conversant in the language. The considerable effort required to include Arabic-language publications is not, therefore, justified in terms of the needs of either Western or Middle Eastern scholars, many of whom are bilingual.

The initial design of the book envisaged a simple system of classification: general references, public administration, economic and social development, and dissertations (listed in chronological order). At a very early stage, however, the need for amendment became obvious. The category "human resources" was introduced to include activities that directly affect people, their development and rights such as training, education, migration, literacy, and status of women. Another change was dictated by the literature on development, as it was widely spread among political, social, and economic perspectives. Finally, a chronological listing of dissertations was abandoned in favor of a functional classification consistent with that of the preceding chapters, i.e., administration, human resources, and development.

Naturally, alternative classification systems are possible and may be justifiable; economic development, for example, may be broken down into numerous subcategories such as industry, agriculture, oil, finance. The classification used, in our judgment, is the most reasonable for a balanced, comprehensive, and interrelated grouping of subjects.

A motivating factor in adopting the classification system is the widely shared view in the Arab world that building administrative capacity is a requisite for the implementation of national development plans. Various pan-Arab conferences (Riyadh, 1978; Baghdad, 1982; Rabat, 1984) on administrative development have consistently stated this thesis. In addition, a review of the literature indicates that development is a more comprehensive process than economic growth; it involves human resources as well as socio-political and economic variables. Thus, the classification categories selected were administration, human resources, and development, which are now discussed in turn.

administration

Contemporary Arab states claim the establishment of competent administrative and organizational machinery as an important national objective. This goal has guided public policies and national development plans for the past two decades.

Thus, countries have made significant investments in the creation of academic programs to offer teaching and training in public and business administration. Enjoying successful faculty recruitment, these units are a fixture of almost every major university in the Arab world. They graduate large numbers of students, many of whom then pursue doctoral-level specialization in Western universities (especially in the United States, as evidenced by the lengthy list of dissertations). In addition, many Arab states have founded institutes of administration to render technical assistance to public organizations, provide training, offer consultation, and conduct research.

Arab governments also extensively employ consultants from industrialized societies to perform feasibility studies, advise on reorganization schemes, and help solve administrative problems. Additionally, states have created such mechanisms for pan-Arab cooperation as the Arab Organization of Administrative Sciences (AOAS), which handles exchange of administrative and development information, technical assistance, training, research, publication programs, and standardization of terminology, data, and modern managerial techniques.

Individually and collectively, then, Arab states recognize the importance of a viable and effective administrative apparatus as a tool of modernization. A compelling objective of research at this stage, therefore, is to take stock of progress (or lack of it) toward meeting the administrative demands of these societies.

The state of research in administration has been under attack from various quarters for four reasons, not only in the Arab world but in the United States and other regions as well. First, as stated earlier, Western scholarship has been more concerned with military/foreign policy issues and strategic economic factors such as oil than with internal developments or social and institutional processes. The leadership style of an Anwar Sadat, for example, or a passing foreign policy decision of a Syrian or Algerian regime can draw more attention than social or administrative dynamics of half a dozen countries.

Second, Arab students of administration and development

face an escalating intellectual identity crisis. Coached in Western-produced theories of management, trained in Western notions of research, they master and mimic Western scholarship, meet Western criteria of evaluation to earn academic degrees or publish in professional journals. When they return home and are immersed in their societies, they question the relevance of their studies—and the utility of their information and methodology—to a traditional environment. In varying degrees, they face a lack of data, hesitant support for research, and an absence of essential freedoms protecting the rights of individuals to evaluate, criticize, and debate public policy issues.

As a result, Arab scholars find more hospitable environments for their professional aspirations outside their places of birth. More than 60 percent of the authors in this English-language compilation have Arabic surnames. Therefore, in a quantitative sense, at least, this book represents scholarship by Arab professionals first, and by Westerners second. This illustrates, at a deeper level, that there are now Arab professionals—scholars and practitioners—who apparently interact with their Western peers on an equal basis. The problem is that they enter into Western culture, learn a Western language, and often deal with Western concepts instead of their own.

Third, administrative research of Arab bureaucracies reveals conservative and traditional organizational and managerial practices with high resistance to efforts of change—characteristics familiar in most public bureaucracies. Donald P. Warwick sums up the critics' views of bureaucracy in the United States by saying that "governmental organizations become the master rather than the servant of the people, stifle initiative, inculcate fear, multiply reporting requirements, circumscribe action, waste time, and deplete the federal treasury."[5] Such dysfunctions of bureaucracies are all the more serious in the context of developing countries, which have become heavily dependent on public sector performance.

An exception to the conventional view of bureaucratic rigidity is conveyed by Clegg (item 28), who reviews the radical processes of workers' self-management in Algeria. Established after independence in 1962 as an essential part of a system of democratic management decentralization, worker committees were soon replaced by rigid forms of centralized state controls. Few such experimental or unorthodox attempts at organizational and managerial practices have been attempted since then in the Arab world. On the conceptual level, however, the literature is rich with innovation and prescriptions, particularly in doctoral dissertations. Hammour (item 487), for example, advocates taking development back to the grassroots village level in Sudan, denouncing the neo-classical (bureaucractic-dominated) approach to development, and abandoning expensive public corporations in favor of village communes and councils. A review of the following chapters indicates a wide range of ideas and perspectives on the issues with varied recommendations on how to deal with them.

Fourth, dissertations indicate just the beginnings of applied public policy-oriented research. Most doctoral research cited here relies on empirical data gathered through questionnaires, field interviews, and examination of official documents. Such activities, while beneficial, are insufficient to stimulate a trend of proactive, empirically based public policy scholarship. Thus dissertations, written in English, tend to remain lodged in American archives.

Utilization of administrative research, however, involves more than translation and printing. Conscious and systematic screening of research findings must be conducted to recognize, accept, and adopt applicable useful information. This is the initial phase of several steps in the utilization process that includes operationalization, implementation, support, and, ultimately, institutionalization of change. Unfortunately, this has not occurred in the Arab world; thus Arab societies are deprived of the benefits of their spending on education in Western universities. Clement Henry Moore (item 118) illustrates this in his work with Egypt's professional engineers. They have not helped the state solve its problems despite achieving high positions in government. Instead, they have retreated to copying ready-made Western technology rather than developing research to deal with specific needs and problems.

In sum, these four points suggest qualitative and quantitative changes in the administrative literature, although the practical impact of such research is not easily ascertained. Stronger links between research and application, however, may be found in the area of human resources, where changes are more visible, in such areas as literacy rate and labor migration.

human resources

This literature indicates a growing interest in the development of Arab human resources. Arab scholars, students, and researchers unquestionably reflect national policies aimed at (a) upgrading educational standards and fighting illiteracy, (b) improving the economic, legal, and political status of women, and (c) dealing with such other issues as labor migration (see Chapters 3 and 5, B).

Many studies raise serious questions and criticize existing educational policies. El-Tom (item 96), for example, blames the Sudanese educational system for teaching skills more suitable to "advanced" countries. Faksh (item 98) describes the limited absorptive capacity of the Egyptian economy to accommodate new, improperly trained graduates, while technical middle-range needs of the job market remain unmet.

Several works suggest a transition stage for Arab women and define the need for a multi-disciplinary social science perspective on research (Abdel Khader, item 76). Baffoun (item 84) relates an important observation from Tunisia, contending that the state—not the rank and file of citizens—takes credit for the proposed emancipation of women. In some Arab countries, the support of the traditional religious establishment is considered critical to the evolution of women's status and rights (Bahry, item 85, Gerner-Adams, item 101).

Economists, administrationists, sociologists, and policy makers, interested in the social implications of labor transfers between "capital-rich" and "capital-poor" Arab states, pay increased attention to the consequences of labor migration on home and host country. Swanson (item 134) identifies inflation, neglect of agricultural lands, and serious shortages of local manpower in North Yemen because of migration of peasants to Saudi Arabia. Birks and Sinclair (items 89 and 91) with Socknat (item 92) discuss Arab manpower in general and in reference to Egypt and the Gulf states. They underline the growing demand for labor to meet developmental requirements in the Gulf region in the 1970s, forcing recruitment of labor from outside the Arab world, particularly from the Indian subcontinent. Also, studies point out that migrant workers do not have consistently positive effects on the economies of their home countries. Some countries must replace their lost workers and deal with fueled inflation because wage remittances are used more for consumption than investment. Keely and Saket (item 110) report such an impact on Jordan because of that country's emigrant workers.

In summary, the range of issues analyzed in this book is not peculiar or even unique to the Arab world. The significance of these problems—and the influence of the literature—extend beyond the confines of any single state or region. The knowledge accumulated here indicates a convergence of experience among Arab states, as well as between them and other Third World nations. This observation is particularly relevant to development, the third major category in this compilation.

development

Development as a concept has not acquired a consistent meaning nor evolved into a widely accepted theory. Even less agreement exists on the practice and processes used to attain development, however it is defined. For the first half of this century, development was viewed as achieving an increase in the national income of the less developed countries;[6] it was equated with economic growth. Achieving this type of development included central planning, control of the economy, and industrialization and urbanization assisted by inflows of foreign capital and technology.[7] Technical assistance and training of the administrative cadre were the essential means for development. The control bias and top-down orientation was obvious.

Several studies of economic development follow this conventional approach (see, e.g., Makdisi, item 377). Focus on growth has the convenience of measuring single factors such as per capita income or percentage increases in gross national product. Narrow, quantifiable economic models also avoid sensitive social and political factors—a relevant concern as discussed earlier.

Yet experience shows that the conventional view of development is simplistic or misleading. Social and political problems prove paramount. The elitist-technocratic perspective of the conventional view created deep tensions and social inequalities.

The consequent shift of focus in the literature to include noneconomic factors has been accompanied by a seeming reorientation of public policy. Sears[8] states a universally acceptable aim of development, "the realization of the potential of human personality." This has three specific, definable, and necessary components—food, jobs, and equality. Development signifies society's struggle against poverty, malnutrition, unemployment, and impediments to equality such as concentration of wealth, and racial and religious prejudices. These goals pose a different challenge: to select processes and develop reliable measures enabling policy makers and administrators to gauge progress.[9]

This change in focus, incorporating social sciences beyond economics, has inspired the emergence of works on social indicators, distributional effects of policy decisions, employment objectives, and other consequences of developmental programs. For Tunisia, Ashford (item 161) reports that its leadership decided to revise development plans to protect political order. Waltz (item 273) expresses dissatisfaction with studies that ask, "How to modernize?" instead of, "What happens to individuals caught in the throes of intense social change?" Economic analysis addresses the rich-poor issue and factors that foster inequality of income distribution between and within Arab countries (Tuma, item 269; Adams and Howell, item 287; and Abdel-Fadil, item 284). Hermassi (item 199) identifies national integration, institutional competence, economic development, and distributive justice as the issues confronting Algeria, Morocco, and Tunisia in the process of transformation. Several studies deal with land distribution in Egypt (Voll, item 415), Syria (Keilany, item 368), and Iraq (Springborg, item 408), and agrarian reforms in other countries not only in terms of growth in economic output, but also in terms of political consequences and social justice. Increasingly, the adjectives "social," "political," and "administrative" have joined "economic" as modifiers of the term development.

Many economists propose unique strategies for development of the Arab world, such as industrial integration to reduce dependence on foreign imports (Ghantus, item 340; Aliboni, item 293; Guecioueur, item 344), among other developmental goals. Ikram (item 356), for instance, discusses strategies for developing various productive sectors of the Egyptian society, with special emphasis on development of human resources.

Increasing dependence on industrial nations for products and technology has necessitated the addition of self-reliance to the objectives of national development. In her study of Kuwait, Ismael (item 357) argues that sustaining an oil economy, dependent upon import of foreign capital equipment, perpetuates underdevelopment. Attendant manifestations of cultural and informational dependence cause serious concerns about cultural identity, values, customs, and the corresponding ability to assert national social, economic, and political practices.

The Arab world endured the struggle for political independence in the 1950s and 1960s, sometimes at high cost (exemplified by Algeria's war with France). Arab states have taken specific measures to enhance economic independence, such as Egypt's 1956 nationalization of the Suez Canal and the recouping of Arab natural resources (particularly oil) completed by the mid-1970s. Consequently, native planners have been better able to formulate comprehensive views of their economies, command their directions, and use financial resources to free themselves from foreign exchange constraints (Hashim, item 351).

Nevertheless, serious economic and social imbalances are

deepening the dependency of Arab societies on Western systems. Imports of industrial products, technology, and foodstuffs are accelerating, leading to economic subordination, creating political and security-related vulnerabilities. Furthermore, the burden of excessive foreign debt in certain countries continues to increase, reaching the threatening level of more than 50 percent of the gross national product (e.g., in Jordan, Egypt, Mauritania, Morocco, South Yemen, Somalia, and Sudan).[10] The situation seems contradictory, considering that oil-producing countries deposit their surplus savings in Western banks that, in turn, lend this money to less well-endowed Arab states at higher interest rates.

In short, recent literature recognizes that the development process is more than an economic exercise in the allocation of scarce resources (Sayigh, item 395). Scholars and practitioners seem to agree on the diagnosis, yet differ on the prescriptions. However, the following imperatives of Arab development appear to be gaining recognition and concern:

—The philosophy and objectives of development must include institutional changes as well as the total mobilization of public and private human and material resources. Development cannot simply be ordained from above. Open discussions and democratic processes of decision-making are essential.

—The reorganization of government departments of statistics, and altering their methods and priorities, is crucial. These agencies must meet the urgent need for useful, reliable data on employment, poverty, external borrowing, inequality levels, impact of various public policies, and other previously neglected variables.

—The analysis and evaluation of development plans must focus on the implementation process and not be limited to economic assumptions, plan objectives, expected results, the planning document itself, and its formulation and approval. With every Arab state promulgating a development plan of its own, the severity of implementation problems is widely recognized. Therefore, managerial techniques essential for implementation become crucial. Among them are: operationalization of goals, needs assessment, analysis of alternatives, impact studies, cost-benefit analysis, and program evaluation. The obstacles facing such investigation and research range from the seemingly unalterable to the trifling. Lack of research tradition, required skills, and incentives are tractable factors, at least in the long run. The political context appears to be the most elusive and least predictable. Vatikiotis (item 414) asserts that, in the absence of capable administrative machinery and reliable data, political motives reduce planning to window-dressing.

—National plans, replete with huge, unreliable aggregates of data, heavily dependent on comprehensive planning, have not fully utilized sectoral planning (focusing on segments of the economy, such as transportation or agriculture) or development projects as the units of analysis. Judging current trends in many Arab countries, greater reliance on sectoral planning is anticipated in the short range.

If development policies purport to better people's lives, successful planning must enhance the confidence and self-reliance of the individual, mobilize communities through effective participation, and install capable, trustworthy leadership. Many of these objectives are reaching the agenda for research and reform in Arab countries for the first time. The experiences of these countries in transforming their aspirations of today into the reality of tomorrow are crucial for societies everywhere.

user's guide

The remainder of this book is organized into five chapters. Entries are listed alphabetically by author, with each item accorded a number. Cross-references, designated by asterisks, have been kept to a minimum.

Chapter 1. Covers books and articles on administration and its subfields, public or private. Main subjects include administrative development, bureaucracy, administrative leadership, civil service systems, training, and so forth.

Chapter 2. Examines human resources with its numerous components and the growing recognition of its significance. Presents research findings on training, education, labor force, employment, population policies, and related topics.

Chapter 3. Explores socio-political factors contributing to or impeding development. Presents articles and books on social or political forces relating to management or modernization of Arab societies.

Chapter 4. Complements the previous chapter by focusing on economic development and national planning.

Chapter 5. Covers doctoral dissertations divided into three concentrations: A. Administration. B. Human Resources. C. Development.

At the end of the book, two indexes facilitate retrieval of information. The Author Index lists items alphabetically by authors. The Country Index classifies books, articles, and doctoral dissertations by country or geographic region (such as Arab world, Gulf states, and so on).

The reader may notice some inconsistency of spelling. A name may occasionally be spelled two ways (such as Osman and Othman, Bahrayn and Bahrain, Nasir and Nasser) due to problems of transliteration. Spellings in titles are presented exactly as they occur in the published work, with standard American spellings used in the annotations. The same holds true for British spellings (such as labour for labor; modernise for modernize). Occasional deviation should not distract from the otherwise high level of consistency.

Journals cited in this volume are listed below in declining order of frequency of citation. All are published in the United States and/or England unless otherwise noted.

The Middle East Journal
Arab Studies Quarterly
International Journal of Middle East Studies
International Review of Administrative Sciences
   (Belgium)
Public Administration and Development
Management International Review (W. Germany)
Economic Development and Cultural Change

introduction   xxvii

Middle Eastern Studies
Public Enterprise (Yugoslavia)
Arab Journal of Administration (The Arab League)
Public Personnel Management
The Journal of Developing Areas
The Journal of Development Studies
Development and Change
Comparative Politics
Economics
American-Arab Affairs
World Development
Comparative Education Review
Middle East Review
Comparative Studies in Society and History
Journal of Development Planning
The Journal of Public Administration Overseas
The Journal of Comparative Administration

The following titles represent a selection of Arabic-language journals (some with sections in English) that focus primarily on problems in administration and development.

Administration and Economics
College of Administration and Economics
Al-Mustansiriya University
Baghdad, Iraq

Arab Journal of Administration
Arab Organization of Administrative Sciences
P.O. Box 17159
Amman, Jordan

Arab Journal for the Humanities
Kuwait University
P.O. Box 26585
Safat, Kuwait

Bulletin of Arab Research and Studies
Institute of Arab Research and Studies
Arab League Educational, Cultural and
Scientific Organization
P.O. Box 1120

Tunis, Tunisia

Bulletin of the Faculty of Commerce, Economics and Political Science
University of Kuwait
Kuwait

Dirasat
Deanship of Research
The University of Jordan
Amman, Jordan

Economic and Business Review
Faculty of Commerce
Ain Shams University
Cairo, Egypt

Faculty of Commerce Review
Al-Azhar University
Cairo, Egypt

Journal of Economics and Administration
Center of Research and Development
King Abdul Aziz University
Jeddah, Saudi Arabia

Journal of Faculty of Commerce
Sana University Publication
Sana, Yemen Arab Republic

Journal of Petroleum Research
Petroleum Research Center
P.O. Box 10039
Baghdad, Iraq

Journal of Administrative Sciences
College of Administrative Sciences,
King Saud University
Riyadh, Saudi Arabia

Journal of the Gulf and Arabian Peninsula Studies
Kuwait University
P.O. Box 17073
Kuwait

Journal of the Social Sciences

introduction xxix

Kuwait University
P.O. Box 5486
Kuwait
Journal of the United Arab Emirates University
Al-Ain
United Arab Emirates
Oil and Arab Cooperation
General Secretariat of the Organization of Arab Petroleum Exporting Countries
P.O. Box 20501
Kuwait
Public Administration
Institute of Public Administration
P.O. Box 205
Riyadh, Saudi Arabia
Research Journal of Aleppo University
Aleppo University
Aleppo, Syria
The Arab Magazine for Information Science
Arab League Educational, Cultural and Scientific Organization
P.O. Box 1120
Tunis, Tunisia
The Iraqi Journal of Economic and Administrative Research
Economic and Administrative Research Centre
The University of Baghdad
Baghdad, Iraq

The need for analysis of policies, processes, and institutions is indispensable at this point in the Arab experience. Administration and development are crucial functions not only because of considerable policy pledges and huge amounts of resources committed, but because the very survival of some of these political systems is dependent on such progress. This bibliography offers information distilled from expert contributions in public administration and many other fields for use by decision-makers, researchers, and informed citizens alike.

Jamil E. Jreisat
University of South Florida

notes

1. Algeria, Bahrain, Egypt, Iraq, Jordan, Kuwait, Lebanon, Libya, Mauritania, Morocco, North Yemen, Oman, Palestine, Qatar, Saudi Arabia, Somalia, South Yemen, Sudan, Syria, Tunisia, United Arab Emirates.

2. Edward Said (item 255) considers Orientalism to be represented by those poets as a mass of writers, poets, novelists, philosophers, political theorists, economists, and imperial administrators, who accept the basic distinction between East and West as the starting point for elaborate theories, novels, social descriptions, and political accounts concerning the Orient, its people, customs, "mind," and destiny.

3. University Microfilms International (Ann Arbor, Michigan).

4. Library of Congress, Near East Section, African and Middle Eastern Division, "Supplement 1975–1981" (Washington, D.C., 1983).

5. *A Theory of Public Bureaucracy* (Cambridge, Mass.: Harvard University Press, 1978), p. 3.

6. Dudley Sears, "The Meaning of Development," *International Development Review*, XIX, 2 (1977), 2.

7. Ponna Wignaraga, "A New Strategy for Development," *International Development Review*, XVIII, 3 (1976), 3.

8. Sears, p. 2.

9. *Ibid.*, p. 3.

10. The World Bank, *World Development Report, 1985* (New York and London: Oxford University Press, 1985), pp. 204, 205.

the bibliography

CHAPTER 1

ADMINISTRATION

This chapter provides references of books and articles in the theory and practice of administration, covering managerial concepts and issues from both the public and private sectors. Main subjects included are administrative development and reform, bureaucracy and its performance, administrative leadership, civil service systems, administrative training, urbanization, and local government.

1. Abtan, A.J.H. "External Control of Public Enterprises in Iraq." **Control Systems for Public Enterprises in Developing Countries.** Edited by Praxy Fernandes. Ljubljana, Yugoslavia: International Center for Public Enterprises in Developing Countries, 1982, pp. 261-279.

   Discusses some methods of controlling public enterprises in Iraq. Examines the role of the Diwan of Financial Control, which, along with other authorities, holds Iraqi public enterprises accountable for performance and attainment of objectives.

2. Abu El-Soud, Ahmed. "Internal Controls Operated Through the Standardized Accounting System in the Arab Republic of Egypt as Tools for Effective Management." **Control Systems for Public Enterprises in Developing Countries.** Edited by Praxy Fernandes. Ljubljana, Yugoslavia: International Center for Public Enterprises in Developing Countries, 1982, pp. 207-214.

4 Administration and Development

Discusses various methods of control in public administration in Egypt. Describes the standardized accounting system and the major public authority, the Central Auditing Organization.

3. Abu-Lughod, Janet L. **Rabat: Urban Apartheid in Morocco.** Princeton, N.J.: Princeton University Press, 1981.

Reviews the development of Rabat, capital city of Morocco, focusing on French colonial urban planning. Argues that policy failures reflect urban planners' decisions to be guided by capitalist elite interests and aesthetics, ignoring continuous social and economic change. Observes that Rabat developed as a conglomerate of quarters, each distinct in ethnic character and function: a fragmented city in which the tiny, powerful, and rich elite enjoys a monopoly over prime urban space and facilities at the expense of the majority.

4. Ajami, Riad. "The Multinational Firm and Host Arab Society: Areas of Conflict and Convergence." **Management International Review,** 20, 1 (1980), 16-27.

Focuses on Arab elites and their attitudes toward the multinational enterprise. Concludes that economic factors (contributions to economic development, industrialization, transfer of technology) are of more concern to elites than political and cultural factors.

5. Al-Araji, Asim. "The Relevancy and the Irrelevancy of the More Advanced Management Educational Programs to Arab Countries' Needs." **International Review of Administrative Sciences,** XLVII, 2 (1981), 105-114.

Discusses domestic needs of Arab administrative systems and available educational opportunities in management at the university level.

6. Al-Araji, Asim M. "'Non-Planning' Approach in Administrative Development Policy-Making in Iraq." **International Review of Administrative Sciences**, XLIII, 4 (1977), 357-364.

   Examines the effect of pre-1972 non-planning approach on the post-1972 planning approach in Iraq. Provides tabulations about administrative changes in state bureaucracy between 1920-72. Notes that the adoption of the planning approach implies emphasis on the processes of goal-setting and implementation.

7. Al-Hegelan, Abdelrahman and Monte Palmer. "Bureaucracy and Development in Saudi Arabia." **The Middle East Journal**, 39, 1 (Winter 1985), 48-68.

   Evaluates six dimensions of the developmental capacity of the Saudi bureaucracy: psychological drive, flexibility, communications, client relations, impartiality, and job satisfaction. Reports that respondents gave the Saudi bureaucracy poor marks in each of the areas, suggesting low developmental capacity. Discusses implications of these findings and whether problems can be corrected.

8. Al-Kubaisy, Amer K. **Administrative Development in New Nations: Theory and Practice with Reference to the Case of Iraq.** Baghdad, Iraq: Al Jamhouriyah Press, 1974.

   Examines administrative development during the mandate and monarchical periods and the performance of the bureaucracy in the face of political revolution. Analyzes the issue of centralization/decentralization and its relevance to managing national development.

9. Al-Nimir, S. and M. Palmer. "Bureaucracy and Development in Saudi Arabia: A Behavioral Analysis." **Public Administration and Development**, 2, 1 (1982), 93-104.

6 **Administration and Development**

Studies and evaluates the developmental potential of public employees in Saudi Arabia, particularly in terms of group perceptions of innovative values and the factors inhibiting the development of innovative behaviors and abilities. Reports low levels of innovative behavior among bureaucrats.

10. Al-Sadhan, Abdulrahman M. "The Modernization of Saudi Bureaucracy." **King Faisal and the Modernization of Saudi Arabia.** Edited by Willard A. Beling. Boulder, Col.: Westview Press, 1980, 75-89.

    Provides description of the evolution of the Saudi bureaucracy and the establishment of certain institutional structures to carry out the essential responsibilities of the central government.

11. Al-Teraifi, Al-Agab A. "Promotion in the Sudanese Civil Service." **Public Personnel Management,** 9, 1 (January/February 1980), 19-24.

    Discusses promotion policies and practices in the Sudanese civil service, pointing to problems such as over-emphasis on seniority (regardless of performance), absence of uniform standards, and predominance of non-achievement criteria. Evaluates 1973 attempts to remedy these deficiencies; finds improvement of problems but not elimination of weaknesses.

12. Al-Teraifi, Al-Agab. "Recent Administrative Reform in the Sudan." **International Review of Administrative Sciences,** XLV, 2 (1979), 136-146.

    Describes the establishment of the Ministry of Public Service and Reforms in Sudan in 1971 as an institutional mechanism for planning and implementing change.

13. Alassam, M. "Regional Government in the Sudan." **Public Administration and Development**, 3, 2 (April-June 1983), 111-120.

    Discusses the reasons for the introduction of regional government in the Sudan and the aims behind this policy. Analyzes the new structure of government following the 1979 transfer of many functions from the central government to province councils. Considers the development of regional government a significant step toward decentralization.

14. Almaney, Adnan. "Cultural Traits of the Arabs: Growing Interest for International Management." **Management International Review**, 21, 3 (1981), 10-18.

    Examines cultural traits and their variation from one Arab country to another. Concludes, that despite economic, social, and political differences among countries, the basic Bedouin traits continue to exert, to varying degrees, certain behavioral influences on all the Arabs. Identifies such traits as emotional responsiveness to language, hospitality, pride, honor, rivalry, and revenge.

15. Altuhaih, Salem and David Van Fleet. "Kuwait Management: A Study of Selected Aspects." **Management International Review**, 18, 1 (1978), 13-22.

    Attributes lack of Kuwaiti managers in companies to complex social and cultural factors (tribe and family systems) rather than to scarcity of educated or skilled domestic managerial talent.

16. Askari, Hossein, John Thomas Cummings, and Michael Glover. **Taxation and Tax Policies in the Middle East.** London: Butterworth Scientific, 1982.

8 Administration and Development

>Discusses taxes in developing countries in general and in the Arab World in particular. Deals with types of taxes, Islamic taxes, tax policies, and tax performance in each Arab country. Offers many tables and statistics.

17. Ayubi, Nazih N.M. "Organization for Development: The Politico-Administrative Framework of Economic Activity in Egypt under Sadat." **Public Administration and Development**, 2, 3 (1982), 279-294.

>Discusses some changes in Egyptian governmental and administrative institutions during the administration of President Sadat resulting from his 1974 "open door" (infitah) policy, and the impact of these changes on development.

18. Ayubi, Nazih N.M. **Bureaucracy and Politics in Contemporary Egypt.** St. Antony's Middle East Monographs No. 10. London: Ithaca Press, 1980.

>Provides a comprehensive analysis of public administration in Egypt over almost three decades. Views bureaucracy as the leading institutional actor in promoting economic development for nationalistic reasons. Discusses political culture, bureaucratic elite, technocrats, informal groups and influences, and bureaucratic reform.

19. Bahroun, Sadok. "Annual Planning in Tunisia." **Journal of Development Planning**, 3. New York: United Nations Department of Economic and Social Affairs, 1971, 60-98.

>Describes the organization of planning in Tunisia, the budgetary organization, and the annual economic budget. Identifies three shortcomings of planning: lack of statistics on employment and labor, lack of representative and accurate price and wage indexes, and lack of measurement of productivity. Concludes that it is not enough merely to draw up a plan; "the most important and also the most difficult thing is to carry it out." Recom—

mends that the plan be discussed at all levels of society and not be limited to a handful of technocrats. Underlines the need for intensive budget programming followed by an annual economic budget as instruments of executing the plan.

20. Bashir, Iskandar. "Training for the Public Sector in Lebanon." **International Review of Administrative Sciences**, XL, 4 (1974), 359-365.

    Provides information about the conditions of training for the public sector prior to and after the establishment of the National Institute of Public Administration and Development in Lebanon in 1959.

21. Blake, G.H. and R.I. Lawless, eds. **The Changing Middle Eastern City.** London: Croom Helm, 1980, and New York: Barnes & Noble Books.

    Compiles twelve articles on cities and urban issues in the Middle East, including urban growth, migration, employment, water problems, and urban planning.

22. Buera, A. and W.F. Glueck. "The Need Satisfactions of Managers in Libya." **Management International Review**, 19, 1 (1979), 113-121.

    Reports on a study of the need satisfaction and need importance of 176 Libyan top executives, applying Maslow's hierarchy of need theory.

23. Buera, A. and W.F. Glueck. "Stage of Economic Development and the Managerial Elite: The Case of Libya." **Management International Review**, 18, 1 (1978), 33-42.

    Reports on Libyan top managers and their characteristics: age, education, training, mobility, political affiliation, foreign travel, foreign language, professional memberships.

10   **Administration and Development**

24. Causey, Margaret Cameron. "Public Enterprise in Algeria: Law as a Bridge Between Ideology and Reality." **Public Administration and Development,** 4, 2 (April-June 1984), 155-170.

    Investigates public enterprise law in Algeria before and after the 1971 reform measures.

25. Chackerian, Richard and Suliman Shadukhi. "Public Bureaucracy in Saudi Arabia: An Empirical Assessment of Work Group Behavior." **International Review of Administrative Sciences,** XLIX, 3 (1983), 319-322.

    Provides an empirical assessment of work group behavior in central ministries in Riyadh using a standardized survey. Covers five conceptual areas: organizational climate, managerial leadership, peer leadership, group process, and satisfaction.

26. Chapman, Richard A. "Administration Reform in Saudi Arabia." **Journal of Administration Overseas,** 13, 2 (April 1974), 332-347.

    Discusses manpower problems with an overview of the Saudi political and economic system. Describes a major administrative problem: government overemployment stemming from a policy of distributing oil wealth through salaries to artificial positions in the bureaucracy.

27. Clarke, John I. and Howard Bowen-Jones, eds. **Change and Development in the Middle East.** London and New York: Methuen, 1981.

    Contains nine papers on development and its administration followed by twelve case studies on specific aspects of development. Emphasizes the importance of geographical realities in the haste to utilize resources. Underlines the significance between "what is feasible and what is desired" in the search for "what is appropriate" in managing development. Includes items 99 and 106.

28. Clegg, Ian. **Worker's Self-Management in Algeria.**
    London: Allen Lane, The Penguin Press, 1971.

    Discusses workers' committees established to manage the industrial, commercial, and agricultural concerns of the French ex-colonialists after Algerian independence in 1962. Emphasizes the committees' role as a system of economic management based on decentralization and democracy in opposition to rigid forms of bureaucratic socialism. Describes how centralized state control replaced self-management within five years.

29. Costello, V.F. **Urbanization in the Middle East.**
    New York: Cambridge University Press, 1977.

    Reviews urban developments in the Middle East from preindustrial to modern society with particular focus on urban growth, rural-urban migration, social adjustment of the city, and urban form and structure.

30. El-Fathaly, Omar and Richard Chackerian. "Administration: the Forgotten Issue in Arab Development." **Arab Resources: The Transformation of a Society** (item 206).

    Identifies various administrative problems facing the Arab world and establishes a typology of administrative systems as a means to consider the range of problems and appropriate administrative solutions.

31. El-Fathaly, Omar I., M. Palmer, and R. Chackerian. **Political Development and Bureaucracy in Libya.**
    Lexington, Mass.: D.C. Heath and Co., 1977.

    Examines various aspects of the political and administrative development of Libya based on a survey administered in a province to more than 600 people. Determines attitudes, beliefs, and political values of citizens and local leaders in the hinterland of a developing country.

12 Administration and Development

32. Elmehrik, Yusef, F.A. Daghestani, Harvey Croze, and Wissam Al-Hashimi, eds. **Environment Monitoring for the Arab World.** Amman, Jordan: The Royal Scientific Society, 1981.

    Incorporates a series of specialized studies on issues related to comprehensive environment monitoring in the Arab countries. Discusses subjects such as pollution, marine pollution, agricultural production, pastoralism, and soil erosion.

33. Ghosheh, Zaki R. "Public Service Ethics in the Arab States." **Ethics in the Public Service: Comparative Perspectives.** Edited by Kenneth Kernaghan and O.P. Dwivedi. Brussels: International Institute of Administrative Sciences, 1983, pp. 121-130.

    Discusses ethical problem areas in Arab public administration. Contends that major ethical problems result from daily interaction between members of the public service and their demanding clientele. Stresses the importance of education and training for public service ethics and the need for a formal code of ethics in each Arab public service.

34. Ghosheh, Zaki R. **Dictionary of Public Administration: English-Arabic.** Amman, Jordan: Al-Tawfiq Press, 1975.

    Compiles approximately 2,000 English public administration terms, providing their Arabic equivalents.

35. Gubser, Peter. "The Zu'ama of Zahlah: The Current Situation in a Lebanese Town." **The Middle East Journal,** 27 (Spring 1973), 173-189.

    Examines the framework within which the zu'ama of Zahlah gather, maintain, and wield political power and authority. Focuses on the religious, economic, social, and administrative relationships between the individual za'im, townspeople, and the electoral district, indicating the shrinking power of the zu'ama.

36. Haddadeen, Muhiba. **Companies in Jordan and Saudi Arabia.** Amman, Jordan: The Jordanian Printing Press, 1984.

    Studies company laws and regulations in Jordan and Saudi Arabia. Emphasizes provisions applying to the formation of limited liability companies and the setting up of joint ventures. Discusses the establishment, registration, income tax, legal representation, management, and internal organization of foreign companies.

37. Ibrahim, Saad E.M. "Over-Urbanization and Under-Urbanization: the Case of the Arab World." **International Journal of Middle East Studies,** 6, 1 (January 1975), 29-45.

    Examines trends of urbanization in the Arab world as they relate to the modernization process. Deals with peculiarities of urbanization and impact on urbanism, economic development, and public policy.

38. Jawad, Shawki. "Management Development in Iraq." **International Perspectives on Management and Organization.** Edited by Roger Mansfield and Michael Poole. Hampshire, England: Gower Publishing Company, 1981, pp. 116-120.

    Discusses the major characteristics of management development in Iraq, focusing on its centralized planning and control.

39. Johnson, Katherine Marshall. **Urban Government for the Prefecture of Casablanca.** New York: Praeger, 1970.

    Studies the municipal organization of one of the largest cities in Africa and the Arab world. Focuses on the institution of urban government and its relations with the central authority. Examines problems of water control, sanitation, mass transportation, housing, education, and social welfare exacerbated by scarce resources and inadequate local power. Lack of commitment by central government hampers city planning and finance.

40. Jreisat, Jamil. **Building Administrative Capacity for Action: The Arab States.** Occasional Papers Series, Second Series, No. 8. Section on International and Comparative Administration, American Society for Public Administration, 1985.

   Examines changing and conflicting demands of Arab administrative systems in an era emphasizing national planning and development. Considers various strategies for administrative change. Presents recommendations for enhancing the administrative capacity of Arab administrative institutions through (1) development of an organizational diagnostic process, (2) design of a performance appraisal model, and (3) development of multi-faceted training programs.

41. Jreisat, Jamil E. "Public Administration Education and Training: Cases from Jordan and Saudi Arabia." **Arab Journal of Administration,** Special Issue in English (April 1982), 54-64.

   Surveys five universities and institutes of public administration in Jordan and Saudi Arabia to determine characteristics of educators and trainees, instructional and training activities, professional relationships, field research and obstacles to field research in these countries. Reports deficiencies and failures in existing programs as well as in the performance of staff.

42. Jreisat, Jamil E. "The Fertile Crescent Countries." **International Handbook on Local Government.** Edited by Donald C. Rowat. Westport, Conn.: Greenwood Press, 1980, pp. 525-534.

Examines the reorganization efforts of local government in Iraq, Jordan, Lebanon, and Syria designed to increase citizen participation, improve administrative performance, reduce financial dependence on the central treasury, and adopt more sophisticated technologies in managing developmental programs. Argues that these reorganization efforts, while perhaps conceptually innovative, have proved less successful than anticipated.

43. Jreisat, Jamil E. "Administrative Change of Local Authorities: Lessons from Four Arab Countries." **Journal of Comparative Administration**, 2, 2 (August 1970), 161-183.

    Compares the administrative structures and functions of local authorities in Syria, Egypt, Lebanon, and Jordan, focusing on problems and issues encountered in implementing alternative models of greater responsiveness to citizen needs and development objectives.

44. Konig, Klaus and Friedrich Bolay. "The Evaluation of an Administrative Co-operation Project in North Yemen and its Significance for German Aid Policy." **Public Administration and Development**, 2, 3 (1982), 225-237.

    Discusses the merits of providing German technical aid to the Republic of North Yemen within the framework of the National Institute of Public Administration in Sana'a, which conducts training programs for improving the administration of the public sector.

45. Koontz, Harold and Mead Johnson. "Effectiveness of Boards of Directors in Socialized Egypt." **Management International Review**, 12, 1 (1972), 27-41.

    Studies the board of directors--a traditional capitalistic device--as the keystone to managing Egypt's public economic enterprise. Concludes that the boards operated with competence and high quality. Recommends more independence from the ministers and greater monetary rewards for good performance.

46. Khuri, Fuad I., ed. **Leadership and Development in Arab Society.** Beirut: American University of Beirut, 1981.

    Contains fourteen papers presented at a 1979 AUB conference exploring problems of leadership and development in Arab societies. Groups papers into categories of (1) cultural unity and socio-political fragmentation, (2) interaction between local leaders and national structures, (3) the capacity of different types of leadership to mobilize for action, and (4) the contradictions of development.

47. Leila, Ali, El Sayed Yassin, and Monte Palmer. "Apathy, Values, Incentives and Development: The Case of the Egyptian Bureaucracy." **The Middle East Journal**, 39, 3 (Summer 1985), 341-361.

    Identifies apathy as the major economic problem facing Egypt today. Assesses the magnitude of the apathy problem in the Egyptian bureaucracy, explores the various reasons for its existence, examines the incentive system, and suggests alternatives. Bases data on a survey of 825 Egyptian civil servants.

48. Long, David E. "The Board of Grievances in Saudi Arabia." **The Middle East Journal**, 27, 1 (Winter, 1973), 71-75.

    Discusses the establishment in 1955 of Diwan al-Mazalim as the principal and highest administrative tribunal--an illustration of the adaptation of a classical Islamic institution to modern needs.

49. Marouf, Nawal. "Administrative Development in Kuwait." **Arab Journal of Administration,** Special Issue in English (April 1982), 30-53.

    Describes the growth of bureaucracy in Kuwait in numbers and costs during the 1960s and 1970s. Points out the large gap between actual standards and capabilities of the administrative units and the needs of the country in order to carry out the responsibilities of national development. Reviews administrative reform efforts in the mid-1970s and the creation of a ministry of legal and administrative affairs in 1976.

50. Marr, Phebe Ann. "Iraq's Leadership Dilemma: A Study in Leadership Trends, 1948-1968." **The Middle East Journal,** 24 (Summer 1970), 283-301.

    Reviews the background of cabinet ministers ten years before and after the Iraqi revolution (1958), using criteria of provincial and ethnic origin, religion, education, occupational background and degree of exposure to the West. Contrasts earlier leaders with their post-revolutionary counterparts, describes emerging leaders, and analyzes the significance for future policy.

51. Mdaghri, Driss Alaoui. "The Limits of State Control over Public Enterprises in Morocco." **Public Enterprise,** 2, 1 (1981), 41-52.

    Discusses government's control over 460 public enterprises. Indicates that intervention by the government is not new and makes the state the leading source of investment and the single most important employer.

52. Micaud, Ellen C. "Urbanization, Urbanism, and the Medina of Tunis." **International Journal of Middle East Studies,** 9, 4 (November 1978), 431-447.

Administration and Development

Summarizes the history of two decades of urban planning for the medina--the old part of the city of Tunis--including attempts to maintain it as an organic part of the metropolitan structure.

53. Mourad, Ahmed A.F. and Sadiq Al-Ayoubi. "Public Projects and Development in the Syrian Arab Republic." **Public Enterprise**, 3, 3 (1983), 49-66.

Discusses public projects and the role of the Syrian public sector in national development. Describes the major characteristics of Syrian public enterprise.

54. Muna, Farid A. **The Arab Executive.** New York: St. Martin's Press, 1980.

Provides analysis based on a survey of fifty-two leading Arab executives from six countries, using semi-structured interviews. Includes topics such as decision-making processes, change, conflict management, and relations to the wider environment.

55. Nakib, Khalil and Monte Palmer. "Traditionalism and Change Among Lebanese Bureaucrats." **International Review of Administrative Sciences**, XLII, 1 (1976), 15-22.

Examines whether the dramatic economic growth experienced by Lebanon since the end of World War II has been sufficient to alter entrenched predispositions toward particularism and inter-group hostility, or whether such predispositions have been able to withstand massive infusions of Western culture and economic modernization. Research is based on questionnaire and interviews with 162 Lebanese civil servants in 1972.

56. Norris, M.W. "Local Government and Decentralization in the Sudan." **Public Administration and Development**, 3, 3 (July-September 1983), 209-222.

Discusses the Sudan's experience in local government from 1951-1981 and the attempt to establish an effective local government system, essential for a country of such size. Describes how the government established district councils in 1951 and, despite financial difficulties in supporting decentralized government, created or developed several other structures in the last thirty years.

57. Nugent, Jeffrey B. "International Instability and the Survival Capabilities of Inter-Arab Public Enterprise Joint Ventures." **Public Enterprise,** 4, 3 (1984), 11-21.

    Discusses the survival capabilities of joint ventures among Arab countries under conditions of instability in international relations. Incorporates examples such as companies operating in Egypt after the Camp David accords, some Syrian-Jordanian companies, and operations of inter-Arab joint ventures in Syria and Iraq.

58. Osman, Osama A. "Formalism vs Realism: The Saudi Arabian Experience with Position Classification." **Public Personnel Management,** 7, 3 (May/June 1978), 177-181.

    Examines the concept of position classification introduced to the Saudi public personnel system in 1970 by American experts reflecting American practices. Points out the hazards of such applications and describes ensuing problems of formalism and rigidity. Underlines the significance of local conditions, including attitudes of decision makers.

59. Othman, Osama A. "Saudi Arabia: An Unprecedented Growth of Wealth with an Unparalleled Growth of Bureaucracy." **International Review of Administrative Sciences,** XLV, 3 (1979), 234-240.

    Describes the developmental bottleneck created by a bureaucracy lacking in tradition and essential qualifications for managing, thwarting capital-rich Saudi Arabia's high expectations for development.

60. Peterson, J.E. **Oman in the Twentieth Century.** London: Croom Helm, and New York: Barnes & Noble Books, 1978.

    Describes the development of Oman and its emerging political and administrative structures. Discusses the development of the administrative system in Chapter Three, including recruitment of officials, finance, and local government. An appendix summarizes sultanate budgets from 1921 to 1947.

61. Rabhi, Mohammed. "Planning in Public Enterprises in the Arab Countries: Problems and Perspectives." **Public Enterprise,** 3, 3 (1983), 33-47.

    A study prepared for a regional meeting of Expert Group in Planning, Kuwait, October-November 1982. Discusses the public enterprises. Calls for openness, consultation, collaboration, and further studies and research.

62. Roberts, M. Hugh P. **An Urban Profile of the Middle East.** New York: St. Martin's Press, 1979.

    Studies urban development and town planning in a period of rapid change in economic and social conditions throughout the Middle East. Provides a variety of case studies for discussion and illustration of future planned communities. Projects growth scales for population, housing, and urban facilities to the year 2000.

63. Roy, Delwin A. "Management Education and Training in the Arab World." **International Review of Administrative Sciences,** XLIII, 3 (1977), 221-228.

Focuses on the experiences of management development institutions, specifically the problems continuing to confront them and their clientele groups. Recommends development of teaching materials, administrative research, focus on high-level functions of administration, experimentation.

64. Roy, Delwin A. "Development Administration in the Arab Middle East." **International Review of Administrative Sciences**, XLI, 2 (1975), 135-148.

    Discusses the establishment of the Graduate Program in Development Administration at the American University of Beirut as a regional program drawing its participants from almost all Arab countries.

65. Sadek, S.E.M. **The Balance Point Between Local Autonomy and National Control.** The Hague and Paris: Mouton, 1972.

    Focuses on the need for local autonomy in Egypt despite the universal tendency toward centralization and control. Recognizes the impressive attempt to reconcile local autonomy with central control by certain statutory safeguards in 1960. Indicates, however, that central interference and control (through appointed state officials, wide powers of inspection and approval, and dualism of functions between state and local bodies) helped to negate attempts at local autonomy. Suggests specific changes to return control to the local level: rigid separation of functions between central and local units, and local control of resources through extended power of tax.

66. Sadik, Muhammad T. "The Road to Enhancing Public Sector Administrative Capability in the Arab Countries." **Arab Journal of Administration**, Special Issue in English (April 1982), 10-22.

    Describes various administrative problems and shortcomings in the Arab world that have kept administrative capacity at a very low level. Argues that the way to develop administrative capability is to improve infrastructure for administrative capability, encourage development planning, strengthen administrative development institutions, and inspire genuine political commitment.

67. Sadik, Muhammad T. and William P. Snavely. "Administrative Problems and Policies." **Bahrain, Qatar, and the United Arab Emirates** (item 254).

    Examines the organization of public administration in Bahrain, Qatar, and Abu Dhabi until 1970. Identifies some basic problems of management of public organizations in these states and the other municipalities that, with Abu Dhabi, form the United Arab Emirates.

68. Salem, Elie Adib. **Modernization Without Revolution: Lebanon's Experience.** Bloomington, Ind.: Indiana University Press, 1973.

    Studies the political, economic, and social forces that have led to the modernization of Lebanon (before the strife that started in 1975). Argues that reforming the Lebanese bureaucracy has been among the important responses of the government to modernization needs.

69. Siegel, Gilbert B. "Performance Appraisal for Development of Human Resources in the Democratic Republic of the Sudan." **Public Personnel Management,,** 13, 2 (1984), 147-155.

    Examines public administration as a catalyst for development. Concludes that public administration in Sudan is not really development oriented, though public servants in general favor the assumption of such a role.

70. Szyliowicz, Joseph S. "Science, Technology, and Development in the Arab World." **Middle East Review**, X, 3 (Spring, 1978), 24-29.

    Presents problems facing the implementation of science and techology policy in the Arab world as an important component of any development effort.

71. Wahba, M.M. "The Egyptian Public Sector: The Control Structure and Efficiency Considerations." **Public Administration and Development**, 3, 1 (January-March 1983), 27-37.

    Describes the problem of control in the public sector and rigidities caused by the imposition of legal controls that leave little latitude in the operation of governmental functions. Illustrates such negative control measures by presenting the numerous steps required for a public firm to obtain finance of its investment plan.

72. Wittington, Dale and Giorgio Guariso. **Water Management Models in Practice: A Case Study of the Aswan High Dam.** New York: Elsevier Scientific Publishing Co., 1983.

    Analyzes the management system of the Nile as a case of water resource management. Provides information on the hydrology of the Nile, its reservoirs operations, and the "real-time" management model in which discharges are computed. Explains how sophisticated modeling exercises are made easy to understand and useful in improving formulation and analysis of policy options.

73. Wright, Peter. "Organizational Behavior in Islamic Firms." **Management International Review**, 21, 2 (1981), 86-94.

    Warns American and Western European multi-national corporations viewing expansion in markets in Islamic countries (particularly those with significant oil revenues) to be aware of the "Muslim way" of doing things. Suggests that managerial attitudes and skills necessary for successful operations in the Muslim world are different from those needed in Europe or America.

74. Zahlan, A.B. **Science and Science Policy in the Arab World.** New York: St. Martin's Press, 1980.

   Provides an overview of the development and management of scientific activity throughout the Arab world. Discusses issues of funding, national policies toward research, and international as well as regional influences on the improvement and expansion of relevant educational and research facilities. Underlines the bureaucratic and financial problems that plague government-sponsored research.

75. Zahra, Shaker. "Egyptian Management at the Crossroads." **Management International Review,** 20, 3 (1980), 118-124.

   Identifies major ideological, economic, social and cultural forces that define the role and nature of Egyptian management. Describes most salient features of that management as bureaucratic, ill-trained, disoriented, and negligent in human resource development.

CHAPTER 2

HUMAN RESOURCES

This chapter focuses on human resources—the means and ends of national development. It provides references of books and articles on critical aspects of the management and development of human resources, such as education, labor force, labor migration, employment, population policies, and status of women.

76. Abdel Khader, Soha. "A Survey of Trends in Social Sciences Research on Women in the Arab Region, 1960-1980." **Social Science Research and Women in the Arab World** (item 138).

    Assesses research trends in social sciences on the status of women in the Arab region from a multi-disciplinary perspective. Discusses transition of the role of women in Arab society through history. Concludes that women during the early centuries of Islam "were active in public life"; attributes seclusion to arbitrary measures developing historically.

77. Abdel-Jaber, Tayseer. "Trends and Prospects of the Brain Drain from Arab Countries." **Arab Journal of Administration**, Special Issue in English (April 1982), 23-29.

    Examines general trends and future prospects of manpower flows within and without the Arab world. Distinguishes between sometimes-temporary intra-Arab flows (as a significant factor in regional economic cooperation and integration) and the more permanent brain drain to advanced countries. Reviews policies formulated by Arab countries to limit the outflow to industrial countries or reverse it. Speculates on future trends and foresees greater efforts by Arab countries in the development and employment of human resources.

78. Abu-Laban, Baha and Sharon McIrvin Abu-Laban. "Education and Development in the Arab World." **The Journal of Developing Areas,** 10, 3 (April 1976), 285-304.

   Examines the tendency of leaders to consider education a tool of social and economic development influenced by practical and theoretical considerations. Argues that in assessing the impact of formal education on development, certain factors must be considered; i.e., implementation of societal goals, balanced institutional change, and legitimate expectations of education.

79. Alessa, Shamlan Y. **The Manpower Problem in Kuwait.** London and Boston: Routledge and Kegan Paul International, 1981.

   Provides comprehensive coverage of manpower problems in Kuwait. Presents data and illustrations on Kuwaiti labor force, foreign manpower, education, and manpower training.

80. Allman, James. **Social Mobility, Education and Development in Tunisia.** Leiden: E.J. Brill, 1979.

   Re-examines the proposition that education is the vehicle for achieving development and modernity. Argues that the problem is not a shortage of educated people, but a surplus of poorly educated citizens with aspirations that cannot be fulfilled, as in Tunisia. Concludes that emphasis on education has not promoted development.

81. Al-Tall, Ahmad Y. **Education in Jordan.** Islamabad, Pakistan: National Book Foundation, 1979.

    Studies the development of the system of education 1950-1977. Emphasizes the relationship between social and economic development and the development of education.

82. Ayubi, Nazih. "The Egyptian 'Brain Drain': A Multidimensional Problem." **International Journal of Middle East Studies,** 15, 4 (November 1983), 431-450.

    Discusses emigration of Egyptians to the Arab world or the West. Relates lack of official policy on the issue to uncertainty over whether brain drain represents a "net curse" or a "net blessing" for the country. Furnishes data on graduates, students abroad, and migrants through the mid-1970s.

83. Badri, Kashif. "The History, Development, Organization and Position of Women's Studies in the Sudan." **Social Science Research and Women in the Arab World** (item 138).

    Surveys the history of women's studies in the Sudan, the nationalist movement, and women's place in society. Discusses the importance of studies on Sudanese women and the organization of such programs. Concludes that studies on Sudanese women would assist the process of social and economic development.

84. Baffoun, Alya. "Research in the Social Sciences on North African Women: Problems, Trends and Needs." **Social Science Research and Women in the Arab World** (item 138).

    Suggests priorities for scientific research. Contends that the state, and not the rank and file, takes credit for the proposed emancipation of women in Tunisia.

85. Bahry, Louay. "The New Saudi Woman: Modernizing in an Islamic Framework." **The Middle East Journal,** 36 (Autumn 1982), 502-515.

    Examines the emergence of Saudi women from the strict social structure of the past into a still-circumscribed role in the changing Saudi dual society of men and women. Investigates such influences as the press, working women, changes in marriage and family life. Concludes that future evolution requires the support of the traditional religious establishment.

86. Belarabi, Aicha. "Research in the Social Sciences on Women in Morocco." **Social Science Research and Women in the Arab World** (item 138).

    Surveys the scope of research during the periods before the protectorate, under the protectorate (1912-1956), and after independence. Discusses conditions of women with respect to education and culture, law, change, the position of the French, paid employment, and other social aspects. Presents suggestions for further research.

87. Behbehani, Kazem, Maurice Girgis and M.S. Marzouk, eds. **Proceedings of the Symposium on Science and Technology for Development in Kuwait.** London: Longman Group Ltd., 1981.

    Contains information on the role of science and technology in Kuwait's development, including their impact on human resources development and finance in private and public service sectors.

88. Birks, J.S. and C.A. Sinclair. "Employment and Development in Six Poor Arab States: Syria, Jordan, Sudan, South Yemen, Egypt and North Yemen." **International Journal of Middle East Studies,** 14, 1 (February 1982), 35-51.

Analyzes employment trends showing the imbalance between job seekers and opportunities, likely to become more pronounced in future years. Contributing to the problem are high population rates and limited creation of jobs as the expansion of civil service becomes a less easy policy. Provides estimates and data on employment and population growth.

89. Birks, J.S. and C.A. Sinclair. **Arab Manpower: the Crisis of Development.** New York: St. Martin's Press, 1980.

   Studies labor transfers in the Arab world and their social implications. Divides countries into regions of capital-rich, capital-poor or in between (Bahrain, Oman, Algeria). Contrasts types of development and change pursued by various countries and the social, political, and economic consequences. Provides official and unofficial data on a wide range of subjects.

90. Birks, J.S. and C.A. Sinclair. "Economic and Social Implications of Current Development in the Arab Gulf: The Oriental Connection." **Social and Economic Development in the Arab Gulf** (item 241).

   Surveys the distribution of wealth in the Arab countries. Examines labor forces, especially in the Arab Gulf region with its growing demand for labor to meet developmental requirements. Contends that the rapid pace of economic development in 1975 transformed migrant labor patterns; shortage of Arab labor in the Gulf forced oil exporters to recruit from the Indian subcontinent.

91. Birks, J.S. and C.A. Sinclair. "Egypt: A Frustrated Labor Exporter?" **The Middle East Journal,** 33 (Summer 1979), 288-303.

   Assesses the impact of labor exportation on Egypt's economy, particularly in alleviating unemployment and providing foreign exchange for internal development. Discusses limited occupational mobility within the rigidly compartmentalized domestic labor market and its effect on migration. Foresees such problems as the need to replace absent migrating workers, workers' wages funneled into consumption rather than investment, and instability of foreign wages in times of political disharmony.

92. Birks, J.S., C.A. Sinclair, and J.A. Socknat. "Aspects of Labour Migration from North Yemen." **Middle Eastern Studies,** 17, 1 (January 1981), 49-63.

    Cites limited economic opportunity and employment in Yemen as reason for that country's becoming the supplier of labor to Saudi Arabia and other oil-wealthy states of the Arab Gulf. Discusses consequences of this human transfer, related policy issues, and the main concern that migration not sidetrack domestic development.

93. Choucri, Nazli. "Migration in the Middle East: Transformation and Change." **Middle East Review,** 16, 2 (Winter 1983/4), 16-25.

    Analyzes the issues of migration in the Arab Middle East, viewing economic development as critically tied to manpower requirements. Places contemporary migration in historical context and reviews changes in migration over the past decade. Offers statistical data on migrant workers by national origin and destination until 1975.

94. Cummings, John Thomas, H.G. Askari, and M. Skinner. "Military Expenditures and Manpower Requirements in the Arabian Peninsula." **Arab Studies Quarterly,** 2, 1 (Winter 1980), 38-49.

    Examines armaments expenditures and their effects on economic development of Middle Eastern countries, not only in terms of competition for funds, but also in terms of diverting trained manpower to less productive sectors. Provides data on military purchases of Saudi Arabia, Kuwait, Qatar, and the UAE.

95. Duguid, Stephen. "A Biographical Approach to the Study of Social Change in the Middle East: Abdullah Tariki as a New Man." **International Journal of Middle East Studies,** 1, 3 (July 1970), 195-220.

    Profiles one of the "new men," the so-called Western-trained technocrats and administrators resolving the conflict among various approaches to social change in the Middle East.

96. El-Tom, M.E.A. "Sudan: The Role of the Educational System in the Migration of High Level Manpower." **The Arab Brain Drain** (item 141).

    Discusses the recent phenomenon of high-level Sudanese manpower emigration and the forces behind it. Blames the Sudanese educational system, which teaches skills more suitable (or relevant) to advanced countries.

97. Entelis, John P. "Elite Political Culture and Socialization in Algeria: Tensions and Discontinuities." **The Middle East Journal,** 35 (Spring 1981), 191-208.

    Describes a conflicting political culture between those who deal with power and have responsibility for governmental decisions, and those who are observers or marginal activists. Finds a balance between the groups traced to the expectation that benefits accruing to the incumbent elites will spread to nongovernmental elites.

98. Faksh, Mahmud A. "The Chimera of Education for Development in Egypt: The Socio-Economic Roles of University Graduates." **Middle Eastern Studies,** 13, 2 (May, 1977), 229-240.

32 Administration and Development

Finds substantial destabilizing consequences in the educational expansion in modern Egypt, not conducive to development. Describes as very limited the absorptive capacity of the economy to accommodate new and improperly trained graduates, while technical middle-range needs of the job market remain unmet.

99. Findlay, Allan M. "Labour Mobility and Manpower Planning in Tunisia." **Change and Development in the Middle East** (item 27).

Discusses labor migration from less favored peripheral regions toward Tunis and other urban cores to achieve social mobility. Observes that development of rural industries offered opportunities for occupational advancement but not social mobility. Examines the threefold nature of labor mobility--spacial, occupational, and social-- and the paradoxical consequences for Tunisian manpower planning.

100. Gallagher, C.F. **Population and Development in Egypt, AUFS Report Nos. 31 and 32.** Hanover, N.H.: American Universities Field Staff Reports, 1981.

Comprises a two-part brief report. Part I presents a statistical analysis of population: birthrates, death rates, natural increase rates, projected death rates for Egypt 1975-2000, projected life expectancy, National Family Planning Program, etc. Part II focuses on the socio-economic future of Egypt. Contends that overall prospects are immeasurably better than they were as recently as two years ago.

101. Gerner-Adams, Debbie J. "The Changing Status of Islamic Women in the Arab World." **Arab Studies Quarterly,** 1, 4 (Fall 1979), 324-353.

Details the position of women in the Arab world according to traditional Islamic law, the development of the feminist movement, educational opportunities, and women's active role in the life of their communities.

102. Hakiki, Fatiha and Claude Talahite. "Human Science Research on Algerian Women." **Social Science Research and Women in the Arab World** (item 138).

    Discusses the period between 1962-1980. Defines three broad problem areas underlying research on Algerian women: problems resulting from transition from traditional to modern modes of life; problems arising from women's participation in political and social life; and conflicting attitudes toward femininity and achievement.

103. Hammam, Mona. "Women and Industrial Work in Egypt: The Chubra El-Kheima Case." **Arab Studies Quarterly**, 2, 1 (Winter 1980), 50-69.

    Studies present-day working women in industry, conditions in the factory, women's perceptions of their role in society, and society's perception of the industrial working woman. Research conducted in a textile factory on the outskirts of Cairo employing 1,150 females out of a work force of 20,000 (148 interviews).

104. Hansen, Bert and Samir Radwan. **Employment Opportunities and Equity in Egypt: A Labour Market Approach.** Geneva: International Labour Office, 1982.

    Studies the Egyptian economy to propose policies, at the request of the prime minister, for productive employment for "all who want to work." Produced in collaboration with ILO mission and Egyptian academicians. Citicizes some liberalization policies of Egypt and--in an attempt to define trends in income distribution and poverty --provides a detailed profile of rural Egypt. Offers a wealth of documentation and data.

34 Administration and Development

105. Hay, Michael J. "A Structural Equations Model of Migration in Tunisia." **Economic Development and Cultural Change,** 28, 2 (January 1980), 345-358.

   Outlines a microeconomic, human capital model of rural-urban migration. Provides an empirical test of the model based on individual survey data gathered in a rural area of Tunisia.

106. Hill, Allan G. "Population Growth in the Middle East Since 1945 with Special Reference to the Arab Countries of West Asia." **Change and Development in the Middle East** (item 27).

   Deals with recent trends in mortality, fertility levels and trends, marriage as a factor affecting fertility, migration, and future demographic prospects. Offers statistical data to the late 1970s.

107. Hinnebusch, Raymond A. "Children of the Elite: Political Attitudes of the Westernized Bourgeoisie in Contemporary Egypt." **The Middle East Journal,** 36 (Autumn 1982), 535-561.

   Explores the political ideology of the Westernized wing of the influential Egyptian bourgeoisie through a study of attitudes of its children. Explains methods of study and social profile of the sample. Concludes that, in developing countries, the Westernized bourgeoisie may be fractured along communal lines, although consensus exists in Egypt in preferring a liberal secular democratic capitalist course and Western political alignment.

108. Hyde, Georgie D.M. **Education in Modern Egypt: Ideals and Realities.** London: Routledge and Kegan Paul, 1978.

   Studies university training, manpower problems, modernization, and the organizational structure and functions of the two ministries specialized in education processes: the Ministry of Education and the Ministry of Higher Education. Discusses basic issues dealing with human resources development in the country.

109. Jones, M.T. "Education of Girls in Tunisia: Policy Implications of the Drives for Universal Enrollment." **Comparative Education Review**, 25, 2 (June 1980), 106-123, Part 2.

    Examines the Tunisian commitment to universal education of girls; a commitment made in the late 1950s after independence as a result of viewing education as an instrument for transforming society. Concludes that after twenty years of growth in enrollment, the goals of universal schooling seem illusive and generate some serious problems, such as the persistent gaps in the drive for universal enrollment and the provision of job-related training. Relates the question of supply and demand to the heart of these issues.

110. Keely, Charles B. and Bassam Saket. "Jordanian Migrant Workers in the Arab Region: A Case Study of Consequences for Labor Supplying Countries." **The Middle East Journal**, 38, 4 (Autumn 1984), 685-698.

    Discusses the role of Jordan as a major contributor of manpower to oil-exporting countries meeting the demands of expanded development. Describes results of survey research by the Royal Scientific Society of Jordan in 1980 gauging the effects of labor migration and remittances at the household level. Focuses on the characteristics of migrants and their households, processes of migration, work abroad, and re-entry into the Jordanian economy. Concludes that migration has had a positive effect, although direct investment and savings have been disappointing.

111. Kelley, Allen C. **Population and Development in Rural Egypt.** Durham, N.C.: Duke University Press, 1982.

36 Administration and Development

Provides analysis of community-level data aimed at developing a population policy balancing the family planning approach and the development (upgrading standards of living) approach. Discusses rural economic, social, and demographic conditions, providing extensive statistical and bibliographic data.

112. Kelley, Allen C., Atef M. Khalifa, and M. Nabil El-Khorazaty. **Population and Development in Rural Egypt.** Durham, N.C.: Duke Press Policy Studies, 1982.

Studies data from the 1979 Rural Fertility Survey and the 1977 Population and Development Project. Uses statistical analysis to clarify interrelationships among desired number of children, child deaths, use of contraceptive methods, and children born. Also deals with education, employment, electricity, and other economic and social indicators and trends.

113. Kettani, M. Ali. "Engineering Education in the Arab World." **The Middle East Journal,** 28 (Autumn 1974), 441-450.

Describes engineering education growth in the Arab world and problems faced. Offers general suggestions for consultation, cooperation, and initiation of a common employment market among Arab states.

114. Kirwan, Frank. "Labour Exporting in the Middle East." **Development and Change,** 13, 1 (January 1982), 63-89.

Examines the movement of labor from Jordan to the Arab countries (and into Jordan from some Arab countries, particularly Egypt) and the impact of this fluctuation of labor on agriculture, industry, services, and the economy in general.

115. Lapham, Robert J. "Population Policies in the Maghrib." **The Middle East Journal,** 26 (Winter 1972), 1-10.

    Examines the population growth policies of Morocco, Algeria, and Tunisia. Lists research problems to consider when examining each country in relation to appropriate methods of family planning under present population policies. Discusses the utility of outside intervention by government or agencies in the process of fertility reduction.

116. McCarthy, Justin A. "Nineteenth Century Egyptian Population." **The Middle Eastern Economy: Studies in Economics and Economic History** (item 214).

    Investigates the reasons for the drastic increase in the Egyptian population during the nineteenth century. Indicates that in 1800, the population (estimated at 7.8 million) was at its lowest point in history, and, by the time of the French expedition, the population had dropped to less than 4 million. Blames wars, plagues, and successions of rulers who destroyed "the civic calm needed for population growth."

117. Meleis, Afaf I., Nagat El-Sanabary, and Diane Beeson. "Women, Modernization, and Education in Kuwait." **Comparative Education Review,** 23, 1 (February 1979), 115-124.

    Discusses progress achieved in women's education and its impact on labor force participation.

118. Moore, Clement Henry. **Images of Development: Egyptian Engineers in Search of Industry.** Cambridge and London: The MIT Press, 1980.

    Studies the engineering profession of Egypt (using survey techniques) as a critical group in

Administration and Development

concert with the leadership of Nasir and, later, Sadat. Concludes that engineers, who have been very highly placed in government, have not helped the state to solve its problems but have relied on Western technology to the detriment of their own research and development.

119. Nagi, Mostafa H. "Internal Migration and Structural Changes in Egypt." **The Middle East Journal**, 28 (Summer 1974), 261-282.

    Examines patterns and trends of internal migration in Egypt between 1937 and 1965. Discusses determinants and effects, including rural-urban migration and its contribution to urbanization (as distinct from industrialization).

120. Nakhleh, Emile A. "Labor Markets and Citizenship in Bahrayn and Qatar." **The Middle East Journal**, 31 (Spring 1977), 143-156.

    Offers suggestions for the development of the two countries, which face similar problems, in three parts: (1) long-range manpower plans to guide development, (2) the need to produce sufficient numbers of trained personnel through a technical/vocational training program, and (3) liberalization of citizenship laws to absorb interested foreign nationals.

121. Omran, Abdel-Rahim. **Population of the Arab World: Problems and Prospects.** New York: United Nations Fund for Population Activities, and London: Croom Helm, 1980.

    Provides an overview of the subject of population in the Arab world and the gravity of its problems; outlines demographic and health contexts and transitions. Describes demographic profiles of Arab populations and brings attention to the potential consequences of excessive fertility and rapid population growth. Surveys existing population policies and offers tables, statistics, and figures.

122. Qubeisi, Hafeth A. "An Approach to the Utilization of Scientific Arab Manpower." **Science and Technology for Development** (item 178).

    Discusses Arab development, transfer of technology to Arab countries, and the importance of carrying out scientific research. Examines Arab scientific human resources, the emigration of researchers and scientists, and the need to attract their return.

123. Rassam, Amal. "Towards a Theoretical Framework for the Study of Women in the Arab World." **Social Science Research and Women in the Arab World** (item 138).

    Suggests a framework within the scope of Islamic and Arab cultures. Contends that the Koran, Hadith, and the various treatises assign women a special status that should be investigated by today's researchers. Discusses sex roles, power differentials, family relations, women, labor and the wage market, and the role of the state.

124. Richards, Alan and Philip L. Martin. "The Laissez-Faire Approach to International Labor Migration: The Case of the Arab Middle East." **Economic Development and Cultural Change,** 31, 3 (April 1983), 455-474.

    Examines the laissez-faire migration policies and theories in respect to the Arab states. Maintains that benefits accrue to individual migrants and individual employers.

125. Saket, Bassam K., Tarik Al-Tell, Sami Zreigat, and Bassam Asfour. **Workers Migration Abroad: Socio-Economic Implications for Households in Jordan.** Amman, Jordan: Royal Scientific Society, May 1983.

    Studies Jordanian migrant workers in the Arab region. Emphasizes social demographic characteristics, Jordanians' decisions to work abroad,

40   Administration and Development

destination countries, remittances, social consequences of international migration for Jordanians, and the increase in wives' decision-making responsibility during and after migration.

126. Sanyal, Bikas C., et al. **University Education and the Labour Market in the Arab Republic of Egypt.** Oxford and New York: UNESCO International Institute for Education Planning/Pergamon Press, 1982.

Explores the links between higher education and employment and provides a wealth of data derived by a group of specialists, based on the International Institute for Educational Planning Study. One of a series conducted by IIEP in a number of countries. Gives an overview of Egypt and offers statistics, methodology, assumptions, limitations, and projections for 1985 and 1990.

127. Serageldin, Ismail, James Socknat, and J.S. Birks. "Human Resources in the Arab World: The Imact of Migration." **Arab Resources: The Transformation of a Society** (item 206).

Discusses international labor migration in the Arab world, focusing on consequences for labor-importing and labor-exporting countries. Provides statistical information.

128. Serageldin, Ismail, et al. **Manpower and International Labor Migration in the Middle East and North Africa.** New York: Oxford University Press, 1983; published for the World Bank.

Presents the results of a World Bank research project by a team of Bank specialists. Concludes that costs and benefits are derived from the changing patterns of labor migration. Underlines disadvantages to labor-exporting countries in terms of needing to replace lost workers and making unsuccessful efforts to channel remittances into productive use. Discusses policy options and implications; provides extensive data.

129. Serageldin, Ismail, James Socknat, J. Stace Birks, and Clive Sinclair. "Some Issues Related to Labor Migration in the Middle East and North Africa." **The Middle East Journal,** 38 (Autumn 1984), 615-642.

Examines the international migration of labor affecting the Middle East and North Africa. Refers to the shifting demographic balance, nature of the migrants, impact on host countries, impact on countries of origin, and impact on migrants themselves. Recommends that countries involved—which have failed to properly address the migration problem—strive to cooperate, do manpower planning, loosen naturalization procedures, and revise terms and conditions of employment.

130. Shaw, Paul R. "Manpower and Educational Shortages in the Arab World: An Interim Strategy." **World Development,** 9, 7 (1981), 637-655.

Discusses major problems Arab countries encounter in trying to meet skilled manpower needs, such as coping with "brain drain" and staffing developmental projects.

131. Shaw, R. Paul. **Mobilizing Human Resources in the Arab World.** London: Kegan International, 1983.

Deals with manpower as it affects the development plans of capital-rich Arab states. Views manpower as the single most important bottleneck in the region. Focuses on problem areas such as construction, agriculture, overpopulation, women and development, manpower deficiencies, and educational planning.

132. Sherbiny, Naiem A. "Expatriate Labor Flows to the Arab Oil Countries in the 1980s." **The Middle East Journal,** 38 (Autumn 1984), 643-667.

Assesses the near-term (1985) and mid-term (1990) prospects for migration in the Middle East and North Africa. Considers economic performance of labor-importing countries (Saudi Arabia, Iraq, Kuwait, United Arab Emirates, Libya) during the 1980s. Contrasts total labor requirements (demand) with domestic or national labor availabilities (supply). Concludes that, barring an economic catastrophe in the oil countries, present migration will likely continue.

133. Sinclair, Clive A. and J.S. Birks. "Manpower in Saudi Arabia, 1980-1985." **Saudi Arabia: Energy, Developmental Planning, and Industrialization** (item 333).

    Discusses the role of labor in contemporary Saudi development with special stress on the Five-Year development plan 1980-1985. Examines manpower growth in relation to the needs of development. Concludes that the Saudi economy and society cannot do without migrant workers.

134. Swanson, Jon C. **Emigration and Economic Development: The Case of the Yemen Arab Republic.** Boulder, Col.: Westview Press, 1979.

    Follows the migration of Yemeni peasants to Saudi Arabia, detailing benefits and losses of such human movement. Identifies negative consequences such as serious shortage of local manpower, inflation of wages and prices, and neglect of agricultural lands. Finds, on the plus side, cash tranfers and higher standards of living in Yemen.

135. Swanson, Jon C. "Some Consequences of Emigration for Rural Economic Development in the Yemen Arab Republic." **The Middle East Journal,** 33 (Winter 1979), 34-43.

    Examines the interplay between agriculture and emigration by considering the economic consequences of labor export for rural Yemen. Concludes that the Yemeni situation is unique because remitted earnings are not translated into wealth and productive enterprises in a country devoid of investment opportunities. Discusses intensive manpower needs of Yemeni agriculture, loss of workers through emigration and the inability of technology to compensate results in rising labor costs, non-use of marginal land, and an overall drop in production.

136. Trebous, Madeleine. **Migration and Development: The Case of Algeria.** Paris: Development Centre of the Organization for Economic Co-operation and Development, 1970.

Documents labor and manpower flow from Algeria to Europe (France in particular), in which one of eight working Algerians lived abroad as of 1966. Deems this labor flow mutually beneficial. Points out that few expatriate Algerians work in managerial or skilled positions, rendering their training of little use upon their return.

137. Tuma, Elias H. "Agrarian Reform and Urbanization in the Middle East." **The Middle East Journal,** 24 (Spring 1970), 163-177.

Assumes that development should precede urbanization and, therefore, rural labor should remain in the countryside until the urban economy is capable of absorption. Inspects the mechanism by which agrarian reform measures have influenced the rate of urbanization. Evaluates compatibility with the objectives of economic development. Suggests alternative measures.

138. UNESCO, ed. **Social Science Research and Women in the Arab World.** Edited by UNESCO. London: Frances Pinter Publishers, 1984.

Contains eight specialized studies of the position of women in Arab societies; based on the proceedings of an "Expert's Meeting on Multidisciplinary Research on Women in the Arab World." Deals with the status of women in Algeria, Egypt, Iraq, Libya, Morocco, Saudi Arabia, Tunisia, and Sudan. Includes items 76, 83, 84, 86, 102, 123.

139. Ward, Richard J. "The Long Run Employment Prospects for Middle East Labor." **The Middle East Journal,** 24 (Spring 1970), 147-162.

    Estimates the extent of unemployment, distribution of the labor force by country, and future employment prospects in several Middle Eastern countries. Describes the employment picture in Jordan, the West Bank, Israel, Gaza, Sinai, Kuwait, and Saudi Arabia, with a brief look at Libya and Lebanon. Sees education as the strongest catalytic agent for employment. Projects 100,000 available jobs in the coming five years within the Middle East. Cites European employment potential.

140. Zaghal, Ali S. "Social Change in Jordan." **Middle Eastern Studies,** 20, 4 (October 1984), 53-75.

    Surveys the demographic change in Jordan, changes in labor force, education, and curriculum. Reports "great changes" in the number of all students enrolled in schools--male and female--and number of dropouts. Covers the period 1961-79 and limits the analysis to the East Bank.

141. Zahlan, A.B., ed. **The Arab Brain Drain.** London: Ithaca Press, 1981.

    Incorporates several studies on selected Arab countries and their national development. Focuses on Arab scientific manpower in the United States, Arab-American professionals and the problem of "brain drain," migration of Egyptians, and aspects of the "brain drain" in Algeria. Includes items 96 and 143.

142. Zahlan, A.B. "The Problematique of the Arab Brain Drain." **Arab Studies Quarterly,** 2, 4 (Fall 1980), 318-331.

    Documents the flow of highly trained manpower from the Arab world to Western Europe and the United States. (In 1976, developing countries lost

fifty percent of physicians, twenty-three percent
of engineers, fifteen percent of scientists.)
Finds causes of outflow more important than actual
loss.

143. Zain, Mohamed Gaffar. "The Brain Drain in the
Context of Social Change in Democratic Yemen and
Problems in High Level Manpower Training at Aden
University." **The Arab Brain Drain** (item 141).

Discusses emigration and brain drain under
British occupation in the People's Democratic
Republic of Yemen after independence. Deals with
the role of Aden University in high-level manpower
education training. Enumerates problems, particularly one relatively common in Arab universities: shortage of qualified faculty members.

CHAPTER 3

DEVELOPMENT: SOCIO-POLITICAL FACTORS

This chapter presents books and articles on the national development of one or more Arab countries from the political and social perspectives. It includes references dealing with subjects such as social class, the military, religion, political institutions, local politics, culture, ideology, and national integration.

144. Abdel-Fadil, Mahmoud. **The Political Economy of Nasserism: A Study in Employment and Income Distribution Policies in Urban Egypt, 1952-1972.** Cambridge; New York: Cambridge University Press, 1980.

    Studies employment and income distribution policies in Egypt during Nasir's era. Covers basic changes in the employment structure in the organized sector, estimates of the size of the "informal sector," public wage policy, distribution of personal income, and equity of the tax system. Provides some analysis of changes in class composition and the growth of "social elites." Includes many tables and figures of data.

145. Abdel-Khalek, Gouda and Robert Tignor, eds. **The Political Economy of Income Distribution in Egypt.** New York and London: Holmes & Meier, 1982.

    Consists of thirteen chapters authored by American and Egyptian academicians analyzing various aspects of Egypt's income distribution experience, macroeconomic forces, tax system, agriculture, urban growth and inequality, education and social mobility, political influences, and foreign economic relations.

146. Abu-Lughod, Janet. "Dependent Urbanism and Decolonization: The Moroccan Case." **Arab Studies Quarterly,** 1, 1 (Winter 1979), 49-67.

    Studies changes in Morocco between 1952 and 1971, i.e., decline of non-Muslim population, increase in urbanization, and the struggle to deal with imbalances created by French and Spanish colonial rule.

147. Ahmad, Eqbal. "From Potato Sack to Potato Mash: The Contemporary Crisis of the Third World." **Arab Studies Quarterly,** 2, 3 (Summer 1980), 223-234.

    Outlines the contemporary crisis of the Third World and suggests requisites for achieving a measure of success in meeting the challenges of legitimacy, independence, development, and distributive justice.

148. Ahsan, Syed Aziz-al. "Economic Policy and Class Structure." **International Journal of Middle East Studies,** 16, 3 (August 1984), 301-323.

    Examines economic policies (land reform, industrial and commercial reform, and foreign trade controls) and their impact on class structure. Asks, who benefitted? who suffered? and what motivated the elites to adopt these policies? Concludes that horizontal cleavages based on social stratification by occupation or income are more pronounced. Finds religious/regional solidarity stronger than class solidarity.

149. Al-Farsy, Fouad. **Saudi Arabia: A Case Study in Development.** London: Stacey International, 1978.

Socio-Political Factors

Provides descriptive and background information about Saudi Arabia and its governmental institutions.

150. Al-Shirawi, Yousuf. "The Impact of Development on Gulf Society and Politics." **The United States, Arabia, and the Gulf** (item 279).

    Discusses the common historical background of the Arab Gulf States and the social and political impact of development on their societies. Deals with the impact of development on Gulf politics and the region's relations with the powers whose economies depend on oil from the Gulf.

*   Almaney, Adnan. "Cultural Traits of the Arabs: Growing Interest for International Management." Cited as item 14.

151. Aly, Abd al-Monein Said and Manfred W. Wenner. "Modern Islamic Reform Movements: The Muslim Brotherhood in Contemporary Egypt." **The Middle East Journal,** 36, 3 (Summer 1982), 336-361.

    Offers a brief historical introduction to the growth and development of modern Islamic reform movements. Uses the Muslim Brotherhood in Egypt to outline important developments. Argues against any Islamic movement's success in gaining power in Egypt because of its lengthy liberal political tradition, close links between middle/intellectual classes and indigenous nationalistic movements, and long-term assimilation of economic change and development.

152. Aman, Mohammed. **Arab Periodicals and Serials: A Subject Bibliography.** New York: Garland Publishing Inc., 1979.

    Contains 2,711 items: daily, weekly, and monthly periodicals in Arabic, English, and French, with subjects ranging from agriculture to archaeology and chemistry.

50 Administration and Development

153. Amin, Galal A. **The Modernization of Poverty.**
Leiden, Netherlands: E.J. Brill, 1974.

Expresses dissatisfaction with Arab economic development, contrary to what is referred to as "over-optimistic literature." Discusses numerous obstacles to future development, particularly the "political factors" that make Arab governments heavily dependent on the good will of some foreign power with regard to foreign policy. Describes economic growth and imbalances; focuses on "new inequalities for old" because economic development neglects the problem of income distribution for most of the Arab countries.

154. Amin, Samir. **The Arab Nation.** Translated by Michael Pallis. London: Zed Press, 1978.

Offers analysis and interpretation of social, political, and economic events in the Arab world before and after the colonial periods. Speculates on possible outcomes of current pressures and movements within the Arab world from a socialist leftist perspective. Will the Arab world be re-united, modernized, rich, and powerful? Or will it be bogged down in an impoverishing traditionalism and prolonged divisions? Predicts the emergence of an invincible revolutionary upsurge by the concentrated, embattled proletariat and vast impoverished peasants against a bankrupt bourgeoisie.

155. Amuzegar, Jahangir. "Ideology and Economic Growth in the Middle East." **The Middle East Journal,** 28, 1 (Winter 1974), 1-9.

Discusses relations between ideology and economic growth in several Middle Eastern countries. Classifies Egypt, Iraq, and Syria under "Arab socialism"; Saudi Arabia and Lebanon under "capitalist" order. Finds no correlation between political ideologies and economic growth; further, finds neither socialist techniques (planning and nationalization) nor the free market mechanism superior in inspiring growth or ensuring the most efficient utilization of resources.

156. Anderson, R.R., R.F. Seibert, and J.G. Wagner. **Politics and Change in the Middle East.** Englewood Cliffs, N.J.: Prentice-Hall, 1982.

   Describes traditional cultures of the Middle East, Islam, Western imperialism, the rise of the state system, modernization, the economic setting, and other aspects of Middle East societies.

157. Anthony, John Duke. **Arab States of the Lower Gulf: People, Politics, Petroleum.** Washington, D.C.: The Middle East Institute, 1975.

   Discusses social, political, and economic conditions in Bahrain, Qatar, and the United Arab Emirates. Develops themes of continuity and change in the Gulf during the period of transition from a simple mode of life to that which is more complex and relatively formalized.

158. Antoun, Richard T. **Low-Key Politics: Local-Level Leadership and Change in the Middle East.** Albany, N.Y.: State University of New York Press, 1979.

   Presents a comparative study of local-level political and change processes in a Jordanian village (Kufr al-Ma). Contends that egalitarianism and solidarity are central ideas not lightly violated, and explicit acts of confrontation and domination are largely out of the question. Describes the presence of a subtle political competition consisting of muted and covert gestures making the function of leadership an art in representing but not commanding or controlling. Describes how local leaders combine traditional patterns of leadership with new sources of power and new attributes of influence.

159. Antoun, Richard, ed., and Iliya Harik. **Rural Politics and Social Change in the Middle East.** Bloomington, Ind., and London: Indiana University Press, 1972.

   Collects papers delivered at a conference on "Rural Politics and Social Change in the Middle East" at Indiana University. Discusses the state of theory and research on the subject and provides seven case studies of local, political, and developmental processes in five Middle Eastern countries.

160. Arkoun, Muhammad. "The Adequacy of Contemporary Islam to the Political, Social, and Economic Development of Northern Africa." **Arab Studies Quarterly,** 4, 1 and 2 (Spring 1982), 34-53.

   Discusses Maghreb's development and its transition from colonial domination to full control of modern means of political, economic, and cultural sovereignty. Links the area's renewal to its geography and history rather than derived from integrationist Islamic or conflictual Occidental models.

161. Ashford, Douglas E. "Succession and Social Change in Tunisia." **International Journal of Middle East Studies,** 4, 1 (January 1973), 23-39.

   Analyzes the situation confronting leaders who undertake rapid development, often by strong state control of the economy and a strongly centered policy. Focuses on the experience of Tunisia and its leadership's decision to revise development plans to protect the political order.

162. Awad, Mohammad H. "The Evolution of Landownership in the Sudan." **The Middle East Journal,** 25, 2 (Spring 1971), 212-228.

   Observes that the military rulers of Sudan in the 1950s did not implement land reform programs as did Egypt, Syria, and Iraq (1952, '58, '59, respectively). Offers a reason: that land reform had taken place in the Sudan nearly half a century before. Chronicles these early changes.

163. Barakat, Halim. "Social and Political Integration in Lebanon: A Case of Social Mosaic." **The Middle East Journal,** 27, 3 (Summer 1973), 301-318.

   Argues for the description of Lebanon as mosaic rather than a pluralistic society. Refers to pluralism as a harmonious relationship between interest, religious, or ethnic groups in a unified social order. Defines a mosaic as comprising groups regulated by checks and balances, but lacking consensus on fundamental issues. Provides seven features of Lebanese society as evidence.

164. Batatu, Hanna. "Some Observations on the Social Roots of Syria's Ruling, Military Group and the Causes for its Dominance." **The Middle East Journal,** 35, 3 (Summer 1981), 331-344.

   States that the present regime's ability to act in concert derives from its common kinship group, which draws strength simultaneous (but in decreasing intensity) from a tribe, a sect-class, and an ecologic-cultural division of the people. Compares Syria to Iraq, which (despite a different balance of ethnic and sectarian forces) displays a similar ruling core, consisting of a minority kinship group of rural origin with army background.

165. Batatu, Hanna. **The Old Social Classes and the Revolutionary Movements of Iraq: A Study of Iraq's Old Landed and Commercial Classes and of its Communists, Ba'thists, and Free Officers.** Princeton, N.J.: Princeton University Press, 1978.

   Examines the ruling system of Iraq after the 1958 revolution. Determines that the most advantaged in the ruling system have been middle-class families who live in the Arab northwestern provincial towns, or who have relatively recently migrated to Baghdad from these towns. Documents how these families, since 1963, have been the principal recruiting ground for decision-makers in government, army, the bureaucracy, and the Ba'th party machine.

166. Bechtold, Peter K. "Military Rule in the Sudan: The First Five Years of Ja'far Numayri." **The Middle East Journal,** 29, 1 (Winter 1975), 16-32.

    Examines the performance of the army coup leaders of the Sudan by concentrating on major issues as perceived by the Numayri regime. Discusses the ways in which the junta attempted to resolve issues, explores its relationships with existing political groups, and compares it with the Abbud regime of 1958-64. Argues that the regime's survival will depend on its willingness to "civilianize" itself or create political institutions outside the military to gain public support.

167. Bechtold, Peter K. "New Attempts at Arab Cooperation: The Federation of Arab Republics, 1971-?" **The Middle East Journal,** 27, 2 (Spring 1973), 152-172.

    Reviews some historical antecedents, major policy considerations, and the viability of the 1971 attempt at greater Arab unity. Concludes that the federation's greatest threats will occur during regime changes in the member states. Barring government upheavals, the federation will be at the mercy of the actors' motivations. Pragmatic domestic considerations may have priority over greater Arab unity. Long-term success will depend on consensus among the political elite and development of citizen loyalty to the federation.

168. Berque, Jacques. **Cultural Expression in Arab Society Today.** Translated by R.W. Stookey. Austin and London: University of Texas Press, 1978.

Reviews images and misconceptions of Arabs in the West. Analyzes various aspects of contemporary Arab society and its culture. Authored by a leading French specialist on the region.

169. Bill, James A. "Class Analysis and Dialectics of Modernization in the Middle East." **International Journal of Middle East Studies,** 3, 4 (October 1972), 417-434.

    Examines stratification by class as an approach to studying political conflict and social change in the Middle East.

170. Bowie, Leland. "Charisma, Weber and Nasir." **Middle East Journal,** 30, 2 (Spring 1976), 141-157.

    Applies Weber's concept of charisma to President Nasir of Egypt and holds the term meaningful if carefully defined. Cautions that--though Nasir was perceived as charismatic by his people--excessive claims should be avoided in the absence of refined techniques of political analysis and survey data.

171. Cantori, Louis J. and Iliya Harik, eds. **Local Politics and Development in the Middle East.** Boulder, Col.: Westview Press, 1984.

    Contains eleven articles discussing the influence of local politics on development in Egypt, Jordan, Lebanon, Syria, Iraq, Tunisia, and North Yemen. Focuses on strategies of rural development, relationships between local and central authorities, and political consequences of roles and positions of such public institutions. Includes items 194, 211, 200, 271.

172. Clements, Frank A. **Oman: The Reborn Land.** New York: Longman, 1980.

    Describes history and geography as well as changes that have taken place since 1970, including the ascendance to power of the current sultan through a British-supported coup and Oman's position as an important exporter of oil.

173. Cole, Donald P. "Pastoral Nomads in a Rapidly Changing Economy: The Case of Saudi Arabia." **Social and Economic Development in the Arab Gulf** (item 241).

    Studies the socio-economic situation of Bedouin tribes and the declining importance of the tribe in a rapidly changing society. Explains that the tribe has suffered in its political stature since the government has begun to administer areas on the basis of localities rather than the traditional tribal divisions.

174. Cooper, Charles A. and Sidney S. Alexander. **Economic Development and Population Growth in the Middle East.** New York: Elsevier, 1972.

    Contains a collection of economic, demographic, and sociological studies financed by the Ford Foundation and implemented jointly by the Rand Corporation and Resources for the Future. Focuses mainly on economic development and population growth in eight Arab countries. Investigates various perspectives and offers statistical data.

175. Cooper, Mark N. **The Transformation of Egypt.** Baltimore: The Johns Hopkins University Press, 1982.

    Focuses on internal pressures and crises that brought the change often referred to as "liberalization." Contends that liberalization is not to be understood as the triumph of Sadat's personal views, but as an outgrowth of the changing relationship of forces among varying political camps. Underlines the beginnings of the shift away from the more doctrinaire socialism under Nasser.

Socio-Political Factors 57

176. Coulson, Noel J. **Commercial Law in the Gulf States: The Islamic Legal Tradition.** London: Graham and Trotman Limited, 1984.

Studies commercial law in the Arab Gulf states within the framework of fundamental principles of Shari'a (Islamic) law. Includes the historical development of commercial contracts. Covers such aspects of contractual relationships as formation, nullity of agreement, dissolution, and freedom of contract.

177. Cunningham, Robert B. "Dimension of Family Loyalty in the Arab Middle East: The Case of Jordan." **The Journal of Developing Areas,** 8, 1 (October 1973), 55-64.

Addresses the process of change in family values as societies move from agrarian to industrially based economies. Focuses on the rate of change in work/job values and social values. Bases inferences on data from Jordan drawn from random samples of students and teachers; makes comparisons with Canadian attitudinal studies.

178. Daghestani, Fakhruddin, Subhi Qasem, and Bassam Saket, eds. **Science and Technology for Development.** Amman, Jordan: The Royal Scientific Society, 1978.

Contains proceedings of Jordan's Science and Technology Policy Conference, Amman, February 1978. Incorporates specialized articles on science, technology, research, and Jordan's socio-economic development during the past twenty-five years. Includes item 122.

179. Deeb, Marius K. and Mary Jane Deeb. **Libya Since the Revolution: Aspects of Social and Political Development.** New York: Praeger Publishers, 1982.

Administration and Development

Analyzes social change and describes the upheavals of oil and political revolution. Addresses five separate aspects of society: urban demographic growth, educational development, the roles of women and of Islam, and social structure. Provides much related data.

180. Dekmejian, R. Hrair. "Marx, Weber and the Egyptian Revolution." **The Middle East Journal**, 30, 2 (Spring 1976), 158-172.

    Examines the impact of Nasir on Egypt through the use of Marxist and Weberian models. Concludes that, in the absence of criteria or performance standards, Nasir must be compared with his political peers. Rates Nasir at the top.

181. Devlin, John F. **Syria, Modern State in an Ancient Land.** Boulder, Col.: Westview/Croom Helm, 1983.

    Profiles modern Syria, its history, environment, change in life style, sectarian communities, and rise of urbanization. Analyzes agricultural development and Syria's approach to planning since 1970. Chronicles the remaking of the economy along socialist lines.

182. Eickelman, Dale F. "Kings and People: Oman's State Consultative Council." **The Middle East Journal,** 38, 1 (Winter, 1984), 51-71.

    Posits the issue of survivability of monarchist regimes in the Middle East in terms of pressures for greater popular participation in decision-making. Views Oman's state consultative council as an institution to alleviate such pressure. Addresses the concept of the council, its beginnings, decrees, and transitional nature. Concludes that Oman is at the crossroads of increasing internal security or providing for long-term stability by effectively widening domestic consultation and participation in decision-making.

183. El-Bushra, El-Sayed. "Some Demographic Indicators for Kartoum Conurbation, Sudan." **Middle Eastern Studies,** 15, 3 (October 1979), 295-309.

 Studies growth, structure, and distribution of population within the urban complex of three cities--Khartoum, Khartoum North, and Omdurman--the triple capital of Sudan and its most dominant area culturally, economically, and demographically.

184. El-Fathaly, Omar I. and Monte Palmer. "Opposition to Change in Rural Libya." **International Journal of Middle East Studies,** 11, 2 (April 1980), 247-261.

 Examines empirically the assumption made by most development theorists that traditional elites are unalterably opposed to rapid social and economic change. Supports the hypothesis with results from study in Libya.

185. El-Rashidi, Galal. **The Arabs and the World of the Seventies.** New Delhi, India: Vikas Publishing House, 1977.

 Discusses the role of the Arab states in terms of oil as a weapon and a means for comprehensive development on the regional and international levels. Focuses on Indo-Arab collaboration, the Arabs, and Third World development. Indicates that the Arabs have played a substantial role in international relations.

*   Entelis, John P. "Elite Political Culture and Socialization in Algeria: Tensions and Discontinuities." Cited as item 97.

186. Erb, Richard D., ed. "The Arab Oil-Producing States of the Gulf: Political and Economic Developments." **AEI Foreign Policy and Defense Review,** 2, 3 & 4, 1980.

60 **Administration and Development**

Contains fifteen papers written by specialists on each of the Gulf countries: Saudi Arabia, Iraq, Kuwait, United Arab Emirates, Bahrain, and Qatar. Divides discussions on each country into two subjects: socio-political developments and economic developments.

187. Esposito, John L., ed. **Islam and Development: Religion and Sociopolitical Change.** Syracuse, N.Y.: Syracuse University Press, 1980.

    Contains a collection of articles that deal with the interaction of Islamic traditional with modernization. Concludes that the role of Islam in sociopolitical change must be studied primarily on a country-by-country basis to avoid stereotypical and outmoded presuppositions.

188. Farah, Tawfic E. "Group Affiliations of University Students in the Arab Middle East-Kuwait." **Political Behavior in the Arab States** (item 189).

    Examines the order of group affiliations among undergraduate students from 13 Arab states at Kuwait University in October 1977. Reports that the random sample of 420 men and women ranked religion first, followed by family, citizenship, national origin, and political ideology.

189. Farah, Tawfic E., ed. **Political Behavior in the Arab States.** Boulder, Col.: Westview Press, 1983.

    Compiles fifteen articles on political behavior in Arab countries, particularly such aspects of political behavior as affiliations, family, religion, social class, socialization and alienation, values, societal development, education, and change. Includes items 188, 233, 234, and 263.

190. Fenelon, K.G. **The United Arab Emirates: An Economic and Social Survey.** London: Longman Group Limited, 1973.

Socio-Political Factors

Describes historical background, oil resources, agriculture and fishing, industrial development, trade, money and banking, national education, health, housing, and other aspects of UAE national development.

191. Fleming, Quentin W. **A Guide to Doing Business on the Arabian Peninsula.** New York: AMACOM-A Division of American Management Association, 1981.

    Provides information to guide Americans doing business in the selected Arab countries of Bahrain, Saudi Arabia, Kuwait, Oman, Qatar, the two Yemens, and the United Arab Emirates. Gives an overview of culture, the legal system, and contract laws. Describes the business climate and the economic viability of the Arabian Peninsula. Lists fifty points in the form of basic facts and recommendations.

192. Garrison, Jean L. "Public Assistance in Egypt: An Ideological Analysis." **The Middle East Journal,** 32, 3 (Summer 1978), 279-290.

    Investigates the history of public assistance, emphasizing the interaction of political change and program development and implementation. Finds that, despite shifts in state ideology, public assistance programs have not changed sufficiently to become a tool to legitimize the regime by demonstrating its humanitarian and progressive nature.

193. Golimo, Frank Ralph. "Patterns of Libyan National Identity." **The Middle East Journal,** 24, 3 (Summer 1970), 338-352.

    Compares the experience of two decades of independent nationhood in Libya with the frequently stated assumption that authority and sovereignty have run ahead of self-conscious national identity and cultural integration. Concludes that preponderant historic, legal, linguistic, and cultural evidence indicates that the bases for Libyan national identity were well established before independence.

194. Gubser, Peter. "New Institutions and Processes in a Traditional Setting: Examples from Al-Karak, Jordan." **Local Politics and Development in the Middle East** (item 171).

    Studies success and failure of new institutions in a traditional setting--the case study being the municipality of Al-Karak and the agricultural cooperative. Describes the work of the two institutions in terms development, their nature, their functions and appropriateness, and the central government's commitment to their role in Al-Karak.

* Gubser, Peter. "The Zu'ama of Zahlah: The Current Situation in a Lebanese Town." Cited as item 35.

195. Gulick, John. **The Middle East: An Anthropological Perspective.** Frederick, Md.: University Press of America, 1983.

    Emphasizes the importance of environment in understanding modern Middle East life. Offers a cultural and social anthropological perspective.

196. Haddad, Hassan S. and Basheer K. Nijim, eds. **The Arab World: A Handbook.** Wilmette, Ill.: Medina Press, 1978.

    Provides a comprehensive description of the geography, history, population, economy, major urban centers, and other aspects of life in each Arab country.

197. Hahn, Lorna. "Tunisian Political Reform: Procrastination and Progress." **The Middle East Journal,** 26, 4 (Autumn 1972), 405-414.

Addresses the questions: Who will succeed Habib Bourguiba? How should the successor be chosen? How should the successor run a government no longer synonymous with Bourguiba? Submits two corollaries: Bourguiba's successor should be chosen institutionally rather than personally and must have fewer absolute powers.

198. Helms, Christine Moss. **The Cohesion of Saudi Arabia: Evolution of Political Identity.** Baltimore, Md.: The Johns Hopkins University Press, 1981.

    Deals with the political development of Saudi Arabia as a sovereign state with fixed boundaries and territorial loyalties. Discusses the use of Islam as a legitimizing force for expansion and control over areas beyond original domain of the ruling family.

199. Hermassi, Elbaki. **Leadership and National Development in North Africa.** Berkeley, Calif.: University of California Press, 1972.

    Discusses issues confronting national societies in the process of transformation. Identifies such issues as national integration, institutional competence, economic development, and distributive justice. Examines emerging patterns of leadership (and the cohesion of these elites) in Morocco, Algeria, and Tunisia.

200. Hinnebusch, Raymond A. "Syria: The Role of Ideology and Party Organization in Local Development." **Local Politics and Development in the Middle East** (item 171).

    Discusses politics and development strategies in Syria, stressing mobilization and development at the base (of the party) and the consequences of Ba'th development strategies. Analyzes the development of bureaucracy and techno-administrative cadres.

201. Hinnebusch, Raymond A. "Syria Under the Ba'th: State Formation in a Fragmented Society." **Arab Studies Quarterly,** 4, 3 (Summer 1982), 177-199.

Examines the weaknesses and strengths of the Ba'th regime. "Overall, the Ba'th authoritarian-populist model has proven much less effective than its architects hoped."

* Hinnebusch, Raymond A. "Children of the Elite: Political Attitudes of the Westernized Bourgeoisie in Contemporary Egypt." Cited as item 107.

202. Hinnebusch, Raymond A. "Local Politics in Syria: Organization and Mobilization in Four Village Cases." **The Middle East Journal,** 30, 1 (Winter 1976), 1-24.

Studies organizational and mobilizational performance of the Ba'th regime. Focuses on local-level linkages, the key to mass mobilization. Describes the regime's efforts to penetrate the village organization through local recruitment; a system that helped undermine attachments to the regime's traditional rivals, legitimize its rule in the countryside, and build peasant support.

203. Hudson, Michael C., ed. **The Arab Future: Critical Issues.** Washington, D.C.: Center for Contemporary Arab Studies-Georgetown University, 1979.

Analyzes problems and prospects of social, economic, cultural, and political development in the Arab world by Arab and American experts on these subjects. Offers perspectives on various issues, such as democracy in the Arab world, economic development, social integration, educational trends, and aspects of cultural change.

204. Hudson, Michael C. **Arab Politics: The Search for Legitimacy.** New Haven: Yale University Press, 1977.

Describes the current malaise in Arab politics, indicated by instability, cynicism, inefficiency, corruption, and repression; identifies it as the result (and, through feedback, the cause) of insufficient legitimacy accorded by the people to ruling structures, ideologies, and leaders. Explains the problem as product of a complex set of historical, social, and cultural conditions, aggravated by imperialism and modernization.

205. Humphreys, R. Stephen. "Islam and Political Values in Saudi Arabia, Egypt and Syria." **The Middle East Journal**, 33, 1 (Winter 1979), 1-19.

Attempts to define a model of cultural behavior in which a set of religiously identified conceptions can create effective political norms. Identifies three elementary religio-political orientations available to contemporary Muslim statesmen in ideal terms: fundamentalism (Saudi Arabia), modernism (Egypt), and secularism (Syria).

206. Ibrahim, Ibrahim, ed. **Arab Resources: The Transformation of a Society.** Center for Contemporary Arab Studies, Georgetown University, Washington, D.C., and London: Croom Helm, 1983.

A collection of papers on human and financial resources, energy, public administration, higher education, political development, and other economic and social developments of the Arab society. Offers cogent analysis of aspects of underdevelopment in the Arab world by highly qualified American, British, and Arab specialists on the region. Especially relevant are pieces by Issawi, Sayigh, and El-Fathaly and Chackerian. Includes items 30 and 127.

207. Ibrahim, Saad Eddin. **The New Arab Social Order: A Study of the Social Impact of Oil Wealth.** Boulder, Col.: Westview Press, 1982.

Examines the impact of oil on Arab society from social and economic perspectives, including the

Administration and Development

effect on inter-Arab labor migration. Focuses on the causes of Egyptian labor migration and its consequences for oil-producing countries, particularly Saudi Arabia.

208. Islami, A.R.S. **The Political Economy of Saudi Arabia.** Seattle: University of Washington Press, 1984.

    Discusses development activities, structure of government, change, potential discontent, and erosion of authority in Saudi Arabia. Produced by the Department of Near Eastern Studies of the University of Washington.

209. Ismael, Jacqueline S. **Kuwait: Social Change in Historical Perspective.** Syracuse University Press, 1982.

    Applies the dependency theory to a case study of social change in Kuwait. Argues that sustaining a primary-commodity export (oil) economy, dependent on importing foreign capital equipment, creates and perpetuates underdevelopment.

210. Ismael, Jacqueline S. "Social Policy and Social Change: The Case of Iraq." **Arab Studies Quarterly,** 2, 3 (Summer 1980), 235-248.

    Describes ideological influences (Ba'th Party constitution) on "social policy" and structured priorities of Iraq, focusing on constitutional changes between 1970 and 1974.

211. Joseph, Suad. "Local-Level Politics and Development in Lebanon: The View from Borj Hammoud." **Local Politics and Development in the Middle East** (item 171).

    Discusses social, political, and economic conditions of ethnic groups living in Borj Hammoud as refugees or victims of regional and international wars. Indicates that local-level development strategies emerged as a result of local, national, and international help. However, the reality of development to these people meant the advancement of "family patron-client or ethnic-sect groupings."

212. Jureidini, Paul A. and R.D. McLaurin. **Jordan: The Impact of Social Change on the Role of the Tribe.** New York: Praeger, 1984.

Analyzes social change and its impact on the tribal structure, considered a major force for stability in the country. Examines the tribal system and its weakening as a result of the demographic, educational, and technological changes of past two decades, with special interest in implications for internal stability.

213. Kay, Shirley. **The Bedouin.** New York: Crance, Russak and Company, Inc., 1978.

Discusses the social and economic development of Bedouin tribes in the Arab countries, including the desert environment and economy, tribal and social structure, and the role of the Bedouin in the modern Arab state. Emphasizes the rich and glorious past of the Bedouin tribes; describes their progress in the modern state and their representation in significant positions in the army, civil service, and the professions of medicine, engineering, and law.

214. Kedourie, Elie, ed. **The Middle Eastern Economy: Studies in Economics and Economic History.** London: Frank Cass and Company Limited, 1977.

Contains seven articles on Middle Eastern economic systems and economic history (includes Iran and Turkey). Discusses nineteenth century Egyptian population, the revolution of 1919, new directions in the economy, and the emergence of local special economic interests. Includes items 116 and 317.

215. Keilany, Ziad. "Land Reform in Syria." **Middle Eastern Studies,** 16, 3 (October 1980), 209-224.

Discusses the slow but favorable impact of land reform on the countryside. Identifies specific results such as government commitment to the redistribution of income in favor of peasants and the emergence of cooperatives for the benefit of small landholders. Indicates that reform does not seem to score highly on the productivity test. Contends, however, that reform plays a critical role in integrating the rural areas with the rest of the country.

216. Kelidar, Abbas, ed. **The Integration of Modern Iraq.** New York: St. Martin's Press, 1979.

Contains a collection of essays by a number of Iraqi and British scholars on the political, economic, and social aspects of the contemporary Iraqi system and its colonial legacy. Focuses on the evolution of the constitutional parliamentary system of government, social conflict and its resolution, pan-Arab nationalist aspiration, the new political elites, civil-military relations, and the impact of oil revenues on the economy.

217. Kerr, Malcolm H. and El Sayed Yassin, eds. **Rich and Poor States in the Middle East: Egypt and the New Arab Order.** Boulder, Col.: Westview Press, and Cairo: American University in Cairo Press, 1982.

The outcome of a Ford Foundation-sponsored study coordinated by the editors. Deals with change and development in Arab societies, particularly in economics and politics. Egyptian and American authors provide analyses of Egypt and Egyptian perspectives of other Arab societies.

218. Khader, Bichara. "The Social Impact of the Transfer of Technology to the Arab World." **Arab Studies Quarterly,** 4, 4 (Summer 1982), 226-241.

Examines technology transfer--a nebulous concept--in terms of development policy, urbanization, elitism, and cultural values. Warns that "technology is not a traveller without luggage." One cannot adopt Western techniques and preserve Oriental cultural purity.

219. Khalifa, Mohammed Ali. **The United Arab Emirates: Unity in Fragmentation.** Boulder, Col.: Westview Press, 1979.

   Discusses the Union of the Emirates, emphasizing political and administrative aspects: federal structure, legislative powers, cabinet structure, and civil service growth. Reviews some phases of social and economic development.

220. Khoury, Enver M. **The Operational Capability of the Lebanese Political System.** Beirut, Lebanon: Catholic Press, 1972.

   Describes the Lebanese political system, its growth, and the environment within which it operates. Details the confessional system, processes of national versus communal socialization, and "primordial leadership groupings" that influence and complicate government decision-making. Asserts that confessionalism "appears to be the best path for stability and equilibrium in a uniquely fragmented communal society." Contains extensive footnotes, numerous diagrams and tables, and a comprehensive index.

221. Khoury, Nabeel A. "The Pragmatic Trend in Inter-Arab Politics." **The Middle East Journal,** 36, 3 (Summer 1982), 374-387.

   States that today's main Arab political groups spring from one of three philosophies: "Islamic revivalist," "radical reformist," or "traditional monarchist." Describes how the latter two emerged in the '50s and '60s, struggling with issues of (1) preferred political system, (2) superpower alliance, and (3) Palestine policy. Submits that, in the '70s, strategic considerations injected a pragmatic element in the relationship between Arab regimes; the gap between "radical reformist," and "traditional monarchist" narrowed on the first two issues. Palestine policy remains problematic, providing fuel for the third force: "Islamic revivalism."

222. Khoury, Nabeel A. "The National Consultative Council of Jordan: A Study in Legislative Development." **International Journal of Middle East Studies**, 13, 4 (November 1981), 427-439.

 Examines the National Consultative Council of Jordan, established in 1978 as an interim replacement for the elected legislature (which was dismissed in 1976).

223. Khuri, Fuad I. **Tribe and State in Bahrain: The Transformation of Social and Political Authority in an Arab State.** Chicago: The University of Chicago Press, 1980.

 Presents a case study of Bahrain in terms of political development and the socio-economic transformation brought about by colonialism and oil.

224. Lawson, Fred H. "Social Origins of Inflation in Contemporary Egypt." **Arab Studies Quarterly**, 7, 1 (Winter 1985), 36-55.

 Relates inflation in contemporary Egypt to political and social factors over monetary or economic ones. Argues that serious outbreaks of inflation have occurred whenever serious political challenges to the ruling coalition have arisen and prevented it from carrying out "a definitive transfer of wealth."

* Leila, Ali, El Sayed Yassin, and Monte Palmer. "Apathy, Values, Incentives and Development: The Case of the Egyptian Bureaucracy." Cited as item 47

225. Levy, Victor. "Cropping Pattern, Mechanization, Child Labor, and Fertility Behavior in a Farming Community: Rural Egypt." **Economic Development and Cultural Change**, 33, 4 (July 1985), 777-791.

Examines cross-sectional evidence on differential fertility in rural Egypt, focusing on the relationship between structural and policy changes in agriculture and fertility and children's schooling. Concludes that variation in labor contributions from children has an appreciable effect on farmers' attitudes toward family size. Indicates that cotton labor intensity is a motivating factor for large families, as mechanization and taxes on cotton growers discourage the use of child labor, reduce birthrate, and increase school enrollment.

226. Liebesny, Herbert J. "Judicial Systems in the Near and Middle East: Evolutionary Development and Islamic Revival." **The Middle East Journal**, 37, 2 (Spring 1983), 202-217.

Examines three dominant trends in legal development: (1) strict application of Islamic principles in legislation and adjudication, giving the religion a constitutional foundation (as in Iran and Pakistan); (2) restraint from changes in basic legal and judicial system (Egypt); (3) dual systems in which shari'a courts apply religious laws while special commissions or courts apply statutory rules (Saudi Arabia, and Afghanistan before the communist coup).

227. Looney, Robert E. **Saudi Arabia's Development Potential.** Lexington, Mass.: D.C. Heath and Company, 1982.

Presents information on Saudi Arabia's development potential, including physical environment, natural resources, political institutions, economics, taxes, monetary and banking policy, development plans, population growth, agriculture, industrial development and policies, the government's industrial program, and so forth.

228. Lutfiyya, Abdulla M. and Charles W. Churchill, eds. **Readings in Arab Middle Eastern Societies and Cultures.** The Hague, Netherlands: Mouton, 1970.

Contains fifty-three papers on various aspects of Arab societies: social organization, culture, social institutions and cultural change, social stratification, the family, urban life, and the role of communication. Offers contributions by Middle Eastern and Western experts representing various social science disciplines and perspectives.

229. Mahmoud, Fatima Babiker. **Sudanese Bourgeoisie: Vanguard of Development?** London: Zed Press, 1984.

Discusses the potential role of the upper economic classes in Sudan in revolutionary change and their alliance with foreign capital. Indicates that the bourgeoisie and landed agricultural capitalists had no major confrontations with the colonialist system and that intellectuals were the core of the nationalist movement. Points out that the bourgeois parties handed over the rule in the post-independence period to reactionary faction of the military as an alternative to a parliamentary system.

230. Mansfield, Peter. **The Arab World.** New York: Thomas Y. Crowell Co., 1976.

Provides a comprehensive review of the Arabs--past and present--with specific discussion of individual Arab states today (the Gulf states, Oman, the two Yemens, Saudi Arabia, Syria, Lebanon, Iraq, Jordan, Sudan, Egypt, Libya, Tunisia, Algeria, Morocco). Concludes with a discussion of the Arabs as viewed by Western eyes as well as the Arabs' own perceptions of issues, problems, and relationships with the West--their former colonizers.

*   Marr, Phebe Ann. "Iraq's Leadership Dilemma: A Study in Leadership Trends, 1948-1968." Cited as item 50.

231. Mason, John P. "Qadhdhafi's 'Revolution' and Change in a Libyan Oasis Community." **The Middle East Journal**, 36, 3 (Summer 1982), 319-335.

     Describes social, economic, and political conditions of the Berber oasis Augila (Awjila) in 1968-70 and changes observed in '77-78. Also discusses the more saliant changes in oasis life in light of Khadafy's socialist Islamic policy, embodied in his **Green Book (al-Kitab al-Akhdar).**

232. Mason, John Paul. "Petroleum Development and the Reactivation of Traditional Structure in a Libyan Oasis Community." **Economic Development and Cultural Change**, 26, 4 (July 1978), 763-776.

     Describes change in Augila oasis society since the petroleum-extraction industry moved to the region in the early 1960s. Modernizing forces not only transform and sometimes maintain indigenous features of traditional society, but also beckon to the past to recall once-viable structures.

233. Melikian, Levon H. and J.S. Al-Easa. "Oil and Social Change in the Gulf." **Political Behavior in the Arab States** (item 189).

     Reports the findings of a study conducted among college students in Qatar between 1974-78. Finds that young married couples prefer to have fewer children than their parents did; women prefer to share in family leadership; and educated women prefer to delay marriage.

234. Melikian, Levon H. and Lutfy N. Diab. "Group Affiliations of University Students in the Arab Middle East." **Political Behavior in the Arab States** (item 189).

74 Administration and Development

Seeks to determine the order of group affiliations among Arab students in the Middle East and the influence on the order of affiliation of sex, religion, political orientation, and background. Examines the effect of social threat or a revolution on affiliation among a sample of Arab students from the American University of Beirut. Ranks the family first, followed by ethnic group, religion, citizenship, and political party.

235. Musa, Omar el-Hag. "Reconciliation, Rehabilitation and Development Efforts in Southern Sudan." **The Middle East Journal**, 27, 1 (Winter 1973), 1-6.

Declares that reconciliation and development in Sudan is contingent on a program of social reform and economic activity for the south, as well as a political solution between the central government and the Southern leadership-in-exile. Argues that long-term help in developing transport systems, agricultural production, communications, and modest industries is crucial for the economic solution.

236. Nakhleh, Emile A. **Bahrain: Political Development in a Modernizing Society.** Lexington, Mass.: Lexington Books, 1976.

Presents a case study of nation-building in Bahrain, especially concerning properties of the political system, the educational system, citizen participation in government, economic development, and related aspects of the government system. Uses systems analysis approach, focusing on what the author calls the crisis of nation-building: identity, integration, penetration, participation, and distribution. Offers numerous statistical tables and much primary-source empirical data.

237. Nakhleh, Emile A. "Political Participation and the Constitutional Experiments in the Arab Gulf: Bahrain and Qatar." **Social and Economic Development in the Arab Gulf** (item 141).

Discusses some prospects of popular political participation in the future of the two countries under family rule. Contends that long-term stability in Arab Gulf societies requires internal political reform, including popular participation in government affairs.

238. Naur, Maja. **Social and Organizational Change in Libya.** Uppsala, Sweden: The Scandinavian Institute of African Studies, 1982.

   Deals with the organization of political power in Libya and the structure of the manufacturing sector. Evaluates the organization of government and the economy in terms of serving the regime's political goals.

239. Niblock, Tim, ed. **State, Society and Economy in Saudi Arabia.** New York: St. Martin's Press, 1982.

   A collection of fourteen articles by scholars of various interests and perspectives who examine recent ideological, religious and political development in Saudi Arabia. Includes articles of special importance on social structure and development, economic and banking changes, and social change after the sudden increase in oil revenues in the 1970s.

240. Niblock, Tim, ed. **Iraq: The Contemporary State.** New York: St. Martin's Press, 1982.

   Contains sixteen articles by Iraqis and Westerners originally presented at a symposium sponsored by the Centers of Arab Gulf States at the Universities of Exeter and Basra. Covers social and economic change, oil, agriculture, progress in education, and change in the status of women.

241. Niblock, Tim, ed. **Social and Economic Development in the Arab Gulf.** New York: St. Martin's Press, and London: Croom Helm, 1980.

Contains twelve articles initially presented to a conference at the University of Exeter, England, 1979. Focuses on Saudi Arabia, Iraq, Kuwait, Oman, Bahrain, Qatar, and the United Arab Emirates. Discusses social, economic, and political development and the challenges it creates. Includes items 90, 173, 237, 256, 412, 418, and 425.

242. Nugent, Jeffrey B. and Theodore H. Thomas. **Bahrain and the Gulf: Past Perspectives and Alternative Futures.** Beckenham, Kent, U.K.: Croom Helm, Provident House, 1985.

    Contains papers resulting from a seminar at the University of Southern California, through formal agreement with the State of Bahrain, on the subject of "Bahrain: After Oil, What?" Covers alternative economic futures, political economy and resource management, and the historical, social and cultural setting.

243. Palmer, Monte, et al. **Survey Research in the Arab World: An Analytical Index.** Cambridgeshire, England: Middle East and North African Studies Press Ltd., 1982.

    Summarizes survey research conducted in the Arab world on political, economic, and social issues. Provides an annotated index of many of the major survey research projects executed in the Arab world.

244. Peterson, John E. **Yemen: The Search for a Modern State.** Baltimore: Johns Hopkins University Press, 1982.

    Studies recent political change and the dynamics of development in North Yemen based on certain elements (tribes, aristocrats, <u>ulama</u>, etc.). Draws from previously untapped sources, such as British Public Record Office and U.S. National Archives.

245. Peterson, J.E. "Tribes and Politics in Eastern Arabia." **The Middle East Journal,** 31 (Summer 1977), 297-312.

Explores the evolution of tribal authority structures and politics in Eastern Arabia (i.e., Bahrain, Qatar, United Arab Emirates, Oman). Discusses the traditional tribal system, tribal components in the development of the modern state, and the erosion of tribal society. Concludes that ruling families will remain dominant for some time despite pressures for broader political participation from radical elements, professional and social groups, and organized labor.

246. Plascov, Avi. **Security in the Persian Gulf: Modernization, Political Development and Stability.** Totowa, N.J.: Allanheld, Osmun and Company, 1982.

Discusses development in the Arab Gulf states, emphasizing effects of rapid modernization on tribalism. Describes changing political priorities, rapid expansion of the education system, and Islam's reaction to such modernization. Also deals with political-military relations, notably among Saudi Arabia, the United Arab Emirates, and Iraq.

247. Polk, William R. **The Arab World.** Cambridge, Mass.: Harvard University Press, 1980.

First published in 1965, this expanded and revised edition analyzes the historical and cultural background of the Arab people. Focuses on the economy of the Arab world and "social change and the new man" in chapter six only; the primary focus is on foreign relations. Special reference is given to relations with the United States.

248. Quandt, William. **Saudi Arabia in the 1980s.** Washington, D.C.: Brookings Institution, 1981.

78 Administration and Development

An overview of Saudi Arabia's relations with the Arab world and other countries, particularly the United States. Discusses developments within the Saudi ruling elites, internal dynamics, and oil policy.

249. Rahman, Fazlur. **Islam and Modernity: Transformation of an Intellectual Tradition.** Chicago: The University of Chicago Press, 1982.

Pinpoints failures of the Islamic system of education from medieval history to the present. Suggests a system of guidelines to redirect the intellectual tradition of Islam to restore the position Muslims once held in the development of human civilization.

250. Reid, Donald M. "The Rise of Professions and Professional Organizations in Modern Egypt." **Comparative Studies in Society and History,** 16, 1 (January 1974), 24-57.

Describes the struggle by professional Egyptians to create professional organizations similar to those of Western countries. The first predominantly Egyptian professional syndicate of lawyers was formed in 1912. Medical, press, and engineering syndicates were established during WWII, and the teachers' syndicate in 1955. Discusses the expansion of education after WWII; in 1965 there were 1,633 law graduates and 1,724 engineering graduates, far in excess of what the country could absorb.

251. Roberts, M. Hugh P. **An Urban Profile of the Middle East.** London: Croom Helm, 1979.

Discusses urban development in Middle Eastern societies (Arab and non-Arab). Describes the various economic motivations for change and includes case studies of towns. Envisages continuation of the process of urbanization in the region.

Socio-Political Factors 79

252. Rodinson, Maxime. **The Arabs.** Translated by Arthur Goldhammer. Chicago: University of Chicago Press, 1981.

　　Attempts to "characterize the Arabs, to describe them" and "to sketch their portrait as a group." Author is a leading French scholar concerned about "demythification" of the subject. Defines the Arab people as those who (1) speak a variant of Arabic and regard it as their natural language, (2) regard as their patrimony the history and cultural traits of the people that has called itself and that others have called Arab, for whom one of those cultural traits has been, since the seventh century, belief in the Muslim religion (which is not limited exclusively to this people), and (3) claim Arab identity, possess an awareness of being Arab.

253. Rugh, William. "Emergence of a New Middle Class in Saudi Arabia." **The Middle East Journal,** 27, 1 (Winter, 1973), 7-20.

　　Examines the "new" Saudi Arabian middle class's influence on the government in areas of economics, society, and politics. Describes this class as the first group to rely on secular, nontraditional knowledge for its positions, free from automatic assignment of class status based on family ties. Speculates that the "new" middle class, still numerically small but expected to increase in size and clout, may clash with conservative traditional forces.

254. Sadik, Muhammad T. and William P. Snavely, eds. **Bahrain, Qatar, and the United Arab Emirates.** Lexington, Mass.: D.C. Heath, 1972.

　　Studies Bahrain, Qatar, and the seven city-states that constitute the United Arab Emirates. Focuses on economic, social, political, and administrative developments in these systems. Provides statistics and background materials. Includes item 67.

255. Said, Edward W. **Orientalism.** New York: Vintage Books, 1979.

Examines assumptions, premises, and images conveyed and perpetrated by Western scholars about the Orient (particularly Arabs and Muslims) during and before the colonial era. Evaluates critically this academic tradition, referred to as "Orientalism" and including writers among whom are political theorists, economists, and imperial administrators as well as poets, novelists, and philosophers.

256. Sakr, Naomi. "Federalism in the United Arab Emirates: Prospects and Regional Implications." **Social and Economic Development in the Arab Gulf** (item 241).

Discusses prospects of federalism among the seven emirates of the United Arab Emirates in the Gulf region, including the evolution of federal machinery, issues related to defense, immigration, finance, and other aspects of the union.

257. Salem, Elie A. "Lebanon's Political Maze: The Search for Peace in a Turbulent Land." **The Middle East Journal,** 33, 4 (Autumn 1979), 444-463.

Examines problems of the Lebanese leadership in attempting to unify diverse religious and political groups into a cohesive political whole. Emphasizes the need for political equality among the actors, enhancement of national identity and loyalty, and rebuilding a national army.

258. Sanger, Richard H. "Libya: Conclusions on an Unfinished Revolution." **The Middle East Journal,** 29, 4 (Autumn 1975), 409-417.

Reviews the achievements of the Libyan revolution over the first five years. Holds that most of its successes were internal and economic; most of its failures external and political.

259. Sardar, Ziauddin. **Technology and Development in the Muslim World.** London: Croom Helm, 1977.

    Discusses the Muslim view of science, cultural and ethnic dimensions of development, and other aspects of the developmental process.

260. Savory, Roger M. "The Religious Environment in the Middle East." **Business and the Middle East: Threats and Prospects** (item 367).

    Discusses the religious environment through historical perspectives. Focuses on Islam as religion, faith, law, tradition, state, and empire. Discusses the impact of the West, beginnings of modernization, and the Muslim intellectual response to Western ideas.

261. Stone, Russell A. and John Simmons, ed. **Change in Tunisia.** Albany, N.Y.: State University of New York Press, 1976.

    Contains a collection of papers on Tunisia, with discussions of a wide range of subjects. Covers emancipation of women, family planning, social mobility, as well as development in general.

262. Stookey, Robert W. **South Yemen: A Marxist Republic in Arabia.** Boulder, Col.: Westview Press, 1982.

    Studies South Yemen, its history, land, people, and colonial rule by the British. Deals, most importantly, with development of the society after independence under Marxist ideology, management of the economy, and the development of political and administrative structures.

263. Suleiman, Michael W. "Values and Societal Development: Education and Change in Nasser's Egypt." **Political Behavior in the Arab States** (item 189).

Administration and Development

Studies the effect of the Egyptian Revolution, 1952, on values, change, and development. Concludes that Nasser's coup was not revolutionary in the realm of values and attitudes of the Egyptian masses, as Egypt has remained a traditionally oriented society.

264. Sutcliffe, Claud R. "The East Ghor Canal Project: A Case Study of Refugee Resettlement, 1961-1966." **The Middle East Journal**, 27, 4 (Autumn 1973), 471-482.

Compares project with nonproject Jordanian farmers in terms of farming methods, land tenure patterns, productivity, income levels, standard of living, and concern with the Palestine problem. Finds East Ghor Canal Project successful, but crucial lack of land reform has prevented the farmer from realizing any economic benefits.

265. Szyliowicz, Joseph S. "The Prospects for Scientific and Technological Development in Saudi Arabia." **International Journal of Middle East Studies**, 10, 3 (August 1979), 355-371.

Discusses difficulties faced in the development of science and technology in Saudi Arabia and the Arab world in general: lack of scientific and technological infrastructure, dependency on external sources, lack of direction that would permit institutionalization, and absence of policy that could lead to needed transformations.

266. Taylor, Alan R. "The Euro-Arab Dialogue: Quest for an Interregional Partnership." **The Middle East Journal**, 32, 4 (Autumn 1978), 429-443.

Recognizes the basic interdependence of the European community and the Arab world on petroleum resources and the transfer of technology. Addresses the impediments to closer working relations in political and economic spheres.

Socio-Political Factors 83

267. Tibi, Bassam. "Political Freedom in the Arab Societies." **Arab Studies Quarterly,** 6, 3 (Summer 1984), 222-227.

   Discusses political freedom lacking as a democratic value (a system of participation of the members of a society at all levels) in the majority of Arab countries. States that a system of structural and institutional frameworks is essential when a state devoid of societal control monopolizes almost all facilities.

268. Tibi, Bassam. "The Renewed Role of Islam in the Political and Social Development of the Middle East." **The Middle East Journal,** 37, 1 (Winter, 1983), 3-13.

   Examines Islam's re-emergence in the political realm from its previous strictly normative role. Attempts to explain the problem of the reintroduction of religious elements into Middle East politics and subsequent impact on the solution of urgent social and economic problems.

269. Tuma, Elias H. "The Rich and the Poor in the Middle East." **The Middle East Journal,** 34, 4 (Autumn 1980), 413-437.

   Suggests that certain historical and environmental conditions have fostered inequality, while ideological and institutional constraints have reduced individual choice. Addresses the nature and magnitude of inequality between and within countries, proposes measures to reduce it, and examines opposing forces.

270. Turner, Bryan S. "The Middle Classes and Entrepreneurship in Capitalist Development." **Arab Studies Quarterly,** 1, 2 (Spring 1979), 113-134.

   Critiques the argument that entrepreneurship is causally important for the emergence of a capitalist production. Rejects the thesis that the missing middle class may explain the relatively tardy industrialization of the Middle East.

271. Tutwiler, Richard. "Taawun Mahwit: A Case Study of a Local Development Association in Highland Yemen." **Local Politics and Development in the Middle East** (item 171).

Describes the evolution of the Development Cooperative--locally known as Taawun Mahwit--in the Yemen Arab Republic. Describes the role of the cooperative movement in the social organizations of Al-Mahwit town and in terms of the central government policies and goals of national development.

272. Vandewalle, Dirk. "Bourguiba, Charismatic Leadership and the Tunisian One-Party System." **The Middle East Journal,** 34, 2 (Spring 1980), 149-159.

Studies the Tunisian democratic/autocratic political system in light of Bourguiba's mixture of political ideology and personal domination. Concludes that Bourguiba's charisma has had a positive historic role in Tunisia, but his retention of power has prevented the development to a truly political society. Greater political participation may depend on the development of workers' unions.

273. Waltz, Susan E. "Antidotes for a Social Malaise: Alienation, Efficiency, and Participation in Tunisia." **Comparative Politics,** 14, 2 (January 1982), 127-147.

Expresses dissatisfaction with most studies of modernization and development that focus on, "How do we modernize?" rather than on the consequences of modernization. Gives attention to a little-asked question in the literature: "What happens to individuals caught in the throes of intense social change?"

274. Wai, Dunstan M., ed. **The Southern Sudan: The Problem of National Integration.** London: Frank Cass and Company Limited, 1973.

   Contains nine specialized articles on the southern Sudan and its problems. Contends that north and south regions are culturally different, each having its distinct historical developments. Discusses the failed efforts of integration into one entity under the colonial system, which has led to the current crisis.

275. Waterbury, John. **The Egypt of Nasser and Sadat.** Princeton University Press, 1983.

   Discusses the political leadership of the country under each regime. Analyzes the emergence of the public sector and its growth and power in the economy. Deals with political and economic order, reform attempts, and governing elites' actions and attitudes.

276. Waterbury, John. **The Commander of the Faithful: The Moroccan Political Elite: A Study in Segmented Politics.** New York: Columbia University Press, 1970.

   Proclaimed as the best volume in English on Morocco and its segmental power structure. Writes from the viewpoint of tension management, conflict regulation, and shifts in interlocking factions of commercial, religious, and regional groups and alliances.

277. Weinbaum, Marvin G. "Egypt's _Infitah_ and the Politics of U.S. Economic Assistance." **Middle Eastern Studies,** 21, 2 (April 1985), 207-222.

Examines the Egyptian economic policy of liberalization (infitah) and the American aid relationship under the Mubarak regime. Criticisms of the liberalization policy increased as evidence mounted of corruption during the Sadat period, resulting in "some romanticization of the values and goals of socialism." Recognizes some subtle economic changes introduced by Mubarak without openly renouncing the infitah policy. Contends that Egypt has no immediate or practical substitute for American financial assistance.

278. Witty, Cathie J. **Mediation and Society: Conflict Management in Lebanon.** New York: Academic Press, 1980.

Presents a conceptual analysis of mediation in a society characterized by political and cultural distance from the law. Studies a Lebanese village in the Biqa Valley, providing comparative analysis with an American urban environment. Covers family organization, conflict management, police and courts, and intermediation.

279. Wolfe, Ronald G., ed. **The United States, Arabia, and the Gulf.** Washington, D.C.: Center for Contemporary Arab Studies, Georgetown University, 1980.

Contains a collection of articles discussing political and strategic matters such as superpower rivalry in the Gulf region, security, stability, and tensions. Deals with aspects of economic integration, change, and development. Includes item 150.

*   Wright, Peter. "Organizational Behavior in Islamic Firms." Cited as item 73.

280. Zahlan, Antoine B. "Constraints on the Acquisition of Technology." **Issues in Development: The Arab Gulf States** (item 426).

Socio-Political Factors

Discusses constraints on acquisition of technology such as manpower shortages, deficiencies in educational systems, and lack of experience by personnel in institutions concerned with such acquisition.

281. Zartman, William, ed., et al. **Political Elites in Arab North Africa: Morocco, Algeria, Tunisia, Libya and Egypt.** New York: Longman, Inc., 1982.

    Attempts to delineate political change in five Arab countries by studying their political elites.

282. Ziadeh, Farhat J. **Property Law in the Arab World.** London: Graham and Trotman, 1979.

    Presents information on the history of real rights in the Arab countries, citing their source as Western or Islamic. Discusses the nature and extent of such rights in the Gulf states, Egypt, Iraq, Jordan, Lebanon, Libya, Syria, and Saudi Arabia. Also covers rights of ownership, real securities, and recent changes in ownership and tenancy.

CHAPTER 4

DEVELOPMENT: ECONOMICS AND PLANNING

Primarily concerned with economic development, this chapter presents books and articles on subjects such as national planning, finance, oil, trade, industrialization, economic integration, land reform, and agriculture.

283. Abdalla, Ismail-Sabri, et al. **Images of the Arab Future.** Translated by Maissa Taldat. New York: St. Martin's Press, 1983.

Aims to focus research on the social, economic, and cultural dynamics that could lead to alternative paths of Arab development. Considered a part of a larger project sponsored by the United Nations University. Examines the way the Arab region is mirrored by global associations such as "The Club of Rome" and OECD. Analyzes Arab strategy documents related to food, energy, education, and "Joint Arab Economic Action" presented to the 11th Arab Summit Conference in Amman, Jordan, November 1980.

284. Abdel-Fadil, Mahmoud. **Development, Income Distribution, and Social Change in Rural Egypt, 1952-1970: A Study in the Political Economy of Agrarian Transition.** Cambridge; New York: Cambridge University Press, 1975.

Analyzes various dimensions of agrarian transition in Egypt during Nasir's era. Surveys the basic changes in the agrarian structure that followed the implementation of the two major land reforms (1952 and 1961). Provides a framework for the process of transition; traces income distribution shifts associated with the new agrarian structure; examines changes in consumption patterns; and discusses governmental policies relating to co-operativisation, pricing, and procurement of farm produce. Rich with statistical tables and figures.

* Abdel-Fadil, Mahmoud. **The Political Economy of Nasserism: A Study in Employment and Income Distribution Policies in Urban Egypt, 1952-1972.** Cited as item 144.

* Abdel-Khalek, Gouda and Robert Tignor, eds. **The Political Economy of Income Distribution in Egypt.** Cited as item 145.

285. Aburdene, Odeh. "U.S. Economic and Financial Relations with Saudi Arabia, Kuwait and the United Arab Emirates." **American-Arab Affairs,** 7 (Winter 1983-84), 76-84.

    Describes the quantity of U.S. financial and economic relations with the three oil-exporting countries. Offers statistics on military services and other exports and the flow of money to the U.S. capital market. Concludes that the economies of these countries will continue to be significant to the United States even after a decline in the flow of investment caused by drop in oil prices and production.

286. Achilli, Michele and Mohamed Khalidi, eds. **The Role of the Arab Development Funds in the World Economy.** London: Croom Helm, 1984.

    Contains twenty-four specialized articles prepared for a February 1983 conference in Milan, Italy. Discusses the role of Arab development funds in the world economy. Includes items 289, 304, 325, 355, 364, 373, 382, 402.

287. Adams, Martin E. and John Howell. "Developing the Traditional Sector in the Sudan." **Economic Development and Cultural Change,** 27, 3 (April 1979), 505-518.

Reviews efforts and failures of development planning 1962-71. Focuses on the Economic Development Plan 1977-83 and the high financial commitment from Arab oil-exporting countries. Examines problems of implementation and inadequate concern for the powerless, threatened traditional farmer.

* Ahsan, Syed Aziz-al. "Economic Policy and Class Structure." Cited as item 148.

288. Al-Abdul-Razzak, Fatimah. **Marine Resources of Kuwait: Their Role in the Development of Non-oil Resources.** London: Routledge & Kagan Paul, 1984.

Describes Kuwait's dependence on oil revenues and the decline of traditional marine activities in importance to the economy. Analyzes the marine and trade sectors as possible sources of economic diversification and development.

289. Al-Humaidi, Bader. "The Kuwait Find for Arab Economic Development: The Loan Grant Policy and Procedure in Favour of Developing Countries." **The Role of the Arab Development Funds in the World Economy** (item 286).

Discusses the basic functions, activities, and organization of the Fund, established in Kuwait in 1961 to support developing countries of varying political and economic systems. Summarizes the projects and financial assistance provided by the Fund to some sixty-one countries.

290. Al-Kuwari, Ali Khalifa. **Oil Revenues in the Gulf Emirates: Patterns of Allocation and Impact on Economic Development.** Boulder, Col.: Westview Press, 1978.

92 Administration and Development

   Deals with growing oil-generated revenues of the Arab Gulf states (Bahrayn, Kuwait, Qatar, United Arab Emirates), underlining the vulnerability of current prosperity as societies orient toward consumerism rather than development. Provides pre-oil history of the region, describes the development of the oil industry, growth of revenues, and impact of allocation on development through 1971. Offers tables, figures, and extensive bibliography.

291. Al-Otaiba, Mana Saeed. **Petroleum and the Economy of the United Arab Emirates.** London: Croom Helm, 1977.

   Discusses economic structure and the petroleum industry from a legal perspective. Examines several related issues, such as oil companies, economic integration, and Gulf and Arab economic integration. Emphasizes the need for developing the non-oil sectors for balance.

292. Al-Sabah, S.M. **Development Planning in an Oil Economy and the Role of Women: The Case of Kuwait.** London: Eastlords Publishing, 1983.

   Examines the dependence of Kuwait on imported heterogeneous labor, viewed as a threat to "social harmony and political stability" and a factor in the "underutilization" of women. Proposes a framework for development planning aiming at a balanced economic base and an equally balanced labor force structure.

293. Aliboni, Roberto. "The Problems of Industrial Development and Arab Economic Integration." **The Problems of Arab Economic Development and Integration** (item 344).

   Examines basic factors relevant to integration, such as the structure of Arab economies, uneven in their levels of industrialization. Emphasizes the diversity of economic policies; some countries have quite conservative monetary and foreign exchange policies, while others (such as Jordan) have relatively liberal policies.

294. Aliboni, Roberto, ed. **Arab Industrialisation and Economic Integration.** New York: St. Martin's Press, and London: Croom Helm, 1979.

Attributes failure of many industrialization plans in developing countries to their pursuit in isolation. Examines Arab efforts to learn from such failures. Focuses on joint Arab sponsorship of industrial projects, labor migration, and inter-Arab and international comparisons of economic data. Includes item 353.

295. Alnasrawi, Abbas. **OPEC in a Changing World Economy.** Baltimore, Md.: The Johns Hopkins University Press, 1985.

Covers the Organization of Petroleum Exporting Countries (OPEC), its members and the management of oil output (price behavior and determination). Analyzes OPEC's relations with industrialized countries and the Third World; examines the rising dependence and interdependence with these regions. Offers tables on oil prices and energy consumption.

296. Alnasrawi, Abbas. "Arab Oil and the Industrial Economies: the Paradox of Oil Dependency." **Arab Studies Quarterly,** 1, 1 (Winter 1979), 1-27.

Points out the increasing economic dependency of the Arab oil-producing countries (Algeria, Iraq, Kuwait, Libya, Qatar, Saudi Arabia, United Arab Emirates) on industrial countries' markets for import-export. Other sectors of the economy are increasingly dependent on the oil sector.

297. Alnasrawi, Abbas. "The Changing Pattern of Iraq's Foreign Trade." **The Middle East Journal,** 25, 4 (Autumn 1971), 481-490.

Describes the change in pattern of Iraq's foreign trade to reflect change in economic structure and new thinking by policy makers. Addresses the volume of trade, composition of trade (exports-imports), spatial distribution, and regional patterns. Primary products dominate exports; consumer goods dominate imports.

298. Aly, Hamdi F. and Nabil Abdun-Nur. "An Appraisal of the Six-Year Plan of Lebanon (1972-1977)." **The Middle East Journal**, 29, 2 (Spring 1975), 151-164.

    Measures the degree of attainment of objectives of the Six-Year Plan in light of historical economic performance. Finds the plan inconsistent and unable to meet its general goals, which appear to be theoretical and lack credibility.

299. Amin, Samir. **The Arab Economy Today.** London: Zed Press, 1982.

    Recognizes the heterogeneous conditions of the Arab economies with extremely varying levels of per capita income, negligible inter-Arab trade, competitive rather than complementary strategies of industrialization, autonomous and varied fiscal systems. Chooses to speak in terms of an Arab economy, primarily for political reasons. Contends that "the decision to move toward Arab unity is probably an historical necessity and may well become a concrete possibility in the foreseeable future."

300. Aperjis, Dimitri. **The Oil Market in the 1980s: OPEC Oil Policy and Economic Development.** Cambridge, Mass.: Ballinger Publishing Co., 1982.

    Presents econometric analysis of the global oil market and underlying motivation for the behavior of oil-exporting countries, especially in terms of development needs as opposed to maximizing revenues.

301. Askari, Hossein and John Cummings. "Food Shortages in the Middle East." **Middle Eastern Studies**, 14, 3 (October 1978), 326-351.

   Examines the likely future agricultural commodity needs of the Arab world from three bases: (1) past and present production, (2) projected regional population increases, and (3) currently indicated adjustments required to meet desirable nutritional levels.

*   Bahroun, Sadok. "Annual Planning in Tunisia." Cited as item 19.

302. Barbour, K.M. **The Growth, Location, and Structure of Industry in Egypt.** New York: Praeger Publishers, 1972.

   Surveys the history of Egypt's industrial development, including the industrial pattern, structure, and concentration in the eras of private capitalism and the socialist revolution.

303. Barnett, Tony. **The Gazira Scheme—an Illusion of Development.** London: Frank Cass, 1977.

   Studies a region in Sudan to test and elaborate a model of dependency theory. Concludes that, in broader historical terms, the Gezira scheme cannot be considered a successful example of development; no worthwhile inprovement can be envisaged.

304. Bassetti, Piero. "International Economic Cooperation and Arab Development Funds." **The Role of the Arab Development Funds in the World Economy** (item 286).

   Points out the need to remedy disorder in the international economic system through efforts of co-financing for development between Arab funds and European institutions. Contends that the European economic system must recover to make Arab financing meaningful in the aid of development projects in the other developing countries.

305. Beblawi, Hazem. **The Arab Gulf Economy in a Turbulent Age.** London: Croom Helm, 1984.

   Studies oil surplus funds and their impact on the Arabian Gulf states and the international monetary system. Focuses on Kuwait and other Gulf states walking a tightrope, balancing their own development with burdens of inflation (exported by developed countries), Reaganomics, and an unstable international monetary order.

306. Boag, Ian. "The Contribution of the EEC to the Development and Integration of the Arab World." **The Problems of Arab Economic Development and Integration** (item 344).

   Discusses inter-Arab economic cooperation and relations of the European Economic Community (EEC) with the Arab states. Views this relationship through the perspectives of the Maghreb-Mashreg agreements, the Euro-Arab Dialogue, the Lome Convention, and other relations involving Arab states and the EEC.

307. Bowen-Jones, H. "Agriculture in Bahrain, Kuwait, Qatar and UAE." **Issues in Development: The Arab Gulf States** (item 426).

   Discusses conditions and characteristics of agriculture in Bahrain, Kuwait, Qatar, and the United Arab Emirates. Isolates climate (hot and humid) as the dominant factor governing agriculture, also complicated by limited water resources and farmers' inability to grow several agricultural items.

308. Bracher, Astrid. "Arab Agriculture: Small is More Productive." **Middle East Review,** tenth edition (Essex, England: World of Information, 1984), 42-44.

Claims that Arab planners have, in the 1980s, been adopting "a more down-to-earth approach to rural development," having discovered from their previous experience that large sums of money alone are not enough to raise agricultural productivity. Shows that the Arab Fund for Economic and Social Development has drawn a three-year plan to participate in twenty small-scale projects in eight Arab countries involving more than $3 billion.

309. Bruton, Henry J. "Egypt's Development in the Seventies." **Economic Development and Cultural Change,** 31, 4 (July 1983) 679-704.

Reviews the performance and management of the economy during the 1970s with focus on change. Discusses the general social and political environment within which the economy had to be managed and development effected. Examines monetary development and exchange rate issues.

310. Carr, David W. "Capital Flows and Development in Syria." **The Middle East Journal,** 34, 4 (Autumn 1980), 455-467.

Investigates the relationship between capital infusion and development within Syria. Addresses the rise in capital flows, impacts on investment levels, changes in national income growth rates, and industrial management. Concludes that long-term potential is high because of expected agricultural improvements from the Euphrates Dam irrigation project, increased petroleum production, and doubling of foreign assistance.

311. Casadio, Gian Paolo. **The Economic Challenge of the Arabs.** Westmead, England: Saxon House, D.C. Heath Ltd. jointly with Lexington, Mass: Lexington Books, D.C. Heath and Co., 1976.

Describes the problems and prospects of economic cooperation between the industrialized West and the Middle East, recognizing the existence of mutuality of needs. Favors a multilateral approach to problems of economic cooperation that would result in the increase of trade and investment opportunities between the two groups of countries.

312. Chaib, Andre E. "Analysis of Lebanon's Merchandise Exports 1951-1974." **The Middle East Journal**, 34, 4 (Autumn 1980), 438-454.

Studies export performance to determine reasons for its growth and diversification. Discusses export structure, destination, and trends in export history, relating growth to the demand in other Arab markets (especially oil-producing countries).

313. Chatelus, Michel and Yves Schemeil. "Toward a New Political Economy of State Industrialization in the Arab Middle East." **International Journal of Middle East Studies,** 16, 2 (May 1984), 251-266.

Discusses the increasing obsolescence of models and patterns applicable to the "development crisis" and the "new ways" of thinking that deny dogmatic approaches. Analyzes the economies of Middle East Arab countries with their numerous imbalances: lopsided growth, food dependency, limited intraregional trade, inefficient investment policies, and low productivity, as they are predominantly "circulation economies" strongly dependent on rent. Calls for non-disciplinary approach for dealing with development of the area.

314. Clawson, Marion, Hans H. Landsberg, and Lyle T. Alexander. **The Agricultural Potential of the Middle East.** New York: American Elsevier Publishing Co., 1971.

Delineates the agricultural potential of the Middle East, providing information on climate, soil, and water resources as these affect agriculture. Outlines the limited state of knowledge about questions of agricultural organization and practice, labor availability, agricultural marketing, farm structure, crop and livestock output, and rural community services. Concludes that much can be done to improve the physical resources of agriculture. Argues that the major obstacle to achieving substantial growth in the agricultural sector is not so much a matter of technology or physical resources but one of establishing more effective social institutions.

315. Cleron, Jean Paul. **Saudi Arabia 2000: A Strategy for Growth.** London: Croom Helm, 1978.

Discusses economic development (in oil and non-oil sectors) and the structure of the economic system through a model that divides it into ten substructures and mathematically describes the various parts. Analytical method is based on the identification and analysis of feedback loops that control the long-term dynamics of the economy. Emphasizes the role of management in Saudi economic development.

*   Cooper, Charles A. and Sidney S. Alexander. **Economic Development and Population Growth in the Middle East.** Cited as item 174.

316. Crane, Robert D. **Planning the Future of Saudi Arabia: A Model for Achieving National Priorities.** New York: Praeger Publishers, 1978.

Discusses the $142 billion five-year development plan (1975-1980). Develops a chart that breaks down the plan by objective and value. Contains analysis of the plan, long-range planning, management, and project implementation.

317. Deeb, Marius. "Bank Misr and the Emergence of the Local Bourgeoisie in Egypt." **The Middle Eastern Economy: Studies in Economics and Economic History** (item 214).

Traces the emergence of "local" bourgeoisie in Egypt as a distinct class at the end of the 1930s, dominated by foreign minorities. Discusses the leadership of Bank Misr (The Bank of Egypt) in agricultural development.

318. Demir, Soliman. **Arab Development Funds in the Middle East.** New York: Pergamon Press for UNITAR, 1979.

Covers three funds engaged in regional development in the Arab world: Kuwait Fund for Arab Economic Development, Abu-Dhabi Fund for Arab Economic Development, and the Arab Fund for Economic and Social Development. Studies institutional means by which some developing countries perform the role of aid-donors. Examines joint efforts of capital-surplus and capital-deficit Arab countries to promote regional development.

319. Dickinson, James M. "State and Economy in the Arab Middle East: Some Theoretical and Empirical Observations." **Arab Studies Quarterly,** 5, 1 (Winter 1983), 22-50.

Describes the growth of the state sector and the new modes of state intervention in the economy, such as nationalization policies and land reform programs. Focuses on Egypt, Syria, and Iraq.

320. Donaldson, William. "Enterprise and Innovation in an Indigenous Fishery: The Case of the Sultanate of Oman." **Development and Change,** 11, 3 (July 1980), 479-495.

Studies Oman's Fishery and the various attempts to introduce innovation into this industry. Emphasizes the general conditions of the country and their influence on the question of technology transfer significant to the fishery industry.

321. Donini, Giovanni. "Saudi Arabia's Hegemonic Policy and Economic Development in the Yemen Arab Republic." **Arab Studies Quarterly,** 1, 4 (Fall 1979), 299-308.

Studies Saudi foreign aid in 1975 and 1976. Describes how Saudi aid to North Yemen has led to growing political and economic influence on that country.

322. Edens, David G. **Oil and Development in the Middle East.** New York: Praeger Publishers, 1979.

    Reviews factors of oil, manpower, and other relevant aspects of development and change in Arab and non-Arab countries. Discusses agricultural and petroleum resources, land reform, economic planning, problems of military spending, revenues and expenditures, designs for progress, oil trade, OPEC, population growth, industrial structure, etc.

323. Edens, David G. and William P. Snavely. "Planning for Economic Development in Saudi Arabia." **The Middle East Journal,** 24, 1 (Winter 1970), 17-30.

    Selects Saudi Arabia as an example of an Arab nation employing deliberate public policies and plans to increase economic welfare in an essentially free-enterprise environment. Examines with the purpose of evaluating the development of formal as well as informal planning in the kingdom.

324. El-Azhary, M.S. **The Impact of Oil Revenues on Arab Gulf Development.** London: Croom Helm, 1984.

    Contains papers presented at the "Symposium on Oil Revenues and their Impact on Development in the Arab Gulf States" at the University of Exeter (U.K.), October 1982. Assesses the region's dependence on oil for development and the urgency of the transition to less oil-oriented economies. Covers topics including state development planning, the Gulf Cooperation Council, prospects of economic coordination, agricultural potential, manpower problems, and the impact of development on society.

102　Administration and Development

325. El-Helw, Mahmoud. "The Role of the Arab Fund for Economic and Social Development." **The Role of the Arab Development Funds in the World Economy** (item 286).

   Introduces the Arab Fund for Economic and Social Development. Discusses its functions and activities as a regional agency established to participate in the development of its member states. Summarizes projects supported by the Fund since it became operational in 1972.

326. El-Khaldi, Ghanem. "The Problems of Agricultural Development and Arab Economic Integration: A Reply." **The Problems of Arab Economic Development and Integration** (item 344).

   Discusses the causes of backwardness of the agricultural sector in the Arab countries. Contends that agricultural integration is imperative for development in countries that have poor systems of production. Arab planning efforts should be focused on a food strategy to ensure meeting future demand for food.

327. El-Kuwaize, Abdulla. "The Gulf Cooperation Council and the Concept of Economic Integration." **American-Arab Affairs,** 7 (Winter 1983-84), 45-49.

   Discusses common conditions of GCC member states and economic reasons for their economic integration. Describes steps proposed for achieving such integration, i.e., establishing free trade zone, unification of economic policy, institutional unification, linkage of principal infrastructures, and implementation of common development projects.

328. El-Mallakh, Ragaei. **The Economic Development of the United Arab Emirates.** New York: St. Martin's Press, 1981.

   Describes the economy of the United Arab Emirates. Presents and analyzes economic problems and supplies practical information on the development process. Offers background materials reflecting the short existence of the federation and recent prosperity due to oil and gas revenues.

329. El-Mallakh, Ragaei. **Qatar: Development of an Oil Economy.** New York: St. Martin's Press, 1979.

 Describes Qatar's economic history, policies, and prospects. Traces the development of the oil industry and underlines its centrality to the overall economy as well as to the future of the country. Claims that continued investment in the development of human capital may be the key to Qatar's self-sustaining development.

330. El-Mallakh, Ragaei. "Economic Requirements for Development, Oman." **The Middle East Journal,** 26, 4 (Autumn 1972) 415-427.

 Postulates that the expansion of the oil industry and the 1970 change in government shifted attitudes toward development. States that the discovery of oil provided government revenues, expanded local markets, offered new employment opportunities, and accelerated Oman's human resource training and basic social services.

331. El-Mallakh, Ragaei. "The Challenge of Affluence: Abu Dhabi." **The Middle East Journal,** 24, 2 (Spring 1970) 135-146.

 Examines the influx of petroleum-based revenues and the resulting impetus for economic development. Addresses the problem of regulating growth via such means as the direction of a Planning Council and use of the Five-Year Development Plan (1968-72).

332. El-Mallakh, Ragaei and Jacob K. Atta. **The Absorptive Capacity of Kuwait: Domestic and International Perspective.** Lexington, Mass.: D.C. Heath, 1981.

104 Administration and Development

Describes Kuwait (free from capital shortage and the exigencies of poverty that inhibit economic growth in most developing countries) as facing factors complicating its ability to create an acceptable return on its oil wealth. Analyzes constraints on absorptive capacity. Offers a model to project future absorptive capacities under alternative scenarios of constraints.

333. El-Mallakh, Ragaei and Dorothea H. El-Mallakh, eds. **Saudi Arabia: Energy, Development Planning and Industrialization.** Lexington, Mass.: D.C. Heath and Lexington Books, 1982.

A collection of papers from an area conference at the International Research Center for Energy and Economic Development in Colorado. American, Canadian, European, and Saudi authors discuss the various aspects of Saudi social and economic development--with special emphasis on recent industries such as petrochemicals. Includes items 133, 334, and 345.

334. El-Mallakh, Ragaei and Dorothea H. El-Mallakh. "The Third Development Plan of Saudi Arabia, 1400-1405 A.H.-1980-1985 A.D." **Saudi Arabia: Energy, Development Planning and Industrialization** (item 333).

Discusses pillars of Saudi Arabia's third development plan, its rationale, objectives, strategies, and patterns. Examines prospects for implementation. Defines the basic priority: to reduce foreign workers in the Saudi labor force.

335. El-Mallakh, Ragaei and Mihssen Kadhim. "Arab Institutionalized Development Aid: An Evaluation." **The Middle East Journal,** 30 (Autumn 1976), 471-484.

Surveys existing major national and regional development institutions in the Arab world, including resources and operation. Analyzes aid objectives, differentiating between political, socio-cultural, economic, and humanitarian motives. Assesses aid quality, project appraisal methods, and the proliferation of aid institutions. Discusses the significance of Arab developmental aid and its potential, especially in light of the decrease in traditional aid sources.

* Erb, Richard D., ed. "The Arab Oil-Producing States of the Gulf: Political and Economic Developments." Cited as item 186.

336. Fahim, Hussein M. **Dams, People and Development: The Aswan High Dam Case.** New York: Pergamon Press, 1981.

Discusses some of the controversies over the building of the Aswan Dam in Egypt and its impact on land, people, urban growth, water policy, and national development.

337. Farley, Rawle. **Planning for Development in Libya.** New York: Praeger, 1971.

Covers a broad spectrum of the Libyan system: geography, history, human resources development, oil and non-oil sectors, and the First Five-Year Plan. Indicates the seriousness of Libyan overdependence on and overestimation of the ability of one factor of production, i.e., capital, to solve the problems of development.

* Fenelon, K.G. **The United Arab Emirates: An Economic and Social Survey.** Cited as item 190.

338. Fouad, Mahmoudi H. "Petrodollars and Economic Development in the Middle East." **The Middle East Journal,** 32, 3 (Summer 1978), 307-321.

Views economic development as dependent on the productive capacities of the people. Development of people is a slow process of education, attitudinal change, and evolution of traditional agricultural and industrial ways. Concludes that Arab oil-producing countries are determined to modernize their economies and improve their people's standard of living and, at the same time, help other Arab countries do the same.

339. Gerner, Deborah J. "Petro-Dollar Recycling: Imports, Arms, Investment and AID." **Arab Studies Quarterly**, 7, 1 (Winter 1985), 1-26.

Discusses various avenues of petro-dollar recycling as a means to consider the effect of surplus capital on interdependence in the international economic system. Concludes that capital-surplus states (notably Kuwait, Qatar, Saudi Arabia, and the United Arab Emirates) are dependent on industrialized countries for imports and investments; thus are vulnerable to changes in the economies of the West.

340. Ghantus, Elias T. **Arab Industrial Integration: A Strategy for Development.** London and Canberra: Croom Helm, 1982.

Suggests integration among certain Arab countries (those in Asia together with Egypt and Sudan) to achieve development and reduce dependence on imports. Emphasizes that pooling of resources would avoid duplication, increase output, and avoid severe economic penalties and losses. Discusses theories of integration, surveys economic conditions in the last three decades, and presents a strategy for integrated Arab industrial development.

341. Ghattas, Emile. "Lebanon's Financial Crisis in 1966: A Systemic Approach." **The Middle East Journal**, 25, 1 (Winter 1971), 31-44.

Examines the impact of the international banking crisis of 1966 on Lebanon's banking structure and the system's response.

342. Glick, Leslie Alan. **Trading With Saudi Arabia.**
London: Croom Helm, 1980.

Studies the development of Saudi Arabia's maritime laws and regulations, development of the Arab tanker fleet, regulation of seaports, harbors, and lighthouses. Discusses international conventions and treaties, requirements pertaining to foreign business operations, tariff, trade and boycott laws, and other legal and commercial matters.

343. Gray, Albert L. Jr. "Egypt's Ten-Year Economic Plan 1973-1982." **The Middle East Journal,** 30, 1 (Winter 1976), 36-48.

Compares Egypt's Ten-Year National Action Program with the two previous five-year plans (1960-65, 1956-70). Contrasts the goals of the current plan with the achievements of the ten preceding years. Examines prospects for the current ten-year plan and elaborates on the outlook for savings, investment, balance of payments, and employment.

344. Guecioueur, Adda, ed. **The Problems of Arab Economic Development and Integration.** Boulder, Col.: Westview Press, 1984.

Contains the proceedings of a November 1981 "Symposium on Problems of Arab Economic Development and Integration" held at Yarmouk University in Jordan. Reviews developmental problems of individual Arab countries on a regional basis. Contends that, given factors of production both at the levels of individual countries and the Arab world as a region, "economic integration constitutes the only way to self-maintained, introverted Arab economic and social development." Focuses on economic development and integration in industry, agriculture, technology, and currency, and reviews obstacles to Arab economic unity. Includes items 293, 306, 326.

345. Hafiz, Talal K. "Technology Transfer to the Developing Nations: The Case of Saudi Arabia." **Saudi Arabia: Energy, Developmental Planning, and Industrialization** (item 333).

Discusses Saudi preparation for technology transfer on the levels of modern institution building and manpower training in several areas where technology is needed, especially in agriculture and industry. Contends that, in the case of Saudi Arabia (which represents a "culturally sensitive situation"), it would be better to stress local training for technology transfer to facilitate adaptation to the country's environment and culture.

346. Hale, Peter B. and Cherie A. Loustaunau. "U.S.-Middle East Trade." **Business and the Middle East: Threats and Prospects** (item 367).

Surveys the history of commercial relations between America and the Middle East since the 18th century. Covers significant dates and agreements related to the development of trade relations. Discusses increasing U.S. strategic interest in the Middle East after World War II, economic development, and aid programs.

347. Hallwood, Paul and Stuart W. Sinclair. **Oil, Debt and Development: OPEC in the Third World.** London: George Allen and Unwin, 1981.

Covers extensive background material on the economic divergencies between developing countries, the changing world economic climate, and the organization of OPEC. Also examines energy price changes and the OPEC aid record in distribution terms.

348. Hameed, K.A. **Enterprise: Industrial Entrepreneurship in Development.** London: Sage Publications, 1974.

Offers a general analysis and some abstract theoretical discussion of economic development. Focuses on Sudan as a case study.

349. Harik, Iliya. "Continuity and Change in Local Development Policies in Egypt: From Nasser to Sadat." **International Journal of Middle East Studies,** 16, 1 (March 1984), 43-66.

Reviews agrarian reform, its economic context, and its consequences of a fixed ceiling on land ownership and state control of the agricultural sector. Discusses obstacles to rural development and the new strategy developed after 1975 to cope with institutional problems and refocus on local government. Examines reform based on decentralization of authority, providing regular sources of income, consolidating local authority and strengthening the representative character of village councils, and disaggregating cooperative functions, placing most of them in the village bank.

350. Haseeb, Khair El-Din and Samir Makdisi, eds. **Arab Monetary Integration: Issues and Prerequisites.** London: Croom Helm, 1980.

Deals with a wide range of economic issues and aspects of Arab economic cooperation. Contains twelve papers presented at a seminar organized by the Center for Arab Unity Studies and the Arab Monetary Fund. Offers critical views of the capital-rich states and financial policies that perpetuate dependency as a result of integration in the capitalist system in the areas of production, trade, capital, and technology.

351. Hashim, J.M. "Arab National Economic Plans: A Look at Some of the Imbalances." **A Society for International Development: Prospectus-1984.** Edited by Ann Mattis. Durham, N.C.: Duke University Press in collaboration with SID, 1983, pp. 233-239.

110   **Administration and Development**

   Reviews accomplishments and failures of Arab national development plans in the 1970s and '80s, particularly in the industrial sector, agriculture, and human resources. Speculates about future challenges.

352. Hazelton, Jared E. "Land Reform in Jordan: The East Ghor Canal Project." **Middle Eastern Studies**, 15, 2 (May 1979), 258-269.

   Describes land reform measures; evaluates their impact on land redistribution and tenure, agriculture output and living standards.

353. Hershlag, Z.Y. "Industrialisation in Arab Countries: Patterns, Options and Strategies." **Arab Industrialisation and Economic Integration** (item 294).

   Discusses Arab industrial development, considered to be still in its infancy. Describes some national industries in Egypt, Syria, Jordan, Iraq, Algeria, Morocco, and Tunisia.

354. Hudson, James. "The Litani River of Lebanon: An Example of Middle Eastern Water Development." **The Middle East Journal**, 25, 1 (Winter 1971), 1-14.

   Addresses the problem of water use confronting Middle East development. Uses Lebanon's Litani River as a case study. Describes geography and geology of the basin, examines the U.S. development plan of 1950, discusses the various proposed project's outputs (electricity, irrigation, household, and industrial water). Suggests that current water policy erroneously emphasizes irrigation over urban supply.

355. Humaidan, Saleh H. "The Activities of the Saudi Fund for Development." **The Role of the Arab Development Funds in the World Economy** (item 286).

Economics and Planning   111

Discusses objectives, organization, activities, and achievements of the Saudi Fund for development since its establishment in 1974, including criteria followed in granting loans to developing countries.

356. Ikram, Khalid. **Egypt: Economic Management in a Period of Transition.** Published for the World Bank. Baltimore: The Johns Hopkins University Press, 1980.

Reports on economic and social development in Egypt, mainly between 1952 and 1978. Prepared for the World Bank by a team of specialists through extensive field work. Discusses strategies and issues of development in various productive sectors of the society, with special attention to development of human resources. Provides data until late '70s.

357. Ismael, Jacqueline S. "Dependency and Capital Surplus: The Case of Kuwait." **Arab Studies Quarterly**, 1, 2 (Spring 1979), 157-173.

Analyzes Kuwait's economic structure through the application of dependency theory. Views contemporary Kuwait as a super-affluent country occupying an anomalous position in terms of theories of development, underdevelopment, and dependency. Kuwait's narrow specialized role in the world division of labor as an oil producer (and its reciprocal role as an exporter of financial capital and market for the commodities of the industrialized world) specifies its dependency.

358. Issawi, Charles. "Growth and Structural Change in the Middle East." **The Middle East Journal**, 25, 3 (Summer 1971), 309-324.

Examines the patterns of economic growth and overall structural change of various countries of the Middle East (countries included are those with available data). Addresses four forces of growth:

Administration and Development

(1) development of infrastructure and human resources, (2) growth of the petroleum industry, (3) foreign aid, and (4) population increase. Discusses areas of structural change: savings and investment, human resources, infrastructure, composition of GNP, agriculture, industry, foreign trade and balance of payments, planning and growth of the government sector.

359. Jalal, Ferhan. **The Role of Government in the Industrialization of Iraq, 1950-1965.** London: Frank Cass and Company Limited, 1972.

    Discusses the role of the public sector in the industrialization of Iraq in the 1950s and early 1960s. Examines major policies and measures that were adopted in support of national industrialization such as protection of private industry, tax exemptions to encourage investment, and licensing of industrial enterprises.

360. Kalkas, Barbara. "Diverted Institutions: A Reinterpretation of the Process of Industrialization in Nineteenth-Century Egypt." **Arab Studies Quarterly,** 1, 1 (Winter 1979), 28-48.

    Explores the development of modern institutions in Egypt during the nineteenth century, concluding that the development of "diverted institutions" impeded modernization attempts in the twentieth century.

361. Kapoor, Ashok, ed. **International Business in the Middle East.** Boulder, Col.: Westview Press, 1979.

    Discusses case studies in international business with involvement by Middle Eastern countries, such as the Kiawah resort project in South Carolina financed by Kuwaiti investment funds and the Arab Potash Company in Jordan financed by several Arab countries.

362. Kavoussi, Rostam M. "Economic Growth and Income Distribution in Saudi Arabia." **Arab Studies Quarterly,** 5, 1 (Winter 1983), 65-81.

Studies how petroleum exports of Saudi Arabia have affected the economy. Asks, who has benefitted from the enormous income generated by these exports? Concludes that income distribution has shifted in favor of the public sector, those with highest incomes, and those with lowest incomes.

363. Kazimi, M.S. and J.I. Makhoue, eds. **Perspective on Technological Development in the Arab World.** The Association of Arab-American University Graduates, 1977.

Covers a wide range of topics related to planning for development of science and techology in the Arab world. Eight papers discuss existing and needed ingredients for such development. Deals (in three parts) with planning for development with focus on manpower planning, sociology of development, and prospects for advanced science applications.

*   Kedourie, Elie, ed. **The Middle Eastern Economy: Studies in Economics and Economic History.** Cited as item 214.

*   Kerr, Malcolm H. and El Sayed Yassin, eds. **Rich and Poor States in the Middle East: Egypt and the New Arab Order.** Cited as item 217.

364. Khaldi, Mohamed. "Arab Aid in the World Economy." **The Role of the Arab Development Funds in the World Economy** (item 286).

Discusses Arab aid to various states, including some from the Third World. Analyzes characteristics and distribution of Arab aid, its volume, and its geographical and sectoral spread.

Administration and Development

365. Khouja, M.W. and P.G. Sadler. **The Economy of Kuwait--Development and Role in International Finance.** London: Macmillan Press, 1979.

   Argues that, aside from oil and oil-related industries, Kuwait's economic advantage is in finance, where Kuwaitis manage their financial assets with a high degree of sophistication.

366. Khouri, Rami G. **The Jordan Valley: Life and Society Below Sea Level.** Longon: Longman Group Limited, 1981.

   Discusses the development of agriculture and the business of farming in the rich Jordan Valley.

367. Kilmarx, Robert A. and Yonah Alexander, eds. **Business and the Middle East: Threats and Prospects.** New York: Pergamon Press, 1982.

   Contains nine articles dealing with social, economic, strategic, religious, security, and political aspects of the Middle East. Provides an overview of Middle East economics, U.S.-Middle East trade, the multinationals, and Arab economic development. Includes items 260 and 346.

368. Keilany, Ziad. "Socialism and Economic Change in Syria." **Middle Eastern Studies,** 9, 1 (January 1973), 61-72.

   Examines ideological and economic changes that have occurred in Syria under the Ba'th rule since 1963. Underlines some radical economic and social measures: agrarian reform, nationalization of industry and trade, and economic planning. Contends that the Ba'th party has completed the conversion of the economy to a socialist one managed by the government. Assesses the impact of change.

369. Knauerhase, Ramon. "Saudi Arabia's Economy at the Beginning of the 1970s." **The Middle East Journal,** 28 (Spring 1974), 126-140.

Examines the West's misconceptions of Saudi Arabian economic conditions. Briefly describes the economy and progress made from 1962 to the beginning of 1972. Observes that important gains have been made, but no sustained broad-front advance has occurred. Points to such hindrances to economic development as continuing conservatism of the religious community and the security of large oil revenues, and places hope for change in the younger, better educated group and in progressive government officials.

370. Kubursi, Atif. **Oil, Industrialization and Development in the Arab Gulf States.** London: Croom Helm, 1984.

Explores the development potential of the Gulf region within the framework of cooperation among countries of the Gulf Cooperation Council and the broader context of the Arab world. Discusses specific problems of water and labor shortages and the future of agricultural development and industrialization.

371. Lackner, Helen. **A House Built on Sand: A Political Economy of Saudi Arabia.** London: Ithaca Press, 1978.

Discusses social, political, and economic development of Saudi Arabia, including analysis of Saudi society in transition, the economic, development plans, and the oil industry. Describes the rapid shift in economic activities away from traditional resources of herding and agriculture.

372. Lees, Francis A. and Hugh C. Brooks. **The Economic and Political Development of the Sudan.** London: The Macmillan Press, 1977.

Provides a general description of the political and economic development of Sudan. Analyzes certain aspects of national development, including population and manpower, agriculture and forestry, transport, power and industry, the financial

116   Administration and Development

system, and external economic relations. Reviews some problems of development planning, prospects, and regional progress; offers recommendations.

373. Lethbridge, Christopher. "European Community Financial Cooperation in the Arab Countries: The Role of the European Investment Bank." **The Role of the Arab Development Funds in the World Economy** (item 286).

Describes the objectives of the European Investment Bank, established in 1958, and its activities in the Arab world. Covers various development projects supported by the bank dealing with roads and railways, agriculture and industry, and deepening and widening the Suez Canal.

374. Mabro, Robert and Samir Radwan. **The Industrialization of Egypt 1939-1973: Policy and Performance.** New York: Oxford University Press, 1976.

Follows a brief historical background of the Egyptian economic experience with concentration on structure and growth of recent manufacturing industry. Discusses productivity and the relationship between industrialization and trade. Compiles extensive statistical information.

375. Makdisi, Samir A. **Financial Policy and Economic Growth: The Lebanese Experience.** New York: Columbia University Press, 1979.

Discusses the Lebanese economy, including objectives, national economic policy, monetary developments, the role of exchange rate policy, and a look for the future. Covers the period before the civil strife beginning in 1975.

376. Makdisi, Samir A. "An Appraisal of Lebanon's Post-War Economic Development and a Look to the Future." **The Middle East Journal,** 31, 2 (Summer 1977), 267-280.

Describes the record of postwar economic development in Lebanon up to 1974. Critically assesses the development record, summarizes the impact of the 1975-76 war, and speculates on the postwar period, which depends on stability and political leadership capable of implementing necessary reforms.

377. Makdisi, Samir A. "Syria: Rate of Economic Growth and Fixed Capital Formation 1936-1968." **The Middle East Journal**, 25, 2 (Spring 1971), 157-179.

Profiles the performance of the Syrian economy as measured by its rate of growth, beginning with the late prewar period. Observes that Syria, a potentially rich agricultural country, has managed to develop at a satisfactory rate. Guided by the private sector to the early 1960s, the economy has been transformed to one firmly controlled by the public sector. Provides statistics on economic indicators.

378. Mazur, Michael P. **Economic Growth and Development in Jordan.** Boulder, Col.: Westview Press, 1979.

Studies the economy of Jordan during two periods: pre-1967 Jordan and post-1967 East Bank. Examines development policies and experiences in the areas of agriculture, industry, and planning. Provides statistical data (mostly pre-1974).

379. Michail, W.M. "A Standard Aggregative Model for the Jordanian Economy." **International Journal of Middle East Studies,** 17, 1 (February 1985), 67-88.

Presents an econometric time-series model designed to use the available Jordanian national accounts statistics. Aims at explaining the structural changes in the economy in the 1970s as well as projecting values of certain macroeconomic variables for the year 1985, the terminal year in the current five-year plan. The model demonstrates that the Jordanian economy is quite stable; will continue to grow even if no remittances were made by Jordanians abroad and no current transfers made to the central government.

380. Moliver, Donald M. and Paul J. Abbondante. **The Economy of Saudi Arabia.** New York: Praeger Publishers, 1980.

Focuses on the development of the economic sector: agriculture, water resources, manufacturing, industry, and other aspects related to national development.

381. Nellis, John R. "A Comparative Assessment of the Development Performances of Algeria and Tunisia." **The Middle East Journal,** 37, 3 (Summer 1983), 370-393.

Compares development strategies of the two countries to discover differences. Discusses the usefulness and validity of the capitalist-socialist distinction. Evaluates the post-independence development efforts of each country. Provides economic statistics. Concludes that the Tunisian economy has grown faster (in terms of GNP per capita) and in a more diversified manner than the Algerian. Reasons, however, that when examining other indicators (distribution), the countries have performed in a roughly similar manner.

*   Niblock, Tim, ed. **Social and Economic Development in the Arab Gulf.** Cited as item 241.

382. Odeh, A.F. "The Canadian International Development Agency and the Arab World." **The Role of the Arab Development Funds in the World Economy** (item 286).

Discusses Canadian-Arab economic cooperation, including co-financing development projects with Arab donors, Canada's relations with Arab aid agencies, and the philosophy and concept of Arab aid. Concludes that Canadian-Arab pooling of sources and information exchange would serve both interests.

383. Oesterdiekhoff, Peter and Karl Wohlmuth, eds. **The Development Perspectives of the Democratic Republic of Sudan: The Limits of the Breadbasket Strategy.** Cologne, W. Germany: Weltforum Verlag, 1983.

    Examines the Sudan's development process. Reviews the limits of agricultural modernization, problems of industrial development, and constraints created by shortages of vocationally educated workers.

384. Penson, John B. Jr. "Synthesis of Optimal Macro Production Plans in Planned Economies: A Syrian Example." **The Journal of Developing Areas,** 16, 1 (October 1981), 31-45.

    Develops a macroproduction planning model that maximizes the gross domestic product of a centrally planned economy subject to the existing engineering capacities of the production sectors and the availability of labor.

385. Pillai, Vel. "External Economic Dependence and Fiscal Policy Imbalances in Developing Countries: A Case Study of Jordan." **The Journal of Development Studies,** 19, 1 (October 1982), 5-18.

    Develops a model to determine the fiscal impact of three factors in a less developed country setting: large-scale public sector outlays, foreign trade, and foreign aid. Finds that, based on the Jordanian experience, the first factor adds more to current expenditures than to domestic revenues (indicating a fiscal imbalance), while the external two factors have positive net fiscal effects. Derives important trade-offs between the growth of public sector investment and future external dependence based on these results.

386. Platt, C.J. **Tax Systems of Africa, Asia and the Middle East: A Guide for Business and the Professions.** Aldershot, England: Gower Publishing Company, 1982.

Summarizes information on the system of taxation (and other relevant material) for the benefit of business companies and other professions. Includes Egypt, Libya, Sudan, and Saudi Arabia. Lists information on taxation, taxes and legislation, individual taxes, and company taxation. Provides information about accounting and tax consultant firms.

387. Poulson, Barry W. and Myles Wallace. "Regional Integration in the Middle East: The Evidence for Trade and Capital Flows." **The Middle East Journal,** 33, 4 (Autumn 1979), 464-478.

Outlines a trend toward economic integration based on evidence of increasing trade flows. Recognizes slow gains and declines in intraregional trade for the most recent years. Acknowledges that impetus for increased regionalism has come from Asian Middle East, while the African Middle East has experienced a decline in such trade.

388. Pounds, Bonnie. "The U.S.-Saudi Arabian Joint Commission: A Model for Bilateral Economic Cooperation." **American-Arab Affairs,** 7 (Winter 1983-84), 60-68.

Describes the objectives of the cabinet-level Joint Commission launched June 8, 1974, as an instrument of cooperation and development. Discusses the operational program and offers a summary of completed projects.

389. Presley, John R. **A Guide to the Saudi Arabian Economy.** New York: St. Martin's Press, 1984.

A general introduction to the country, with emphasis on macroeconomic information, economic development, education, health, and business.

Economics and Planning 121

390. Richards, Alan. **Egypt's Agricultural Development 1800-1980: Technical and Social Change.** Boulder, Col.: Westview Press, 1982.

Analyzes Egypt's agricultural development. Includes a section on technical and social change from 1890-1914. Discusses agriculture under the Nasir and Sadat administrations, along with the various reform programs.

391. Richards, Alan. "The Agricultural Crisis in Egypt." **The Journal of Development Studies,** 16, 3 (April 1980), 303-321.

Argues that origins of the current agricultural crisis can be traced to policy choices and political decisions made during the administrations of Nasir and Sadat. Suggests that the economy continues to fall between the approaches of socialism and capitalism; class structure, distribution of resources, and the social basis of the regime have blocked either path. Finds the regime unwilling to mobilize the peasantry or provide decentralized incentives for farmers. Attributes the current problem of rural Egypt to contradictions of state capitalist agriculture.

392. Ronall, J.O. "Banking Developments in Kuwait." **The Middle East Journal,** 24, 1 (Winter 1970), 87-90.

Examines the previous national banking system and reasons for its restructuring. Discusses national currency, the Central Bank of Kuwait, and regulation of the banking system. Gives an overview of commercial banking's history.

393. Sadik, Ali Tawfik. "Managing the Petrodollar Bonanza: Avenues and Implications of Recycling Arab Capital." **Arab Studies Quarterly,** 6, 1 and 2 (Winter/Spring 1984), 13-38.

Discusses OPEC's challenges, the growth of oil revenues in nominal and real terms, and the existing model for recycling Arab capital. Analyzes recent developments and their implications. Utilizes mathematical formula in the analysis.

394. Sayigh, Yusif A. **The Determinants of Arab Economic Development.** New York: St. Martin's Press, 1978.

    Discusses conceptual and methodological issues of development in twelve Arab countries and the Arab region as a whole. Emphasizes the diversity of development thinking and the multiplicity of avenues that can lead to development.

395. Sayigh, Yusif A. **The Economics of the Arab World.** New York: St. Martin's Press, 1978.

    Provides a voluminous, comprehensive study of developmental achievements and failings in twelve Arab countries. Constitutes one of a two-volume study on the subject. Expands the analysis of development beyong the restricted economic growth notions measured in terms of annual rate of increase in GNP.

396. Sayigh, Yusif A. "Problems and Prospects of Development in the Arabian Peninsula." **International Journal of Middle East Studies**, 2, 1 (January 1971), 40-58.

    Describes development in the region, not only in terms of natural resource development (oil), but in areas where changes in techology, discovery of new resources, development of manpower, and change in organization provide needed dynamism. Satisfaction of these conditions has gone furthest in Kuwait and Saudi Arabia; elsewhere, the situation is different.

397. Schliephake, Konrad. **Oil and Regional Development: Examples from Algeria and Tunisia.** New York: Praeger, 1977.

Economics and Planning 123

Provides information on regional development based on hydrocarbons in Algeria and Tunisia. Discusses effects of the oil industry on different economic systems and political attitudes of oil-exporting countries during the "energy crisis."

398. Searby, Daniel M. "The Hidden Side of the Kuwaiti Economy: A Rapidly Growing Industrial Base." **The International Essays for Business Decision Makers.** Edited by Mark B. Winchester. Amacom: A Division of American Management Association, published for the Center for International Business, Houston, Texas, 1978, pp. 105-110.

Discusses aspects of the Kuwaiti economy, stressing rapidly growing industry and problems of industrial growth. Emphasizes labor as the resource in shortest supply. Observes that the economy, normally thought of in terms of oil export, has an impressive industrial sector.

399. Seymour, Ian. **OPEC, Instrument of Change.** New York: St. Martin's Press, 1981.

Discusses the rise of oil governments to positions of control over their valuable commodity. Provides a history of OPEC; gives financial analysis from the perspective of an economic journalist.

400. Sharif, Walid. **Oil and Development in the Arab Gulf States: A Selected Annotated Bibliography.** London: Croom Helm, 1985.

Surveys literature on oil in the Arab Gulf region, with emphasis on the Gulf Cooperation Council countries (Bahrain, Kuwait, Oman, Qatar, Saudi Arabia, and the United Arab Emirates). Covers sources during the decade 1973-1983.

401. Shaw, John A. and David E. Long. **Saudi Arabian Modernization: The Impact of Change on Stability.**

124 **Administration and Development**

>Washington, D.C.: The Center for Strategic and International Studies, Georgetown University, 1982.

>Analyzes the problems and potentials of economic development efforts. Assesses their stabilizing and destabilizing impact on various societal groups (the royal family, military, students, merchants, etc.). Indirectly reflects a series of conferences and commissioned papers on Saudi Arabia's development.

402. Sid Ahmed, A.K. "Arab Development Agencies and South-South Cooperation." **The Role of the Arab Development Funds in the World Economy** (item 286).

>Discusses assistance provided to Third World countries, including the extent of Arab financial assistance, its objectives, its impact on South-South cooperation, and prospects for South-South cooperation.

403. Simmons, Andre. **Arab Foreign Aid.** East Brunswick, N.J.: Fairleigh Dickinson University Press, 1981.

>Describes the bilateral aid programs of six major Arab donors--Iraq, Kuwait, Libya, Qatar, Saudi Arabia, and the United Arab Emirates--and six largely Arab-sponsored multilateral institutions, including the Arab Bank for Economic Development in Africa and the Arab Fund.

404. Simmons, John L. "Agricultural Cooperatives and Tunisian Development (Part I)." **The Middle East Journal**, 24, 4 (Autumn 1970), 455-465.

>Examines the Tunisian experience in cooperative management, which, by 1961, became a national synonym for economic progress and development. Describes the agricultural cooperatives in their historical context of development (status quo, gradualism, crisis). Provides data on land under

state management in 1968 in terms of production units, livestock cooperatives, polyculture cooperatives, et al.

405. Simmons, John L. "Agricultural Cooperatives and Tunisian Development (Part II)." **The Middle East Journal**, 25, 1 (Winter 1970), 45-57.

Observes that after fifteen years experience in the management of cooperative farms, Tunis abandoned the system in 1969. Describes how serious political and economic repurcussions of land reform and management provoked a political crisis, leading to resolutions that agricultural land management be restored to private control. Identifies factors in failure such as lack of cost-benefit analysis, mismanagement, vague objectives, nonexistent methodology, a period of extensive structural alterations in all national institutions, lack of on-the-job training, and political context.

406. Skold, Melvin D., Abdel Atty El-Shinnawi, and Nasr Lotfy. "Irrigation Water Distribution along Branch Canals in Egypt: Economic Effects." **Economic Development and Cultural Change**, 32, 3 (April 1984), 547-567.

Evaluates some of the economic costs of inadequate water distribution for agricultural projects and points out the need for improved systems of irrigation to meet present and future food requirements.

407. Smith, Tony. "The Political and Economic Ambitions of Algerian Land Reform, 1972-1974." **The Middle East Journal**, 29, 2 (Summer 1975), 259-278.

Examines the Algerian government's use of land reform to dramatically increase agricultural production, lay a base for internal market consumption for national industry, and create a structure for popular participation in political life. Foresees great economic gains in demand for industrial goods from more productively employed peasantry. Argues that for the system to achieve stability, it must disperse power and create constitutional linkages throughout the country through party structure and organized interest groups.

408. Springborg, Robert. "New Patterns of Agrarian Reform in the Middle East and North Africa." **The Middle East Journal**, 31, 2 (Spring 1977), 127-142.

    Surveys general criticisms of present land tenure systems, various proposals for improvement, and the resultant conflict. Concludes that the current heterogeneous character of tenure systems will be preserved, possibly becoming further mixed because of political factors such as appeasement of varied segments of the public, desire to attract foreign aid, and the recognition that no one pattern of ownership is universally successful.

409. Stephens, Robert. **The Arabs' New Frontier.** Boulder, Col.: Westview Press, 1976.

    Studies the Kuwait Fund for Arab Economic Development in the context of economic and social backgrounds of Arab countries. Concludes that if increased development funds from oil are to be used effectively, they need serious, intelligent, and incorruptible management for inter-Arab institutions.

410. Suliman, Ali Ahmed. **Issues in the Economic Development of the Sudan.** Khartoum: Khartoum University Press, 1975.

    Discusses questions of labor, finances, planning, and development strategy, including matters related to agriculture, transport, industry, technology, and education.

*   Swanson, Jon C. "Some Consequences of Emigration for Rural Economic Development in the Yemen Arab Republic." Cited as item 134.

411. Tetreault, Mary Ann. **The Organization of Arab Petroleum Exporting Countries: History, Policies, and Prospects.** Westport, Conn.: Greenwood, 1981.

    Provides compendious information on OAPEC and its problems. Supplements discussion of oil economics and politics with data on trade patterns, military spending, and cultural homogeneity.

412. Townsend, John. "Problems Confronting the Establishment of a Heavy Industrial Base in the Arab Gulf." **Social and Economic Development in the Arab Gulf** (item 241).

    Discusses problems of rapid transformation of the Arab Gulf states into an industrial region. Identifies problems such as reluctance of international companies to make joint ventures with Gulf companies, poor regional coordination of industrial plans, and dependence on foreign labor.

413. Tuma, Elias S. "Population, Food and Agriculture in the Arab Countries." **The Middle East Journal**, 28, 4 (Autumn 1974), 381-395.

    Assays the interdependence between population and agriculture under various demographic and agricultural conditions. Deals with population control, family planning policies, and the results of agricultural policies. Explores areas of priority for research and policy implementation. Concludes that a viable balance between population and economy may be difficult to attain country-by-country but feasible on a regional basis.

*   Turner, Bryan S. "The Middle Classes and Entrepreneurship in Capitalist Development." Cited as item 270.

414. Vatikiotis, P.J. "The Modernization of Poverty." **Middle Eastern Studies**, 12, 3 (October, 1976), 193-204.

Questions basic assumptions about planning as an instrument of change and development. Explains certain consequences of planning, such as enhanced state controls and direction. Examines various planning problems in the Arab states, particularly political motives that reduce planning to window-dressing in the absence of capable administrative machinery and reliable data.

415. Voll, Sarah P. "Egyptian Land Reclamation Since the Revolution." **The Middle East Journal**, 34, 2 (Spring 1980), 127-148.

Reviews land reform in Egypt since 1952 and problems of reclamation and cultivation. Views land reform as necessary but insufficient to alleviate rural poverty. Reclamation aims to increase domestic agricultural and provide an adequate livelihood for landless rural population. However, new lands consumed forty to sixty percent of agricultural expenditures but returned less than one percent of total agricultural production. Only 56,000 of more than a million and a half landless families received reclaimed land. Nevertheless, commitment to land reclamation will continue for political and ideological reasons.

416. Waterbury, John. **Public Versus Private in Egyptian Economy,** Northeast Africa Series. Hanover, N.H.: American Universities Field Staff, 21, 5, 1976.

Finds a proper assessment of public sector performance over the past twenty years of state capitalism difficult because of inaccurate or incomplete data. Contends, however, that there are no examples of outstanding public management, and the major ills plaguing the public sector are labor redundancy, slipshod and inconsistent accounting techniques, idle capacities, faulty sectoral organization, and management techniques.

* Weinbaum, Marvin G. "Egypt's Infitah and the Politics of U.S. Economic Assistance." Cited as item 277.

417. Weiss, Dieter. "Urban Agglomeration Problems and National Housing Policy in Egypt." **Economics,** 24 (1981), 109-120.

    Contends that housing is the first most important basic requirement after food. Considers high increase in population a major contributing factor to the housing crisis.

418. Wilkinson, J.C. "Changes in the Structure of Village Life in Oman." **Social and Economic Development in the Arab Gulf** (item 241).

    Discusses reasons for the collapse of the traditional structure of village life in Oman. Argues that the collapse is caused, partly, because of importing foodstuffs; the relative rejection, by villagers, of traditional products (dates, camels); and the development of an alternative economy by national efforts.

419. Wilson, Rodney. **Banking and Finance in the Arab Middle East.** New York: St. Martin's Press, 1983.

    Surveys the development of banking and financial systems. Discusses traditional banking practice, the emergence of modern banking, growth of Arab financial expertise, Islamic banking in principle and practice, the role of commercial banks, and aid and development assistance agencies.

420. Wilson, Rodney J.A. "Egypt's Export Diversification: Benefits and Constraints." **The Developing Economies,** XXII, 1 (March 1984), 86-101.

    Studies Egypt's recent experience in export diversification, designed to exchange historical dependence on its cotton crop. Analyzes problems and consequences of the effort, which took two forms: (1) substitution of manufactured cotton goods such as yarn, thread, and woven cloth, and (2) substitution of alternative crops for new cotton, such as potatoes, onion, citrus, and rice.

421. Wilson, Rodney J.A. **The Economies of the Middle East.** New York: Holmes and Meier Publishers, 1979.

Offers a general economic survey of the entire Middle East, including three non-Arab states.

422. Wohlers-Scharf, Traute. "The Developmental Role of OPEC/Arab Funds and International Arab and Islamic Banks." **Public Enterprise**, 4, 1 (1983), 23-40.

Examines the contribution of the recently established OPEC/Arab funds, as well as the role of the international commercially oriented Arab and Islamic banks and their efforts to support development in Third World countries in the '80s.

423. Wynn, R.F. "The Sudan's Ten-Year Plan of Economic Development, 1961/62-1970/71: An Analysis of Achievement." **The Journal of Developing Areas**, 4, 5 (July 1971), 555-576.

Describes the Sudanese economy prior to the ten-year plan published in March 1962 (the first attempt at comprehensive planning). Reviews the framework and execution of the plan (in 1970), when departures from the plan's projections had become sufficiently serious that the formulation of a new plan for 1969-73 seemed appropriate. Points out factors contributing to failure, relating either to plan implementation or incorrect assessment of the economy.

424. Young, Arthur N. **Saudi Arabia: The Making of a Financial Giant.** New York: New York University Press, 1983.

Discusses modern Saudi Arabia from social, political, and economic perspectives. Describes the political system, wealth from oil, approaches to reforms, the founding of the monetary system, relationship with OPEC, and other subjects related to development. Describes the country's transformation from a desert land into one of the world's leading economic and financial powers.

425. Zahlan, Rosemarie Said. "Hegemony, Dependence and Development in the Gulf." **Social and Economic Development in the Arab Gulf** (item 241).

Provides a historical survey useful in guiding the formulation of socio-economic strategies for the development of the Arab Gulf states. Discusses the pre-oil period, transition to oil, repercussions of the oil agreements. Gives a perspective on the post-oil era.

426. Ziwar-Daftari, May, ed. **Issues in Development: The Arab Gulf States.** London: Research and Services, Ltd., 1980.

Contains a collection of economic studies by Arab and English scholars and government officials. Classifies subjects covered as "bottlenecks," "case studies," and "viewpoints." Investigates a wide range of economic issues. Covers banking, industry, labor, and agriculture. Includes items 280 and 307.

CHAPTER 5

DOCTORAL DISSERTATIONS

This chapter presents selected doctoral dissertations divided into three groups: A. Administration, B. Human Resources, and C. Socio-economic Development. All are Ph.D. dissertations unless otherwise noted.

A. Administration

427. Abalkhail, Sulaiman Saleh. "Public Enterprises and Development in Kuwait." Claremont Graduate School, 1979.

States that government has been compelled to enter economic enterprises that would otherwise be in private hands. Observes that the aggregate economy is almost totally dependent on the oil industry, while economy outside oil is heavily dependent on government. The government-public enterprise link in development is based on growing government financial ability, rather than any particular ideology or design.

428. Abdalla, Elhadi Abdal-Samad. "Development Administration and Regionalism: Towards a Communalist Approach to Decisional Process in the Sudan." University of Pittsburgh, 1981.

Criticizes traditional development administration as "fixated on control philosophy derived from the dominant rational-central-rule approach." Explores the case of Sudan as an illustration of

Administration and Development

negative consequences of an administrative system preoccupied with control while lacking capacity to govern.

429. Abdeen, Adnan Muhammad. "The Role of Accounting in the Economic Development of Syria." D.B.A. dissertation. Mississippi State University, 1974.

    Reports results of interviews with Syrian accountants, managers, and public officials, and a structured questionnaire to registered statutory accountants. Describes the expanded role of accounting resulting from complex regulations and comprehensive economic planning. Points out need to improve diverse accounting practices and reports. Recommends professional organization, coordination with government, and increased contacts with accountants in other countries.

430. Abdelrahiem, Zahir Hamad. "The Long-Term Growth of Government Expenditure and Economic Development of the Sudan: 1956-1980." Syracuse University, 1982.

    Describes the long-term growth of public expenditures. Considers whether the traditional demand, cost, fiscal policy, and disruption explanations for expenditure growth hold for Sudan.

431. Abdelrhman, Mohamed Bushara. "Bureaucracy and Development: A Study of the Civil Service in Sudan." Florida State University, 1983.

    Explores attitudes of senior civil service administrators toward change based on responses to a questionnaire. Tests 205 respondents' views on friction, communication, responsibility, and emigration, correlating attitudes with independent variables of social status, education, work organization, and family influence. Indicates conservatism among senior administrators, dissatisfaction, and lack of commitment to their work.

Dissertations/Administration 135

432. Abdo-Khalil, Zeinab M. "Public Sector Administration in Egypt." Claremont Graduate School, 1983.

    Studies productive enterprises in Egypt owned and/or operated by the government with the explicit objective of accelerating economic and social development. Examines environmental factors, organization and accountability, management of public enterprises, the boards, problems of motivation, assessment of performance, and other management problems.

433. Abusin, Ahmed Ibrahim. "Administrative Reform in Sudan: A Human Resource Perspective." University of Southern California, 1977.

    Aims to (1) elaborate on the interaction of independent variables influencing reform and to develop a conceptualization for a reform strategy, and (2) focus on human resources in terms of planning, development, and retention. Assumes that administrative reform is a subsystem of the social milieu, dependent on the two main social variables of reform: leadership and environmental factors. Concludes that reform must work to change the educational and personnel systems of the Sudan in order to produce an employable and motivated manpower force compatible with national development needs.

434. Abussuud, Alawi Nuri. "Administrative Development and Planning in Saudi Arabia: The Process of Differentiation and Specialization." University of Maryland, 1979.

    Illustrates the evolution of the Saudi bureaucracy toward a more functionally specific bureaucratic structure. Employs Fred Riggs' Prismatic Model as a tool of analysis (descriptive and analytical). Concludes that, despite problems, the bureaucracy has attained "a certain degree of rationality ... illustrated by a number of tangible achievements."

Administration and Development

435. Ahmed, Elamin Abdalla. "The Sudan's Experience in Local Government: An Evaluation Study." Claremont Graduate School, 1983.

Describes the system of local government under British rule and the introduction of a new system by the People's Local Government Act of 1971. Critically evaluates the application of this Act, hailed, at its inception, as revolutionary, advancing people's participation, decentralizing power and authority, and encouraging development planning and implementation.

436. Ahmed, Rafia Hassan. "Central Personnel Growth in Expenditure and Size of the Sudanese Government." Claremont Graduate School, 1980.

Asserts that over-staffing and under-utilization in the central personnel system thwart efficiency and productivity. Finds that thirty percent of central expenditure goes annually to central personnel salaries and wages (using quantitative methodology). Discusses efficiency, productivity, effectiveness, and capability of central personnel compared with other countries. Finds socio-economic services weak and most development projects incompletely financed. Recommends hiring freeze, redistribution of central personnel (including transfer to regional and local governments), in-service training, and reorganization of the system.

437. Al-Arrayed, Thuraya Ebrahim. "An Analysis of the Development of Administrative Structure in the Bahraini System of Education, 1919-1974." The University of North Carolina at Chapel Hill, 1975.

Studies stages of development of the public education system from an organizational perspective. Draws on Ministry of Education documents and primary source data as well as results of a questionnaire measuring attitudes, knowledge of organizational practices, and orientation (professional or bureaucratic) of the administrative staff. Concludes that current policies are justified in giving more weight to educational qualifications and less to sex and length of service in deciding hiring and promotion. Questions the practice of promoting clerical staff to administrative positions on the basis of long service.

438. Al-Awaji, Ibrahim Mohamed. "Bureaucracy and Society in Saudi Arabia." University of Virginia, 1971.

Deals with the interrelationship between the bureaucracy and four environmental factors: geohistorical, social, economic, and political. Underlines the important position occupied by bureaucracy, its competition for control of various benefits, and its institutional leverage in the allocation and distribution of various tangible and intangible economic benefits. Discusses organizational and behavioral characteristics of bureaucracy, with data resulting from a questionnaire administered in 1970. Consists of 79 items formulated in light of several propositions about interaction between the bureaucracy and its human ecology and with special reference to some aspects of F.W. Riggs' "Sala Model."

439. Al-Dabbagh, Taher Hussien. "Analysis of Managerial Training and Development Within Saudi Arabian Airlines." North Texas State University, 1980.

Surveys and critically examines the management development program (MDP) of the Saudi Arabian airline. Bases data on personal interviews with 33 top Saudia executives and a questionnaire returned by 112 (of 130) managers, staff managers, and supervisors. Finds that "MDP was far from achieving its objectives" as it did not change the behavior of participants. Cites misunderstanding of Saudi Arabian culture and circumstances; lack of manpower analysis; lack of cooperation, coordination, and communication between training department and other departments; and lack of formal plans for management succession.

Administration and Development

440. Al-Falah, Fouad Abdul Samad. "Fragmentation and Administrative Integration in Public Agencies: A Clinical-type Study of Administrative Practices in Kuwait National Petroleum Company." The American University, 1975.

Applies Kaufman's concepts of "forces of fragmentation" and "strategies of integration" to the Kuwait National Petroleum Company. Collects data from documents, reports, manuals, and charts, and via interviews with top executives in Kuwait, London, and Tokyo. Identifies absence of clear mandate and declared written policy, weak information and feedback system, and geographical dispersion. Counteracting strategies include centralization, Kuwaitization, reorganization, high pay, inspections, and training.

441. Al-Ghamdi, Abdullah Abdulghani. "Action Research and the Dynamics of Organizational Environment in the Kingdom of Saudi Arabia." University of Southern California, 1982.

Deals with the unpredictability of change introduced with development; also with the deficiencies of existing research in public administration that characterizes a rigid bureaucratic structure often incompatible with Saudi culture. Finds current research following the western positivist model--abstract and stressing cognitive and mechanistic approaches. Favors an "action research paradigm" based on epistomological and methodological praxis, hermeneutics, existentialism, phenomenology, and pragmatism to address the deficiencies that exist in the Saudi public administration system. Hopes to increase competency, creativity, and problem-solving processes.

442. Al-Hegelan, Abdelrahman Abdelaziz. "Innovation in the Saudi Arabia Bureaucracy: A Survey Analysis of Senior Bureaucrats." Florida State University, 1984.

Surveys 231 individuals in 10 ministries to assess the innovative capability of Saudi senior bureaucrats. Uses factor analysis, frequency distribution, and cross tabulation to analyze data. Attributes lack of innovation to low skills. Reports a significant relationship between innovation and appropriateness of education, job satisfaction, fear of mistakes, income, delegation of authority, decision making, centralization, social participation, and organization size.

443. Al-Jibouri, Sadia Jabouri Joudi. "Size, Technology and Organizational Structure in the Manufacturing Industry of a Developing Country: Iraq." D.B.A. dissertation. Mississippi State University, 1983.

Examines the relationship among structure, technology, and size of organizations in Iraq and compares them with organizations in Jordan. Describes methods of testing in the sample of twenty-seven companies (public, mixed, and private ownership) and reveals methods of testing and results of analysis of six hypotheses involving multiple-item scales, structural variables, and correlations with size, technology, workflow adaptability, etc.

444. Al-Khaldi, Abdullah Motad. "Job Content and Context Factors Related to Satisfaction and Dissatisfaction in Three Occupational Levels of the Public Sector in Saudi Arabia." Florida State University, 1983.

Explores the degree of job satisfaction and dissatisfaction in Saudi Arabia via a questionnaire administered to 800 public employees (civilian) at low, middle, and high occupational levels. Concludes that employees are motivated by work itself: i.e., such factors as achievement, relationship with peers, and working conditions. Found satisfaction highest among employees in high positions and older employees. Found employees in the Ministry of Foreign Affairs significantly more satisfied than those in other governmental agencies.

140 Administration and Development

445. Al-Kubaisy, Amer K. "Theory and Practice of Administrative Development in New Nations with Reference to the Case of Iraq." University of Texas at Austin, 1971.

Examines the significance, meaning, and approaches of administrative development. Applies concepts to Iraq and concludes that level of performance in developing administration "has not reached a satisfactory stage" because of the neglect of both the monarch and the Republican elites in terms of considering the effects of ecological factors. Recommends education, resocialization, and decentralization as means to remove factors that hamper effectiveness of Iraq public administration.

446. Al-Mazroa, Suliman Abdullah. "Public Administration Trends and Prospects in the Context of Development in Saudi Arabia." Claremont Graduate School, 1980.

Considers development drive of administrative origin because the administrative system is the most organized body responsible for initiating, financing, promoting, and supervising the implementation of development. Reviews some aspects of administration and suggests changes.

447. Al-Mizjaji, Ahmad Dawood. "The Public Attitudes Toward the Bureaucracy in Saudi Arabia." Florida State University, 1982.

Surveys the Saudi public's receptivity to change, trust in bureaucracy, and satisfaction with public agencies and services: hospitals, postal, telephone, price control, and utilities.

448. Al-Neaim, Hamad Abdulaziz. "An Analysis of the Recruitment of Foreign Employees in the Civil Service of Saudi Arabia." North Texas State University, 1980.

Studies Saudi Arabian strategy to alleviate manpower needs in civil service by recruiting foreign employees. Bases data on review of literature and documents; personal interviews with civil service officials; and questionnaire returned by 90 (of 116) Saudi civil service personnel who recruit foreign employees. Describes recruiting, finding evidence of procedural delays. Recommends matching people with the right jobs, exploring all sources of qualified potential applicants, and instituting an orientation program to reduce turnover among foreign employees.

449. Al-Nifay, Abdullah Musleh. "An Assessment to Redesign In-Service Training Programs for Paraprofessionals Employed in Military Hospitals Under the Jurisdiction of the Saudi Arabian Ministry of Defense." University of Pittsburgh, 1981.

Examines training and skills of hospital employees to determine the extent of in-service training needs. Uses the results of this needs assessment plus review of literature to design an in-service training program focusing on objectives, techniques, materials, participants, and evaluation methodology.

450. Al-Okush, Fawzi Abdallah Ahmed. "Technology Transfer to a Developing Country, Jordan: A Decision-Making Study." Syracuse University, 1978.

Studies the decision-making process involved in technology transfer; particularly, how decision to use the technology was made. Selects three public agencies for the case method approach. Uses information collected through interviews, official documents, and other published materials. Confirms the central role of public agencies in imparting and using new technologies; suggests the creation of a unit to cater to technology transfers.

451. Al-Omar, Jasem Ebraheem. "A Comparison of Values and Job Satisfaction Among American and Arab Managers." D.B.A. dissertation. United States International University, 1984.

Compares levels of job satisfaction of American male middle-level managers with those from the Arab Gulf States to determine the relationship between job satisfaction and values. Derives data from questionnaires to U.S. and Arab managers; both groups were attending school in southern Califorina. Findings are simplistic: similarity in job satisfaction and differences in group values.

452. Al-Sabban, Aidros Abdullah Srour. "The Municipal System in the Kingdom of Saudi Arabia: A Case Study of Makkah." Claremont Graduate School, 1982.

Describes the Saudi municipal system, identifies administrative problems, and suggests some solutions. Focuses on the municipality of Makkah.

453. Al-Shaibi, Hameed A.M. "An Analysis of the Perceptions of Personnel Directors in the Public Sector in Iraq Concerning the Importance of Their Managerial and Organizational Functions." The University of Iowa, 1979.

Defines the perceptions of sixty-five personnel directors in the public sector based on a sixty-nine-item questionnaire. Asserts that directors do not give a high enough degree of importance to managerial and organizational functions. Recommends that personnel directors devote greater attention to managerial subfunctions, particularly those employing the principle of planning.

454. Al-Shuaib, Shuaib Abdulla. "Accounting and Economic Development in Kuwait: Description and Analysis." University of Missouri-Columbia, 1974.

Contends that the development of accounting in Kuwait has become "more responsive to the economic development needs of the country." Draws on literature, interviews, corporate financial statements, and a questionnaire survey answered by sixty-four percent of Kuwait's licensed accountants. Reports that the capital market operates without financial information; "investors buy and sell on the basis of rumors and guesswork." Also reports that the development planning process lacks basic needed information and suffers from short implementation time. Recommends establishment of a stock exchange; cooperation among accountants, educators, and the Ministry of Commerce and Industry; and generation of information for macro planning.

455. Al-Tawail, Mohammed Abdulrahman. "Institute of Public Administration in Saudi Arabia: A Case Study in Institution Building." University of Pittsburgh, 1974.

Assesses the institution-building process of the Saudi Institute of Public Administration (IPA), established in 1961. Analyzes the IPA's capacity using the conceptual model developed by the Inter-University Research Program in Institution Building, examining variables such as leadership, doctrine, resources, and internal structure. Identifies the IPA's most recent five years as the period during which it achieved a higher degree of institutionality; offers reasons based on analysis of documents, questionnaires, and interviews with IPA trainees, their supervisors, and the IPA's top administrators and faculty members.

456. Al-Teraifi, Al-Agab Ahmed. "Administrative Reform in the Sudan with Special Reference to Personnel Aspects." University of Pittsburgh, 1978.

Evaluates recent administrative reform, focusing on aspects of the public personnel system (classification, recruitment, promotion, training). Relies on primary data, government records, interviews, and literature. Identifies problems; offers a plan of action for administrative reform as a component of the development process.

144 Administration and Development

457. Al-Thubaity, Awad Mastour. "Department Chairpersons' Perception of Their Position Regarding the Requirements and Process of Selection, the Major Responsibilities, and the Requirements for Job Satisfaction in Saudi Arabian Universities." Michigan State University, 1981.

Based on a questionnaire administered to 152 chairpersons at three Saudi universities. Finds that most chairmen are new in their departments, new in their positions, or new in the country. Reports significant differences in research background and publication as well as (at two of the universities) concern with teaching.

458. Alhumaid, Abdulrhman I. "An Empirical Study of the Characteristics of the Governmental Budgetary Process in Rich and Uncertain Environments: The Case of Saudi Arabia." The Louisiana State University and Agricultural and Mechical College, 1981.

Uses library research, interviews, and empirical testing of quantitative budgetary data to examine the characteristics of the governmental budgetary process. Describes the process as nonincremental, with supplemental budgeting one of the major attributes. Reports that "spending agencies tend to exaggerate their estimates" knowing the Ministry of Finance will alter them. Observes lack of well defined decision criteria, qualified personnel, and modern data-gathering techniques at all levels.

459. Ali, Abbas J. "An Empirical Investigation of Managerial Value Systems for Working in Iraq." West Virginia University, 1982.

Explores the value system patterns of Iraqi managers and their relationship to organizational and demographic variables. Uses six value system descriptions as dependent variables: tribalistic, ego-centric, conformist, manipulative, socio-centric, and existential.

460. Ali, Amal Eltigani. "Sudan General Petroleum Corporation: A Study of the Evolution of its Organization." D.B.A. dissertation. The George Washington University, 1984.

Investigates the evolution of the General Petroleum Corporation and how it relates to government strategy toward the petroleum sector. Gathers data from official records of the corporation and several ministries. Finds that the organization, macro and micro, tends to change in response to changes in government strategy, particularly certain political and economic factors affecting the strategy.

461. Alnimir, Saud Mohammed. "Present and Future Bureaucrats in Saudi Arabia: A Survey Research." The Florida State University, 1981.

Includes the results of two surveys of attitudes, one of 500 bureaucrats in eight ministries, the other of 600 students preparing for government careers. Finds among bureaucrats (1) unacceptability of work-related mobility, (2) reluctance to work in rural areas, (3) monetary incentive not a factor in job choice, (4) conservative attitudes toward development programs, (5) unwillingness to take risks in decision making, (6) low tendency toward innovative behavior. Reports significant differences between bureaucrat and student behavior only in willingness to work in rural areas, attitude toward ascriptive values, and attitude on social issues.

462. Alrayes, Tarik Mohammad. "Authority and Influence in the Government Civil Service in the State of Kuwait." Claremont Graduate School, 1979.

Studies the nature of the relationship between non-Kuwaiti administrators in the civil service and their Kuwaiti subordinates. Finds non-Kuwaitis form just over half of the population, but seventy percent of the labor force; they hold sixty percent of civil service jobs, but only ten percent of administrative positions. Finds--based on four months of interviews in Kuwait--that non-Kuwaiti administrators do not assume full authority over their subordinates, have no job security, relinquish some legal authority rather than risk dismissal; and the Kuwaiti subordinate knows he is being groomed for the non-Kuwaiti's position.

463. Amer, Abdulgader Ayad. "Managerial Effectiveness of State-Owned Firms: An Empirical Study of State-Owned Firms in Libya." Oklahoma State University, 1974.

Evaluates problems of state-owned firms and explores managerial effectiveness in terms of planning, education of managers, size of firm, production technology, and goals. Randomly samples fourteen of Libya's seventy-six such firms, using personal interviews. Tests several hypotheses; offers guidelines urging more government emphasis on education, and adoption of new technology and application of cost-benefit analysis tools by management.

464. Amry, Mohammed-Abdullateef Yousuf. "Program Budgeting Model for Saudi Arabian Elementary Education: An Emphasis on Program Costs for Decisions." The University of Arizona, 1976.

Examines the current budgetary system, emphasizing the line-item approach and limited to input costs estimates. Recommends a general program budgeting system that can provide input-output information relevant to planning as well as to controlling. Emphasizes the inclusion of three different kinds of quantitative information: quantitative objectives, quantitative outputs, and the cost of achieving these outputs and objectives.

465. As'ad, Ibrahim Ahmad. "Government Budgeting and its Control in Saudi Arabia." Claremont Graduate School, 1982.

Discusses structures involved in the budget process since the first Saudi budget was published in 1948. Describes various organizations created to control the public finance and to monitor the budget's execution.

466. Askar, Samir Ahmed. "Personal Value Systems of Egyptian Managers." D.B.A. dissertation. Mississippi State University, 1979.

    Studies the value systems of 236 Egyptian managers based on questionnaires measuring personal values and behavioral measures. Classifies forty-nine percent of managers as moralistic, thirty-six percent pragmatic, and three percent affect. Managers placed the highest behavioral relevance scores on high productivity, organizational stability, and organization efficiency. In terms of personal goals, managers placed higher value on dignity, prestige, influence, and power.

467. Atieh, Sulayman Hassan. "A Proposed Model for the Audit and Evaluation of the Objectives and Accomplishments of Jordanian Governmental Expenditure Programs." The University of Arizona, 1975.

    Offers a model for Jordan's Audit Bureau to evaluate efficiency and efficacy of government programs. Identifies constraints on the application of the model, such as uncontrollable political and cultural factors and lack of trained auditors and an adequate governmental accounting system. Recommends training auditors in evaluation methodology and establishing a data bank for public programs.

468. Ayoubi, Zaki Mousa. "Technology, Size, and Organization Structure in the Industry of a Developing Country: Jordan." Indiana University, Graduate School of Business, 1975.

    Explains the linkage of technology and size with organization structure in industrialized and developing countries. Gathers data on thirty-four industrial organizations using the Aston standard schedules (developed in the U.K.) and tests their validity for a developing country. Concludes that organization size is the strongest explanatory variable of variance in functional specialization, standardization, formalization, percent of employees in administration, etc.; and that degree of government ownership is the strongest explanatory variable of variance in centralization of decisions. Demonstrates the feasibility of applying a multivariate methodological approach in the study of organizations in developing countries.

469. Badawi, Abobakr Abdeen. "An Analysis of Job Tasks in Selected Occupations as Related to Vocational School Curriculum in Egypt." Ed.D. dissertation. Indiana University, 1982.

Aims to examine the relationship between vocational program offerings and Egyptian labor market by investigating the perceptions of vocational school graduates, their employers, and supervisors regarding variables of tasks performed on the job.

470. Badawi, Ibrahim Mohamed. "Organization and Administration of Public Enterprises for Socio-Economic Development: The Egyptian Experience, 1805-1975." New York University, 1977.

Studies the theoretical foundations and practical applications of public enterprises for social and economic development. Deals with the public enterprise device as a developmental alternative. Discusses the common features and major problems of three selected organizational models of public enterprises. Traces the origin, evolution, and collapse of public enterprises in the Egyptian economy from 1805-1952 and their subsequent re-emergence and expansion. Examines the organizational and administrative arrangements and institutional changes of public enterprises.

Dissertations/Administration 149

471. Badi, Yousef Mohamed. "Regional Growth Impact of Libyan Development Budget Expenditures." University of Nebraska-Lincoln, 1982.

Constructs a regional growth model to be used in regional planning in Libya and to take account of government development expenditures.

472. Badran, Sanaa Mohamed. "An Investigation of the Egyptian Auditor's Perceptions of the Independence of the Auditor." University of Arkansas, 1983.

Attempts to provide empirical evidence concerning the perceptions of auditors' independence within the Egyptian accounting profession and to determine whether Egyptian Chartered Accountants' perceptions of auditor/client independence differ from the positions of the SEC on that issue.

473. Bashaireh, Ahmed Suleiman. "Centralization and Decentralization in Educational Administration: Implications for Jordan." Indiana State University, 1982.

Investigates the desired levels for administrative decision-making relative to functions of public schools as perceived by educational administrators in Jordan and the United States. Questionnaire distributed to administrators at the state and local levels in both countries.

474. Binsaleh, Abdullah Mohammed. "The Civil Service and its Regulation in the Kingdom of Saudi Arabia." Claremont Graduate School, 1982.

Describes the considerable attention paid by the government to developing the public personnel system through reorganization. Deals with the issuance of the 1977 Civil Service Regulations to set procedures and techniques for the estabished merit system and offers recommendations.

150 Administration and Development

475. Buera, Abubakr Mustafa. "The Libyan Managerial Elite in the Private and Public Sectors." University of Missouri-Columbia, 1975.

Develops, based on data from a sample of 176 managers, a profile of the typical Libyan manager. Typically, the manager is male, a college graduate, married with children, has been educated (college) outside Libya, knows one or two foreign languages, is from an urban area, belongs to the Arab Socialist Union (the sole political organization), supervises ten or fewer subordinates, and has worked for only one or two enterprises.

476. Busniena, Saddeg Mansour. "A Comparative Study of the Need for Achievement Among Managers of Public vs. Private Organizations in the Libyan Arab Republic." The Louisiana State University and Agricultural and Mechanical College, 1977.

Investigates the relationship between the type of organization and achievement among Libyan managers. Reveals through statistical analysis that the "n" achievement is higher among managers of private business organizations than among managers of either profit-oriented or nonprofit public organizations. Concludes that, in the process of economic development, the Libyan government should not depend solely on the public sector unless efforts are made to raise the "n" achievement level of public organizations.

477. Canjar, Riec Eileen Iwiritzt. "A Structural Comparison of Spacial Organization in Conventional and Unconventional Military Systems: The Case of the 1958 Algerian Revolution." University of Michigan, 1983.

Uses the Algerian Revolutionary War to reconsider space as an organizing concept in human behavior and to direct the attention of military sociology to the study of field operations.

Dissertations/Administration 151

478. Durra, Abdel Bari. "Development Redefined: Human Resources Perspective for Developing Countries. Its Implications for Jordan." University of Southern California, 1975.

Explores themes of reconsideration of development models in view of national experiences and problems, particularly as they relate to human resources. Questions the relevance of capital accumulation, regarded as "the critical element in economic growth." Also criticizes political science and sociological perspectives for the dominance of structural functionalism. Suggests an interdisciplinary "human resources perspective of development."

479. El-Faki, Salah El Din Hamid. "An Environment-Based Performance Appraisal System for the Public Service in the Sudan." University of Southern California, 1983.

Argues that the performance appraisal system in the Sudanese public service does not, and cannot, work because the values of this system are antithetical to those of the culture in which it functions. Suggests an appraisal system compatible with the organizational-cultural environment.

480. El-Hindi, Adnan Hassan. "Reforms in Jordan's Budget System." Syracuse University, 1976.

Proposes improvements in Jordan's budgetary system, which is characterized by excessive budgetary fragmentation, multiplicity of budget categories, emphasis on line-item structure, and an inadequate link with development plans. Proposes to restructure the system to avoid such deficiencies, measure governmental impacts on the economy, serve economic analysis, and be attuned to development planning. Criticizes the use of the current and development expenditure classification, a distinction that--under the old budget structures--was neither realistic nor systematic. Indicates that the growing financial pressures of the last six years resulted in the recommendation of a Planning Programming Budgeting System for Jordan's budget.

481. El-Rawi, Mohamed F. "The Political Role of Bureaucracy in Contemporary Egypt." Southern Illinois University, 1975.

    Applies Fred W. Riggs' "imbalance" theory regarding bureaucracy and representative institutions, and Alfred Diamant's "developmental movement regimes" model to post-1952 Egypt. Examines Egypt's political and administrative development, finding bureaucratic institutions relatively more developed than representative ones. Traces bureaucracy's political activities not to "imbalance" but to administrators' close relationship with Egypt's president. Finds bureaucratic performance effective vis-a-vis agrarian reform laws, the High Dam project, and operation of the Suez Canal. Concludes that the Diamant model is closer to Egyptian political reality than Riggs' theory. Suggests augmenting representative institutions (Arab Socialist Union and National Assembly) via the prestige of the presidency.

482. Eldahry, Ahmed Kamal. "Budgeting and Policy Analysis: The Egyptian Case." State University of New York at Binghamton, 1981.

    Explicates the relationship between public policy, the political system, and other systemic variables as reflected in the budget. Notes the close relationship between centralized political authority and economic development prevalent since Pharaonic times. Analyzes the 1962-63 reforms, identifies institutional and sociopolitical factors, and presents a flow chart describing budget formation.

483. Eljazz, Awad Ahmed Mohammed. "Managerial Motivation for Organization Effectiveness in the Sudan." University of Southern California, 1982.

Dissertations/Administration

Investigates theoretical concerns of motivation and organization effectiveness and empirically analyzes the situation in Sudan regarding the motivation of managers and overall organization effectiveness.

484. Fadaak, Tarek Ali. "Urban Housing Policy Evaluation in the Kingdom of Saudi Arabia." Portland State University, 1984.

    Uses data collected from official government documents, field visits, and interviews to evaluate the urban housing policy of Saudi Arabia. Argues that public sector involvement in housing is most effective when indirectly applied through subsidies to the private sector.

485. Ghosheh, Zaki Rateb. "The Process of Administrative Change in Jordan: 1921-1967." Southern Illinois University, 1970.

    Describes the process of administrative change in Jordan between 1921 and 1967, taking into account economic conditions lacking viability and dependent on external assistance. Identifies training and education of personnel as an "instrumental and essential feature" of administrative improvement.

486. Halta, Salim Sulieman. "A Plan for Organizing a Training Program for Medical Auxiliaries in the State University of Jordan." The Florida State University, 1977.

    Focuses on educational legislation expressing governmental policies for the development of higher education, particularly the development of the University of Jordan and its health-related faculties. Examines health services and the Ministry of Health's organization and administration, budget allocations, and health facilities. Outlines a prototype for a program to train medical auxiliaries to provide first-line comprehensive health care to family members.

487. Hammour, Mirghani Abdelaal. "The Public Corporation As a Tool of Management and Development (with special reference to the Sudan)." University of Pittsburgh, 1979.

Describes developing countries' use of the public corporation to implement quick developmental programs. Argues that assumptions about the cost effectiveness of the public corporation--and its high responsiveness to public needs and demands--collapse in many developing countries because of differences in sociopolitical environment. Points to Sudan's lack of democratic institutions to provide public accountability and scrutiny, and the feeble position of its private sector. Describes jealousy, administrative conflict, and attempts at obstruction and sabotage by other government institutions. Proposes taking development back to the village and grass-roots level, denouncing the neo-classical approach to development, and abandoning the public corporation in favor of village communes and councils.

488. Hanna, Nagy Kamel. "Towards a Methodology for Planning Models. Case Study: Transportation Planning in the Sudan." University of Pennsylvania, 1976.

Identifies basic elements of a methodology for the construction and use of models in planning. Tests the effectiveness of the conventional approach to modeling (analytic) compared with an emerging alternative (systemic). Constructs a set of models (econometric, prioritization, simulation, process-flow, conceptual) to address aspects of transportation planning, contrasting the effectiveness of the analytic and systemic approaches. Reports that evidence supports the systemic strategy as a planning process that is more imaginative about the future, more adaptive to evolving needs, and more responsive to institutional building requirements. By comparison, the analytic strategy is more sensitive to the immediacy and urgency of current problems and to the pressures of short-term payoffs. Redesigns specific criteria for the selection of both strategies, develops recommendations for their alternative use, and designs a mixed strategy involving simultaneous or sequential applications.

489. Harrim, Hussein Mahmoud. "Public Administration Development in Jordan: An Integrated Approach." University of Southern California, 1976.

Asserts that the "real problems and causes of ... deficiencies and poor performance of the public administration system have seldom been attacked." Cites sporadic, consultant-centered efforts at structural/procedural improvements. Asserts that subjectivity, traditionalism, favoritism, nepotism, lack of regard for the public, absence of an "inquisitive, experimental mind," and pessimism "permeate the public administration system"; largely the product of dominant values and social institutions. Attributes bribery and corruption, in part, to low pay. Suggests a framework for developing public administration emphasizing "the interdependent social and technical subsystems of the administrative system.

490. Howeedy, Mostafa Abd el-Razzak. "A Study Suggesting Contemporary Urban Design Guidelines Using the United Arab Emirates as an Illustrative Case." D.E.D. dissertation. Texas A&M University, 1978.

Attempts to develop contemporary urban design guidelines for the central area of the city of Dubai. Reviews the literature of urban design and methodologies of selected North American cities. Reviews the growth patterns in the seven Emirates; recommends continued research.

491. Istasi, Cecile Wesley. "Planning Guidelines for a National Scientific and Technical Transformation System in the Sudan." University of Pittsburgh, 1976.

156 Administration and Development

Proposes goals, objectives, functions, and prerequisites of a national information system. Includes a subsystem of information for industry, its operational requirements links with other national and international systems, and the priorities and obstacles of implementation. Includes opinion poll of professional librarians in Sudan and a framework to guide other efforts to develop national information systems.

492. Jadallah, Salih Mahmoud. "Performance Auditing and Program Evaluation in Government--Saudi Arabia as a Field of Application." D.B.A. Texas Tech University, 1978.

Describes a conceptual framework for monitoring government programs to provide managers with information that promotes efficient and effective management. Develops a generalized performance audit model, selecting the area of procurement to assess applicability of the model to Saudi system of public administration. Describes research methodology, which entailed review of literature; structured interviews at the GAO in Washington, D.C., and the Exchequer and Audit Department in London; and a field study in Riyadh to delineate current program monitoring and determine needs for performance auditing and program evaluation.

493. Jarawan, Eva Muawwad. "Development and Verification of Role-Specific Competencies for Hospital Administration in Lebanon." Georgia State University, 1984.

Identifies competencies necessary for the effective hospital administrator in Lebanon and determines the degree of importance attached to each one. Develops actual and ideal role-specific competencies as perceived and rank-ordered by hospital administrators, faculty, and students respectively.

494. Khalifa, Ali Mohammed. "The United Arab Emirates: Unity in Fragmentation--A Study in Ministate

Integration in a Complex Setting, 1968-1976." University of California, 1978.

Traces the background, consummation, and development of the UAE as a federal entity in a primarily tribal culture. Identifies hindrances to integration (tribalism, paternalism, territorial disputes among states, and the "immigrant phenomenon" and many countering influences. Bases research on review of literature, documents, surveys and interviews with members of federal and local governments, and inerviews with "prominent members of the intelligentsia and the private sector." Concludes that the UAE came into being as the result of elites' perceptions that states were unable, individually, to assume responsibilities of statehood with meager material and human resources.

495. Khashoggi, Hani Yousef. "Local Administration in Saudi Arabia." Claremont Graduate School, 1979.

A descriptive-analytical study of the Saudi local administration system. Focuses on the central-local relationship. Relies on documentary evidence, review of literature, observation of operations, and interviews with central and local officials. Finds a significant gap between concept and practice. Attributes failure of attempts to devolute powers to local administration to lack of local capabilities, lack of coordination between local administrations, and lack of guidelines for local functions. Finds local-national cooperation on planning nonexistent.

496. Kheir, Abubaker Mustafa M. "A Conceptual Model of Computer-Based Information Systems Requirements for a Governmental Department in a Developing Country." D.B.A. George Washington University, 1979.

Deals with computer transfer of experience from a government agency in an industrialized nation to a like agency in a developing country. Develops a CBIS requirement framework, rated by U.S. government experts, then re-evaluated by international experts using criteria emphasizing the framework's suitability to government agencies in developing countries. Results have been used to develop a new CBIS framework for the Sudanese Department of Statistics (modeled on the U.S. Census Bureau).

497. Kordi, Khalil Abdulfuttah Khalil. "The Major Characteristics of the Accounting Information Systems in Some Selected Saudi Industrial Businesses: A Critical Analysis." The University of Arizona, 1979.

Examines major characteristics of internal accounting services to management in twenty-four medium to large-scale industrial firms. Asks, how much effort are Saudi accountants devoting to applying advanced cost accounting techniques? Concludes that the controllership function is more preoccupied with recording financial transactions and keeping accurate records than serving management's need for information. Also concludes that management--unwilling to make extensive use of accounting information in decision-making--shows little interest in sponsoring efforts to enhance information systems' effectiveness.

498. Madi, Mohammed Abdullah F. "Developmental Administration and the Attitudes of Middle Management in Saudi Arabia." Southern Illinois University, 1975.

Reports results of a 1974 field study in Riyadh consisting of interviews and a questionnaire administered to 252 middle managers. Identifies middle managers and analyzes social, educational, and occupational backgrounds; examines perceptions about responsibility, authority, supervision, participation in planning, training policies, and other administrative problems. Asserts that middle managers are not so passive as upper management believes; they "felt they were given only limited authority to get the job done" and "indicated their strong willingness to assume more responsibility ... if given the chance to participate in the planning process." Recommends a training plan based on a new concept of training.

499. Matejka, Jacqulin Cranfill. "Political Participation in the Arab World: The Majlis Mechanism." University of Texas at Austin, 1983.

Argues that the majlis is the major instrument of political participation in the Arab world and that informal mechanisms and procedures limit the power of Arab leaders. Points out some ways in which the West unnecessarily misunderstands Arab political behavior. Discusses advantages and disadvantages of participation via the majlis, which is inadequate for modernizing Arab society.

500. Milyani, Hisham M. "The Budgetary Process in Saudi Arabia." The Florida State University, 1983.

Explores the budgetary process by examining budgetary recommendations, participants and their roles, steps, and information sources.

501. Misallati, Abdalla Salem Omer. "Tripoli, Libya, Structure and Functions as an Arab-Islamic City." University of Kentucky, 1981.

Analyzes Tripoli's urban structure in terms of location and association of land use, land values, population densities, morphological aspects, and urban movement patterns.

502. Mohammed, Adam Azzain. "Regional Resource Allocations in the Sudan: 1971-1980." The Florida State University, 1981.

Uses 1971-1980 budgetary data, particularly grants to regions and regional shares of developmental projects, to evaluate charges of regional inequality. Concludes that the pattern of allocation of resources serves neither the objectives of rapid economic development nor those of distributive justice. Recommends investment in the agricultural sector and the distribution of grants according to a criterion acceptable to recipients.

503. Mohammed, Hassan Yousif. "The Impact of the Transfer of Agricultural Technology on the Sudan." Boston University, 1983.

    Suggests that Sudan's political and bureaucratic elite have limited their options by utilizing the existing technology package. Argues that elite's power, status, and income depend on the maintenance of a centralized administrative system. Focuses on the Gezira Scheme--one of the largest public agricultural corporations in the Sudan.

504. Mohammed, Shamil Kamil. "Leadership Behaviors of Youth Center Superintendents in Iraq as Perceived by Selected Staff Members." Ed.D. dissertation. University of Northern Colorado, 1983.

    Describes the characteristics of the present leadership of youth center superintendents in Iraq as recognized by the administrative staff, faculty, and superintendents themselves. Relies on data collected from forty-six randomly selected youth centers. Finds significant differences between groups concerning leadership and leaders' behavior. Argues that tolerance of freedom and integration are highly valued behaviors in leaders.

505. Moneef, Abdullah Ali. "The Attitude of the Saudi Citizens Toward the Imposition of Individual Income Tax." University of South Carolina, 1981.

    Argues that the imposition of an income tax would aid resource allocation and income redistribution, stabilize the economy, and enhance political awareness. Describes the 1950 income tax cancelled on religious grounds. Uses the Likert scale in a questionnaire administered to

700 government employees in five agencies and 204 Saudi graduate students in the United States (with respective response rates of 68 percent and 47 percent). Finds civil servants under age 50 in favor of an income tax. Civil servants over age 50 and graduate students oppose it, with opposition related to finances, not religion.

506. Murshid, Talal Asad. "Saudi Arabia: Administrative Aspects of Development." Claremont Graduate School, 1978.

    Reviews the general development of Saudi Arabia with a focus on administrative development in the period 1932-75. Examines the indicators of development, utilizing the "ecological model" of development advanced by Fred Riggs. Argues that development and modernization in Saudi Arabia in the past quarter century give good evidence that the transition will be made efficiently and effectively.

507. Nusair, Naim Ogleh. "Regional Development and Planning in Jordan: Jordan Valley Authority, 1973-1980." D.P.A. dissertation. State University of New York at Albany, 1982.

    Examines the institution of the Jordan Valley Authority and identifies causes of poor performance, such as over-centralization, lack of central political control, poor coordinaion with other institutions, and lack of citizen involvement.

508. Park, Thomas Kerlin. "Administration and the Economy: Morocco 1880 to 1980: The Case of Essaouira." University of Wisconsin, Madison, 1983.

    Studies the administration and economy of a town and region of Morocco using Arabic archival material and interviews. Evaluates Moroccan financial policies, assesses the administrative system, and estimates the degree of involvement of rural producers in the capitalist market.

Administration and Development

509. Pasha, Hafiz Ahmed. "Seasonal Housing Markets: A Model of Pilgrim Housing in Makkah." Stanford University, 1984.

   Examines the policy question of how to organize efficiently the provision of accommodation during the peak period of pilgrimage, when the population swells from .5 million to 1.3 million. Offers a model empirically applied to data collected from housing surveys carried out in 1981 by the Hajj Research Center, Ummal Qura University, Saudi Arabia.

510. Salih, Siddig Abdelmageed. "The Impacts of the Government Agricultural Policies on Domestic Wheat Production in the Sudan." Duke University, 1984.

   Examines Sudanese government policies in the wheat market, i.e., multi-tier pricing, compulsory procurement of part of the domestic productions, and government monopoly of wheat imports. Indicates cheating among farmers by underreporting production as a consequence of policies. Calls for correcting or even abandoning current policies and argues for domestic production of wheat as a policy.

511. Samman, Nizar Hasan. "Saudi Arabia and the Role of the Imarates in Regional Development." Claremont Graduate School, 1982.

   Describes the system of local authorities, their training needs, relations with national ministries, and the creation of a Supreme Council for Regional Development.

512. Shadukhi, Suliman Mohammed. "Application of Organization Development (OD) in Saudi Arabia's Public Organizations: A Feasibility Study." The Florida State University, 1981.

   Identifies the organizational problems of two Saudi public organizations and suggests appropriate OD techniques for solutions. Describes the management system as authoritarian, with the nature of the problems hierarchical, indicating a low degree of effectiveness. Recommends improving organizational climate, managerial leadership, peer leadership, and group process. Also suggests adapting the Survey of Organizations to Saudi organizations and culture.

513. Tawati, Ahmed Mohmed. "The Civil Service of Saudi Arabia: Problems and Prospects." West Virginia University, 1976.

    Evaluates the role of the public personnel system in Saudi society vis-a-vis four interrelated objectives: (1) critical analysis of the evolution of personnel administration from the emergence of modern Saudi Arabia to the present, (2) critical analysis of the various functions of the current personnel system, (3) examination of the impact of the economic boom on the civil service, and (4) explanations via a comparative perspective on administration. Draws data from published material, government documents, interviews with political officials and government managers, and literature on administrative development in changing societies.

514. Tikriti, Mwafaq Haded. "Elites, Administration, and Public Policy: A Comparative Study of Republican Regimes in Iraq, 1958-1976." The University of Texas at Austin, 1976.

    Undertakes an in-depth examination of the various background characteristics of political elites. Attempts to determine factors influencing their attitudes and behavior in deciding public policy on modernization and political development. Includes study of original Arabic sources, national and international publications, and interviews with some prominent Iraqi political personalities and administrators. Underlines the reciprocal relationship between the elites' background, the bureaucracy, and public policy performance.

164　Administration and Development

515. Turki, Hedi. "A Study of Management's Budget-Oriented Behavior in Tunisian Business Enterprises." University of Illinois at Urbana-Champaign, 1981.

    Conducts a field study of six organizations (representing about three quarters of the chemical industry) to determine the extent to which budget-oriented behavior of managers is dependent on individual, organizational, and environmental factors. Shows the predominance of the control and evaluation aspects of budgeting, suggesting that the control and performance-measure aspects of budgeting offer a richer field for investigating managers' behavior than the participation aspect. Indicates the importance of centralization, organization structure, personality, and demographic factors in explaining managers' budget-oriented behavior.

516. Yacoub, Suheil A. "The Eight Formal Organizational Variables in Hage's Axiomatic Theory Applied to Teacher Training Institutes in Iraq." Ed.D. dissertation. The University of Akron, 1981.

    Administers a questionnaire to obtain three-year data from eleven teacher training institutes. Concludes that Hage's Axiomatic Theory is not general enough to be functional, with explanatory capacity limited to internal factors in organizations. Asserts that social, political, and economic factors influencing organizational behavior should be considered.

517. Yahya, Mahmud Mohamed. "Management Education and Training in Somalia: The Case of Somali Institute of Development Administration and Management." University of California, Los Angeles, 1984.

    Investigates the status of the Somali Institute of Development Administration (SIDAM) with focus on the period 1974-1984, using the institution building model developed by Esman and Blaise as the guiding theoretical framework. Identifies a set of problems facing SIDAM and makes specific recommendations.

518. Young, Jerome Edward. "Municipal Government and Politics in the West Bank." University of Cincinnati, 1984.

Studies the municipalities of the West Bank (under Israeli occupation since 1967) and the impact of the 1976 elections. Concludes, based on field interviews in eight major West Bank towns, that municipalities evolved from Western influences dating to Ottoman rule over Palestine. Describes Israeli occupation's constraints on conduct of municipal business; municipal planning, budget, and delivery of services are made extremely difficult.

519. Zarouq, Hassabelrasoul Hussein Ahmed. "Citizen Participation: The Experience of Sudanese Local Government." University of Southern California, 1983.

Focuses on the concept of citizen participation in local government: its dimensions, goals, and role. Evaluates effectiveness in administering local affairs and suggests improvements. Uses conceptual, experiential, and experimental approaches based on data collected through questionnaires, interviews, and examination of government records. Argues that factors retarding participation are related to dominance of bureaucratic institutions, failure to delegate power, financial limitations, and quality of membership.

520. Zarrugh, Omar Salem. "Developing a Training Program for Civil Service Employees, A Model Training Program for the Socialist People's Libyan Arab Jamahiriya. Ed.D. dissertation. Ball State University, 1981.

Investigates the effectiveness of training programs and the possibilities for improvement.

166 Administration and Development

Suggests need for a master plan to organize and supervise training programs, as well as identifying training needs and developing a central training unit.

B. Human Resources

521. Abdelghany, Abdelghany Mohamed. "School Life Tables and a Comparative Study in Demographic and Educational Development in Egypt." The Florida State University, 1979.

Uses the school life table technique to determine whether the education system has achieved its most significant goals, i.e., producing citizens fully educated physically and spiritually; being accessible to citizens regardless of income; and helping build a "new society based on democratic socialism." Explores such issues as the success of the policy of compulsion, differences between enrolled population and total population, and eradication of illiteracy.

522. Abdelhamid, Nimer Kamal Kamel. "The Role of Women's Organizations in Eradicating Illiteracy in Jordan." The University of Michigan, 1983.

Attributes the drop in illiteracy in Jordan from 67.3 percent in 1961 to 34.6 percent in 1982 largely to the increase of literacy among women. Focuses on the Women's Association for Combating Illiteracy as the leading organization working on the problem of female illiteracy.

523. Abdelmagid, Mohamed Hassan. "Sudan's Outflow of Human Capital: The External Labor Migration, Magnitude, Causes and Effects." Claremont Graduate School, 1983.

Examines labor outflow to Arab petro-countries and its negative impact on national development because of the loss of the educated and skilled.

524. Abegaz, Berhanu. "Modeling Manpower in Development Planning: Methodological and Empirical Problems with Sudanese Illustrations." University of Pennsylvania, 1982.

Suggests that formulation of important national policies concerning investment in education and income distribution require reliable projections of manpower requirements linked to development plan targets or econometric forecasts of sectoral output.

525. Abou-Helwa, Ahmad Essam. "Macro-Planning of Post-secondary Education: A Strategic Plan for Egypt's Human Resource Development in a Period of Transition." Kansas State University, 1984.

Investigates Egypt's post-secondary education planning with respect to human resource development using analytical-descriptive methods. Concludes that: (1) rapid expansion in higher education led to unbalanced growth in various disciplines, both quantitatively and qualitatively; (2) discrepancy exists between graduate supply and manpower demand; (3) higher education suffers from lack of planning and coordination with developmental programs; (4) scant criteria exist for judging supply or shortage of graduates in specific fields. Recommends a strategic plan to link higher education with socioeconomic development projects.

526. Abu Ras, Abdullah Said. "Factors Affecting Teachers' Utilization of Elements of Educational Technology in Saudi Arabia." Indiana University, 1979.

Studies the status of educational technology in elementary schools through a questionnaire to one hundred and sixty-seven elementary teachers and seventy-three principals in Al-Baha (a typical rural area) as well as interviews with decision-makers in the Ministry of Education and the District Educational Directorate. Finds audio-visual equipment and materials less available than

168 Administration and Development

prescribed by the Ministry, with fewer than three percent of teachers familiar with such equipment. Concludes that educational technology programs are not meeting educational needs.

527. Ahmed, Hashim Moinuddin. "The Al-Ain (United Arab Emirates) Adult Literacy Program: A Study of Student, Teacher and Program Goals." Ed.D. dissertation. University of Toronto, 1983.

Assesses the adult literacy program as an example of a national literacy effort. Examines its implications for learner's needs. Uses a sample of two hundred students, twenty-four teachers, and five administrators in the Adult Basic Education Program. Finds substantial disagreement on program goals. Offers recommendations to integrate the literacy program (and education in general) to national goals.

528. Akkad, Adnan Abdulhamid. "The Development of Indigenous Manpower in Saudi Arabia." Colorado State University, 1983.

Presents a descriptive hypothesis on the volume and consequences of the presence of foreign manpower. Deals with demographic, economic, and social consequences of the large influx of foreign labor. Makes recommendations for maximizing indigenous manpower development.

529. Al Moulla, Eisa Ali. "A System for Evaluating the Administration and Effectiveness of Vocational Education Programs in Saudi Arabia." Ed.D. dissertation. University of Trinity College (Canada), 1980.

Advocates the adoption of a systematic evaluation system for vocational education programs to alleviate problems in meeting manpower demands and to replace trial-and-error with continuous assessment and modification. Examines well-known U.S. educational models, lesser known vocational education models, and literature. Studies vocational education programs in Saudi Arabia; presents a model for evaluating such programs. Defines explicitly the roles and tasks of planners, decision makers, and evaluators.

530. Al-Abdalwahed, Ahmad Murtada. "Human Resource Development and Manpower Planning in Saudi Arabia." Claremont Graduate School, 1981.

Examines and analyzes human resource development and manpower planning in qualitative and qualitative dimensions. Evaluates economic, social, and organizational environments and their implications for the performance of educational and manpower planning systems. Describes the higher education system, establishment of the Central Planning Organization, and manpower development aspects of national development plans.

531. Al-Abdulkader, Ali Abdulaziz. "A Survey of the Contribution of Higher Education to the Development of Human Resources in the Kingdom of Saudi Arabia." University of Kansas, 1978.

Surveys the effectiveness of the Saudi higher education system to meet skilled manpower needs, relying on documentation and a questionnaire administered to Saudi high school seniors. Identifies critical issues such as limitation of public kindergarten, high drop-out rate (particularly at the higher education level), limitation of evaluation process, acute teacher shortage, and limited outputs of higher education that impact development of manpower. Finds most high school seniors subsequently enrolling in agriculture, commerce, engineering, and medicine.

532. Al-Alloush, Khaled Mahmoud. "Labor Migration and Income Distribution: The Case of the Arab Region." The Johns Hopkins University, 1981.

Indicates that labor migration within the Arab region has become increasingly significant in the 1970s, involving large numbers of workers, large sums of money, and cutting across all occupations.

Attempts to examine the question within a multi-sector macro-economic/demographic model that traces the effects of migration of different labor categories on income distribution in the sending countries.

533. Al-Baadi, Hamad Muhammad. "Social Change, Education, and the Roles of Women in Arabia." Stanford University, 1982.

Investigates the relationship among social change, modern education, and the roles of women. Uses four methods of research: analysis of ethnographic data, content-analysis of women-related writings in Arabian newspapers, official data, and a survey. Concludes that urbanization resulted in a diminution of women's traditional role in production. Suggests that the rise in women's educational attainment will likely lead to resentment of sex-segregationist restrictions.

534. Al-Ghamdi, Mohammed Said Dammas. "The Impact of Ecological Factors Upon the Attitudes of Saudi Students Toward Work Values: A Search for Development Approach." The Florida State University, 1982.

Investigates the impact of four ecological factors upon the attitude to Saudi students toward work values. Classifies ecological factors into two types: informational factors consisting of education and mass media consumption, and societal factors consisting of religious commitment and tribal attachment. Examines work values of local mobility, occupational mobility, impartiality, technical skills receptivity, and time importance.

535. Al-Hareky, Saad M. "A Study of the Effectiveness of Modern Educational Technology on the Mathematics Performance of Elementary Students in Saudi Arabia." Pennsylvania State University, 1983.

Evaluates the effectiveness of two types of modern educational technology--computer-based instruction and instructional television--as devices for increasing achievement in mathematics among elementary school students. Studies student and teacher attitudes, using classes of twenty males and twenty females in each application. Reports positive attitudes by all toward the new techology.

536. Al-Hashil, Ismail Lazim. "The Formulation of Goals in the Educational Planning Process in Iraq." University of Pittsburgh, 1977.

Attempts to determine how educational goals are formulated within the context of national development planning. Finds that educational goals, objectives, and targets were formulated at top ministerial and administrative levels; national development planners influenced politicians more than educators in setting targets; educational goals were associated with manpower needs and lack of research and evaluation capabilities.

537. Al-Ibrahim, Abdul Rahman Hassan. "Toward a Conceptual Model for Curriculum Development: The Case of Qatar." State University of New York at Buffalo, 1980.

Uses a normative survey of public school teachers and administrators to construct a conceptual model of curriculum development processes as they might be organized for effective change and introduction of educational innovations. Demonstrates that educational problems of developing countries such as Qatar are too serious and too extensive to be left to traditional methods to resolve. Finds heavy demands for staff development to overcome the handicaps that insufficiently trained personnel experience; severe overcrowding in schools; morale of teachers and administrators suffering "as much from lack of information" about planned changes as from

172 Administration and Development

existing conditions. Finds research and development not well understood; and no consistend means of matching manpower needs with student abilities.

538. Al-Jallal, Abdulaziz A. "Evaluation of the Vocational Schools in Saudi Arabia in Social and Economical Context." University of Colorado, 1973.

Measures the proportion of vocational graduates making the "proper use" of their vocational training. Studies the social, economic, and cultural factors associated with the success or failure of the Saudi vocational program. Finds, based on questionnaire administered to 237 graduates, that majority of graduates report having jobs related their training, but the degree of relationship between jobs and training is not very strong. Concludes that the achievement of manpower requirements is beyond the capacity of existing vocational schools. Recommends the coordination of planning, implementation, and placement of graduates.

539. Al-Jenabi, Muhamed Nassif Jasim. "Manpower Planning for Agricultural Development: The Role of Agricultural Higher Education Institutions in Iraq." University of Pittsburgh, 1981.

Attempts to establish the magnitude of the shortage of professional and technically skilled agricultural workers; recommends approaches to resolve the shortage.

540. Al-Jumaily, Fathia H. "Rural Migration and Juvenile Delinquency in Iraq: A Case Study of Medenat Al-Thowrah in Baghdad." State University of New York: Buffalo, 1984.

Examines, for the first time, juvenile delinquency among urban immigrants and nonimmigrants in two selected areas, using official records of 923 cases. Finds delinquents of Al-Thowrah different in many ways from those of Baghdad, i.e., more likely to be older, more unskilled, and more are illiterate. They committed more serious offenses, received heavier sentences, planned their activities, smoked and drank more, and had a higher percentage of recidivism.

541. Al-Kandari, Jasem Yousef. "Alienation in the Workplace: A Comparative Study Between Kuwaiti and Non-Kuwaiti Workers." University of Colorado at Boulder, 1983.

    Investigates the relationship between worker characteristics and measures of work alienation, job involvement, job satisfaction, and social alienation among three hundred and thirty-three male blue-collar workers from the Kuwaiti oil industry.

542. Al-Kufaishi, Hassan Abdul-Razzak. "Education as a Vehicle for National Development in Iraq." University of Southern California, 1977.

    Examines the role of education as a catalyst to promote progress and change. Concludes, based on statistical data, that planning is essential to meet needs and achieve a balance among educational concerns. Offers recommendations designed to enhance the role of education in national development.

543. Al-Mehawes, Mohammed Abdulrahman. "Saudi Arabia Graduate Returnees: Their Adjustment, Stress and Coping to Adapt and Re-integrate into Saudi Arabia." University of Denver, 1984.

    Studies cultural, social, educational, and professional readjustment and associated stress and coping strategies of students returning home after studying in the United States. Derives data from a survey of 354 Saudi students who spent two or more years in the United States. Recommends professional help, pre-departure orientation programs, and coordination with American host institutions.

174 Administration and Development

544. Al-Moammar, Abdallah Abdulaziz. "The Manpower Dilemma of Saudi Arabia." University of California-Irvine, 1983.

Examines development spurred by huge oil revenues. Details tensions created, manpower problems, and threat to traditional values by foreign workers and technology transfers. Assesses the role of government and education in arriving at solutions.

545. Al-Musallam, Bassama Khalid. "Women's Education in Kuwait and Its Effect on Future Expectations: An Ethnography of a Girl's Sex-Segregated Secondary School." State University of New York at Buffalo, 1984.

Delves into processes of education in a girls' secondary school to detect the type of socialization that could lead to attitudes of inequality in future gender relationships. Bases data on observation and interviews. Documents high educational and occupational aspirations; students tend to postpone marriage and set premarital conditions stipulating completion of education before child rearing and homemaking force them to give up working.

546. Al-Nima, Sameer Khayri. "The Mass Literacy Campaign in Iraq: A Critical Analysis." University of Missouri, 1982.

Studies the mass adult illiteracy eradication campaign mounted by Iraq in the late 1970s. Explores the historical, political, social, and economic background of the campaign and its broader ideological framework.

547. Al-Obaid, Abdullah Salih. "Human Resources Development in Saudi Arabia: Case of Technical Manpower Programs and Needs." Ed.D. dissertation. Oklahoma State University, 1979.

Focuses on technical manpower programs and the potential contribution of technical education to human development. Attempts to determine the status of technical manpower programs via interview/questionnaire, but concludes "there is no systematic way of determining the exact technical manpower needs in the kingdom." Urges reexamination of all education programs and agencies, national planning, and development strategies in terms of a comprehensive plan.

548. Al-Sabban, Mariem Abdullah. "Career Patterns of Girls' Elementary School Principals in Saudi Arabia: in the Cities of Makkah and Jaddah." University of Colorado at Boulder, 1983.

Examines the career patterns of girls' elementary school principals to distinguish sequences of jobs leading to the principalship. Compares subjects of the two cities, investigates background, and identifies barriers. Derives data from questionnaire distributed to 150 female elementary school principals.

549. Al-Shami, Ibrahim Abdullah. "Tradition and Technology in the Developmental Education of Saudi Arabia and Egypt." The University of Michigan, 1977.

Studies the concerns of the Saudis and the Egyptians with technological education for modernization and industrial development. Portrays the Egyptian policy as radical, whereas Saudi policy is adaptive in coping with the demands for social change and technology.

550. Al-Tarrah, Ali Ahmad. "Economic Development and the Structure of the Kuwaiti Labor Force." Michigan State University, 1983.

Investigates factors contributing to uneven distribution of the indigenous labor force since

Administration and Development

the discovery of oil. Examines two specific and related factors that have shaped the structure of the labor force: Kuwait as a supplier of a single primary product, and the effects of class structure on the domestic labor market.

551. Alghofaily, Ibrahim Fahad. "Saudi Youth Attitudes Towards Work and Vocational Education: A Constraint on Economic Development." The Florida State University, 1980.

    Develops a 121-item survey administered to a random sample of 200 Saudi academic students, 200 vocational students, and 200 illiterates, with the respondents equally split between urban and rural. Uses SPSS Factor analysis and cross-tabulation analysis to test the hypothesis concerning attitudes toward manual labor and other attitudes toward work. Finds "low acceptability" of manual labor, private jobs (versus government), mobility of work, economic incentive, preferences for rural work, and employment by stranger rather than relative. Recommends promoting positive work attitudes and skills, promoting the image of vocational education, and controlling employment in government agencies.

552. Almana, Aisha Mohamed. "Economic Development and its Impact on the Status of Women in Saudi Arabia." University of Colorado at Boulder, 1981.

    Describes historical socio-economic and political conditions in order to understand the current position of Saudi women. Examines women's educational opportunities, labor conditions, and social welfare and health services available to women.

553. Ameziane, Ahmed. "A Study of the Implementation of Educational Objectives in Morocco Since 1956 with Implications for Administrators." Marquette University, 1983.

Examines educational practices in Morocco and the discrepancies between objectives and implementation. Indicates inequality and selectivity of education in favor of males and residents of urban areas. Underlines the importance of two objectives: adaptation of education to socioeconomic needs, and development of technical education.

554. Andriamananjara, Rajaona. "Labor Mobilization and Economic Development: The Moroccan Experience." The University of Michigan, 1971.

   Attempts to review and evaluate the performance of the 10-year-old Promotion Nationale program. Employs a cost-benefit analysis of 10 projects, surveys 251 workers and utilizes a linear programming model. Finds that while the program effects an income transfer from richer to poorer provinces and has a favorable impact on immediate employment, it has "not performed adequately" in imparting the worker with status-improving skills. Classifies the Promotion Nationale as a moderate success.

555. Arntsen, Andrea. "Women and Social Change in Tunisia." Georgetown University, 1977.

   Examines the efforts of the Tunisian elite and government to define women's equality for an independent Tunisia and to create an environment and institutions in which Tunisians can learn new values, attitudes, behavior, and roles. Describes the traditional system of gender differentiation and its modification during the French protectorate. Examines the Tunisian elite's perception, interpretation, and application of egalitarianism to women in areas of legal rights, education, occupational life, political participation, and modern associations. Concludes that women remain a marginal group in politics and the economy and that gender differentiation persists despite the elite's stress on equality.

Administration and Development

556. Askar, Ali G. "A Study of Teachers Job Satisfaction in Kuwait." The University of Michigan, 1981.

Studies satisfaction, the importance of professional needs, factors influencing career decisions, and needed improvements in the educational system as perceived by 926 teachers responding to a questionnaire. Finds problems including: "school environment is not conducive to teachers' professional growth" and "little cooperation exists between home and school." Recommends adopting a unified pay scale, instituting programs to professionally upgrade teachers, and increasing community involvement in educational matters.

557. Assad, Soraya Wali El-Deen. "Women and Work in Saudi Arabia: A Study of Job Satisfaction in Higher Education." Colorado State University, 1983.

Explores women's feelings toward work to determine job satisfaction and explain factors contributing to it. Relies on results of questionnaire with 258 respondents and interviews at the women's branch of King Abdul-Aziz University and Girl's College in Jeddah.

558. al-Rahim, Salah Mahmood Abdul Karim. "Educational Development and Human Resource Planning in Iraq: An Analysis of Trends During the Republican Period." University of Texas at Austin, 1978.

Attempts to show that "the lack of socio-economic development in Iraq results in part from the lack of attention given to educational planning and to the development of human resources." Discusses the origin of the Iraqi educational system, its present curriculum structure and administration. Analyzes critically the expansion in education and problems that must be dealt with to provide human resources needed for national development and modernization.

559. Bagader, Abubaker Ahmed. "Literacy and Social Change: The Case of Saudi Arabia." The University of Wisconsin-Madison, 1978.

Offers content analysis of six textbooks used in adult literacy campaigns involving nine hundred and thirteen themes. Describes an "ideal type" represented by the texts: a modern man only in subjugating nature to his needs, conscious of present times, oriented toward "doing" but hindered by dependence on traditional authority and non-openness to new experiences.

560. Carami, Mohamed Salim Gasim. "Development and Proposed Reorganization of Educational Administration in Saudi Arabia." Ed.D. dissertation. University of Cincinnati, 1978.

Describes the development of the educational system from 1926-1977 and proposes reorganization. Includes sources such as official documents, literature, field observation, and interviews (1975-76). Maintains that the major factors affecting the system are region, socio-cultural values, politics, and economics. Recommends several structural and administrative changes in the present system, including consolidation and establishment of standards of practice.

561. Dughri, Abdurrazzagh Mahmud. "Human Resources Development and Educational Policy in Libya." University of Pittsburgh, 1980.

Calls the shortage of skilled manpower the "bottleneck" in Libya's socio-economic development. Uses an economic model to project economic growth for the next two decades along with a student flow model to match educational output with manpower requirements. Shows the country will continue to suffer from manpower shortages throughout the next twenty years, with demand overwhelmingly greater than supply. Identifies wastage in education (vocational, women's, adult)

180   Administration and Development

and teacher qualifications. Considers (1) capital substitution for labor, (2) increasing productivity level, (3) following a better policy of using foreign labor, (4) establishing manpower training programs. Emphasizes Libya's need to use "all possible and available ways and means to development its human resources."

562. El-Amin, Ahmed El-Sheikh. "A Comparative Study on Human Resources, Basic Needs Performance, and Economic Development with Special Emphasis on the Sudan." University of Southern California, 1981.

Classifies 115 countries into levels of development according to an index comprising the GNP per capita and the physical quality of life to determine the relationship among human resource development, basic needs performance, and economic development. Focuses on Sudan, asking why Sri Lanka and India score better on physical quality of life despite lower GNP per capita. Concludes that development should be judged not on attained growth, but on how growth has benefitted the satisfaction of human needs. Calls for restructuring the education system to integrate it with "the whole learning system and training policies ... and an economy building on labor-intensive approaches."

563. El-Ghannam, Taher Ahmed Mohamed. "A Model for a Developmental Approach to Educational Planning for the Purpose of Realizing the Goal of Universal Compulsory Schooling in Developing Countries: An Application to the Nine-Year Compulsory Education Mandate in the Arab Republic of Egypt." State University of New York at Buffalo, 1979.

Designs a planning model for expanding compulsory education in developing countries. Includes social as well as economic considerations, taking into account poverty, illiteracy, peer influence, and relevance of curriculum. Applies the model to Egypt's educational expansion. Suggests that compulsory universal education may be possible to achieve.

564. El-Huni, Ali Mohamed. "Determinants of Female Labor Force Participation: The Case of Libya." Oklahoma State University, 1978.

Ascertains the most important determinants of female labor force participation, assessing the "magnitude and direction" of factors affecting decisions to seek employment. Includes personal interviews based on a random sample of eight hundred households in Tripoli City. Provides labor market data on 1,957 women aged 15 or over. Uses two multiple regression equations: one for married and one for single women. Studies age, number of children, home ownership, family size, number of labor-saving devices, and employment of head of household.

565. Elbadri, Sadat Abdurrazagh. "Education in Libya: An Historical Review and Report on the Status of Curriculum and Curriculum Planning." Ed.D. dissertation. State University of New York at Buffalo, 1984.

Focuses on attributes and impact of school curriculum on learners and society. Interprets and synthesizes the educational and curriculum policies followed by successive governments in charge of education in Libya over nearly a century, from 1895-1981. Argues that before independence in 1951, education served colonial interests; after, education suffered qualitative underdevelopment. Compares the two periods.

566. Elsayed, Mohamed Salah Eldin. "Worker Participation in Management in the Experience of the Arab Republic of Egypt." D.B.A. dissertation. The George Washington University, 1972.

182 Administration and Development

Attempts to determine the extent to which worker participation in management has affected industrialization in Egypt, the decision-making process of industrial firms, and status of workers. Includes results of questionnaire and interviews with workers, management, union officials, elected representatives, and government officials. Concludes that worker participation in management, as expressed in relevant laws, "has not fulfilled its objectives"; attributes this to failure in practice resulting in no contribution to the industrial decision-making process, dissatisfaction among workers, and no increase in productivity.

567. Galal, Khamis Abd-el Mohsen. "Manpower Development and Educational Trends in Egypt since the 1952 Revolution: Problems and Prospectives." University of Pittsburgh, 1979.

Investigates manpower development as affected by imbalanced quantitative educational expansion since 1952, which created a shortage of critical skills and a surplus of graduates without jobs. Asks, how can training in the educational system be matched to manpower needs? Offers analysis of literature and official statistics as well as interviews with students and officials. Finds educational expansion directed by social and political considerations rather than economic needs. Recommends major policy changes: consolidate general, technical, and vocational secondary schools into comprehensive schools; use scholarships at the university level to distribute students by fields of study; provide pay-scale incentives to encourage manual labor and teaching technical and primary education. Also recommends tying short-term manpower forecasts to the five-year cycle of educational planning.

568. Gummed, Amer Ali. "High-Level Manpower Requirements for Economic Development in Libya." Oklahoma State University, 1979.

Attempts to determine manpower requirements to plan the educational system to fill them. Finds existing enrollment not attuned to the economy. Calculates shortages and surpluses by fields of specialization. Recommends that colleges of sciences, engineering, and economics and commerce be given highest priority for enrollments.

569. Hassan, Abdel-Salam Hassan. "Population-oriented Development: A Proposed Model for Egyptian Village Government." The University of North Carolina at Chapel Hill, 1977.

Addresses the ineffectiveness of population-control activities (as well as other developmental activities at the village level) to bring about substantial changes in either population or developmental indicators. Examines aspects of ideological foundations, regulatory legislation, structural relationships between and among programs, and the actual functioning of programs in the villages. Recommends reliance on "Islamic ideology, its theory of government, and its principles pertaining to human development."

570. Helmy, Eglal Ismail M. "Alienation Among Industrial Workers in Egypt: A Comparative Study of Weaving and Motorcycle Assembly Operations." The Pennsylvania State University, 1979.

Tests level of alienation of 212 industrial workers at two companies. Employs a five-item Guttman scale to test anomie among workers; compares results with findings in several other countries. Finds a curvilinear relationship between level of mechanization and index of alienation. States that alienated workers tend to be poor, uneducated rural migrants who occupy the bottom rung of the occupational ladder.

571. Ibrahim, Barbara Lethem. "Social Change and the Industrial Experience: Women as Production Workers in Urban Egypt." Indiana University, 1980.

Reassesses accepted generalizations concerning the labor force participation of Arab women. Uses

184 Administration and Development

historical, observational, and interview data on Egypt's urban working class. Uses an interactionist perspective and elements of dependency theory to balance cultural explanations with structural factors of market demand for labor and familial division of labor. Asserts that wife's earnings are "increasingly seen as essential for the realization of family goals." Describes factory work environments as "agents for social change" because they provide "a context in which young girls are socialized into cohesive female work groups." Describes the impact of employment on marriage, fertility, and self-image.

572. Issa, Mahmoud Sayed Abdou. "Modernisation and the Fertility Transition, Egypt: 1975." University of Pennsylvania, 1981.

Uses data from the 1974-75 National Fertility Survey to analyze fertility trends and patterns of socio-economic and regional differentials. Studies potential number of surviving children in the absence of birth control, relating this and other variables to modernization. Attributes decline in fertility to "motivation" arising from a high potential supply of children, small desired family size, and low costs of birth control.

573. Jallad, Saud Saadeh. "The Role of an Educational Technology Center in the Development of Teacher Education in the Yemen Arab Republic." Ed.D. dissertation. The Catholic University of America, 1981.

Determines needs for pre-service and in-service teacher training in educational technology, analyzes goals, and prepares a three-to-five-year plan for development and implementation of an educational technology center. Bases plan on information derived from interviews with randomly selected decision-makers in the Ministry of Education, teachers/instructors and student-teachers; documents; and analysis of qualitative data. Reports government request for funds from the World Bank to implement the plan.

Dissertations/Human Resources

574. Khalfallah, Ramadan Araibi. "Migration, Labor Supply and Regional Developments in Libya." The University of Oklahoma, 1979.

Identifies the relationship between interregional migration and regional labor supply. Divides the country into labor deficit and surplus regions. Statistically analyzes census data and reports results of data collected from a survey of immigrants in Tripoli and Benghazi. Recommends a more interventionist planning policy stressing need for more decentralized industrial strategy.

575. Khuthaila, Hend Majid. "Developing a Plan for Saudi Arabian Women's Higher Education." Syracuse University, 1981.

Gathers data on women's higher education, explores the nature of problems confronting women seeking such education, recommends improvements in the existing structure, and suggests a plan. Bases conclusions on review of literature, structured interviews with students and staff, and a questionnaire administered to 140 seniors, 23 faculty members, and 37 administrators. Advocates elimination of separating men and women, "at least at the administrative and faculty levels"; diversification of curriculum; upgrading of facilities and equipment; redefining admission systems; giving priority funding to undergraduate programs.

576. Kisnawi, Mahmoud Mohammed. "Attitudes of Students and Fathers Toward Vocational Education: The Role of Vocational Education in Economic Development in Saudi Arabia." University of Colorado at Boulder, 1981.

Administers a scaled questionnaire to 486 students and fathers in Riyadh, Mecca, and Jeddah based on a random selection from three general intermediate schools and three general secondary schools from each city. Among intermediate students, a majority revealed negative attitudes toward vocational-industrial education and manual occupation (but fathers expressed positive attitudes). Both secondary students and fathers favorably viewed vocational-industrial education (but not manual occupations). Advocates use of mass media to stress value and dignity of manual work.

577. Khangi, Abdelrahman Abdalla. "The Impact of the Six Year Development Plan (1977/78-1982/83) on Public Education in the Democratic Republic of the Sudan." Ed.D. dissertation. University of Northern Colorado, 1980.

Identifies major implications of the educational development plan, finding that successful implementation will lead to improvements in planning for educational expansion, curriculum, teacher training, and educational innovation. Bases findings on review of literature and documents from the Ministries of Education, National Planning; National Council for Higher Education; UNESCO.

578. Kukhun, Amin Bader Ali. "A Strategy for Implementing Accountability in the Jordan System of Public Education." Michigan State University, 1975.

Develops an accountability model based on goals and problems of the education system and determines a strategy for implementation. Draws on UNESCO and AID documents, Ministry of Education statistics, and information culled from conferences with Michigan education specialists. Concludes that an accountability system should be implemented in all administrative offices at elementary and secondary levels, that in-service education is essential for implementing the model, and that such problems as high dropout rate and illiteracy provide the foundation for the development of such accountability.

579. Mahmoud, Mahgoub El-Tigani. "The Impact of Partial Modernization on the Emigration of Sudanese Professionals and Skilled Workers." Brown University, 1983.

Argues that new formulations of political organization, educational programs, and agricultural mechanization have aggravated uneven development in Sudan and provoked massive migration from rural to urban areas--even to other countries (particularly Saudi Arabia). Recommends changes to advance popular participation in decision-making with respect to processes of development and migration.

580. Makhamreh, Muhsen Abdullah. "Determinants of Labor-Management Disputes and their Settlement in the Private Sector in Jordan." The Ohio State University, 1981.

Investigates the determinants of labor-management disputes in the private sector as well as the effectiveness of the settlement system. Finds that size of the total employment and degree of unionization are the major determinants, followed by socio-political variables such as family and tribe protection, political affiliation, class discrimination, and economic variables such as wage level.

581. Makli, Adnan Hussain. "Proposed Theoretical Framework for Planning Farmer Training Programs for Rural Development in Iraq." The University of Wisconsin, Madison, 1983.

Defines the major constraint on the growth of agricultural production in Iraq as the shortage of adequately trained manpower. Seeks to develop a theoretical framework of planning processes for farmer training programs using the rational approach and techniques of analysis, synthesis, and modeling.

582. Mansour, Taha A. "International Labor Migration: The Case of Jordan." University of Cincinnati, 1983.

Develops a labor migration model incorporating the special features of the pattern of migration

188 Administration and Development

from Jordan. Reports that labor migration is positively related to income differential between Jordan and oil producing Arab countries, political tension in Jordan, high literacy rate in Jordan, and presence of relatives and friends in oil-producing countries. Predicts changes in the pattern of migration in the near future.

583. Morsy, Mohamed A. "Selected Demographic Characteristics and Perceived Reasons for the Nonreturn of Egyptian Missions Members who Secured their Ph.D.'s in the U.S." University of Virginia, 1980.

Compares a sample of 100 missions members who returned to Egypt after completing advanced degrees with 100 who did not to identify demographic factors. Bases conclusions on a questionnaire and interviews. Identifies political freedom, political stability, and academic factors as important. Describes the nonreturnees as mostly within ages of 31-40, married, with family educational backgrounds higher the Egyptian standard; more than 50 percent worked in medicine, engineering, science, or business.

584. Mussa, Safi Imam. "Problems of Human Resources Development in Saudi Arabia." University of Southern California, 1975.

Views the problem of human resource development as one of ability (lack of skills) and willingness (unfavorable attitudes toward certain occupations). Points out that the "willingness dimension" involves modifying the value system and calls for a program to enlighten and "create favorable attitudes toward all productive activities." Argues that reform and reorganization of Saudi administration are "a crucial requisite for any purposeful developmental effort."

585. Nabti, Farid George. "Manpower, Education, and Economic Development in the Kingdom of Saudi Arabia." Stanford University, 1980.

Studies expansion of the school system, development, and female participation in the labor force to determine the reliance of the country on foreign labor in the year 1990. Predicts continued low participation of females, combined with continued dependence on foreign teachers and administrators in an expanding school system, will produce "heavy reliance on foreign labor...in the target year." Notes, however, that if 75 percent of females ages 15-65 participate in the work force, and government slows development to implement 60 percent of projects, the country would have a labor surplus.

586. Nama, Ahmad Mohammed. "Human Resources Development: The Case of Qatar." Claremont Graduate School, 1983.

Describes the country's wealth of natural resources (oil and gas), emphasizing its need to fully develop human and physical resourses.

587. Osman, Mohamed. "Evaluating the Population and Development Program Impact on Family Planning in Rural Egypt." Cornell University, 1984.

Focuses on the degree to which prevalence of contraceptives can be attributed to the Population and Development Program, designed to implement national population policy by integrating development and population programs in rural areas. Concludes, based on national rural fertility survey of 1979, that the program took right direction but had small impact. Gives little support to the development approach to fertility reduction, at least in the short run.

588. Redjeb, Mohamed Salah. "A Longitudinal Study of the Determinants of Success in the Tunisian Labor Market: Socio-schooling." Stanford University, 1977.

Analyzes empirically the relationship that determines level of schooling acquired and how schooling, together with socio-economic background, is valued in the Tunisian labor market. Derives estimates from a recursive model based on the human capital approach to investments in education. Suggests, on the basis of empirical results, that socio-economic background is a major determinant of level of schooling but exercises virtually no effect on labor market success. Similarly, measured ability is a significant factor in the schooling model but has limited effects in the labor market. Finds a "diploma effect" playing a major role in terms of earnings and waiting time for the first job.

589. Sabie, Ahmed. "Industrial Manpower Needs in Iraq with Implications for Industrial Education." University of Missouri-Columbia, 1979.

Analyzes government data, identifies industrial occupation areas where technical personnel are needed, determines skilled manpower needs based on 1976-80 National Development Plan, and identifies program areas industrial schools must provide to meet manpower need. Concludes that educational programs depend on the country's stability; skilled manpower shortages will continue unless the academically oriented primary and secondary schools offer industrial education; and increased cooperation from private sector is necessary for needed expansion of industrial education programs.

590. Salama, Galal Ahmed. "Attitudes Toward a Student-Oriented Meaningful Lecture Method, Self-concept, and Locus of Control of Egyptian Science Teachers With and Without Professional Education Training." Indiana University, 1981.

Matches a group of eighty science teachers with and without professional educational training based on number of years of teaching experience. Finds that teachers with professional training exhibit "more desirable attitudes" toward the lecture method, more positive self-concept, and a greater external locus of control. Advocates enhancement of these attributes via professional education courses at institutions of higher education.

591. Shahatit, Kamel Farhan. "The Contribution of Human Capital to Economic Growth and Development: The Case of Jordan." University of Pittsburgh, 1983.

    Stresses the importance of human capital as a major factor in the process of growth and development in general (and Jordan in particular). Measures the contribution of education to economic growth and development in Jordan. Tests the relationship between human capital development and economic development.

592. Sharma, Rabinder Kumar. "Fertility Determinants in Urban Morocco." University of Pennsylvania, 1975.

    Uses Esterline's framework to study determinants of reproductive behavior. Hypothesizes that "in a pre-modern...society with limited voluntary fertility regulation, observed fertility is largely determined by natural fertility." Finds support for the hypothesis subject to limitations of inadequate measuring devices and underreporting of contraception and abortion.

593. Stuart, Madeleine Fisher. "Developing Labor Resources in the Arab World: Labor Activity Effects from School Attendance and Socio-economic Background Among Women in the East Jordan Valley." University of Southern California, 1981.

    Attempts to identify factors that contribute to the economic activity of rural women, such as school attendance and socio-economic background. Reports that interviews with 210 women from three villages reveal no consistent relationship existed.

594. Taha, Abdel-Rahman El Tayib. "The Sudanese Labor Movement: A Study of Labor Unionism is a Developing Society." University of California, Los Angeles, 1970.

Describes structure and function of the labor movement (beginning in 1946-47); explains it in terms of Sudan's socio-economic and political environment. Views the movement as "a universal phenomenon emerging as a reaction to industrialization." Includes data from labor department and trade union reports, and interviews with union members and leaders. Attributes politicization and radicalization of the movement to underdevelopment of the country, policies of the ruling elite, and the influence of communism.

595. Talafha, Hussain Ali. "Supply of Labor in Jordan." Syracuse University, 1983.

Investigates the ability of Jordanian education networks to efficiently supply skilled manpower to meet increasing demands. Utilizes a recursive model to relate enrollment to labor market. Includes three equations: wage determination, freshman determination, and graduate determination.

596. Toboli, Abulkasem Omar. "An Economic Analysis of Internal Migration in the Libyan Arab Republic." Oklahoma State University, 1976.

Investigates factors expected to determine migration behavior and per capita income differentials in Libya. Employs a simultaneous equations model to test certain hypotheses about migration behavior and expected income differentials. Estimates the model using published data for two periods (1954-64 and 1964-73). Indicates that internal migration occurs in response to expected per capita income differentials.

597. Ware, John Alex. "Housing for Low-Income Rural Families in Less Developed Countries: A Case Study, Jordan." Syracuse University, 1978.

Deals with housing for low-income rural families. Focuses on two problems of Arab agricultural settlements in semi-arid East Jordan Valley: (1) housing policy formulation, and (2) determination of a house construction system to enable families to help provide themselves with permanent shelter. Evaluates government and private agency housing programs. Recommends policies to help low-income families acquire permanent housing. Endorses a simple permanent house construction system using materials readily available in the valley.

598. Zahrani, Saeed A. "The Education of Allied Health Personnel in Saudi Arabia." University of Pittsburgh, 1983.

Identifies problems and issues faced by the Allied Health Personnel Education caused by acceleration in development demands. Offers results of a questionnaire to administrators, faculty, and students of seven allied health institutions. Recommends remedial actions in recruitment, education, and research.

599. Zalatimo, Farouk Rushdi. "The Development of the Educational System in the State of Kuwait since 1961." Southern Illinois University at Carbondale, 1977.

Describes the educational system, the administrative structure of the Ministry of Education, the development of formal education in Kuwait from 1961-1976, and factors affecting educational development (religion, financial prospects, nationalism, etc.). Recommends periodic studies to diagnose and assess projected needs and translate them into plans; also urges limiting the Ministry of Education to establishing broad policies, leaving detailed directions to those directly involved.

600. Zalatimo, Yasira Najati. "Curriculum Design for a Developing Society: A Vocational Business and

Administration and Development

Office Education Program for Women in Saudi Arabia." Southern Illinois University at Carbondale, 1981.

Designs a program for vocational business and office education for Saudi women (no such program currently exists) who have completed high school. Includes fifty-four hours of foundation courses plus specialization in accounting, secretarial administration, insurance management, data processing, or banking. Points to large numbers of foreign women currently employed in such areas.

601. Zarroug, Khalid Hassan. "The Sudanese Experience in Graduate Education for Public Service Employees Abroad: An Evaluation Study." University of Southern California, 1980.

States that legislation has mandated evaluation, but training programs "have not included the concepts, technology, and procedural methods for meaningful evaluation." Seeks to evaluate the efficiency and effectiveness of graduate study abroad. Concludes that benefits accruing from graduate study abroad exceed costs. Identifies factors reducing effectiveness of such study, including "difficulties encountered in utilization of knowledge" and "organizational climate." Shows a "strong inverse relationship" between job satisfaction and brain drain.

C. Development

602. A-Shami, Hashim Gamal. "The Impact of Cotton on Economic Development of Egypt, 1952-1976." The University of Wisconsin-Madison, 1979.

Provides a detailed analysis of the contributions of cotton to Egypt's economic development. Measures financial contributions, creates a model to measure resource transfer, and examines foreign exchange earnings, domestic resource costs, labor intensity, and income distribution.

603. Abbadi, Suleiman Mahmoud. "Monetary Policy in LDCs with Special Reference to the Middle East." The University of Texas at Austin, 1981.

Investigates monetary policy in developed countries and in LDCs, focusing on the ability of monetary authorities in the Middle East to control the money supply and conduct monetary policy. Discusses Jordan, Egypt, Kuwait, and Saudi Arabia, arguing that a "well defined and stable demand for money function must exist for the monetary authorities...to achieve the objectives of monetary policy." Finds that the demand for real money balances in the four countries is a function of real income and the expected rate of inflation. Makes recommendations to help commercial banks control the money supply more effectively.

604. Abdalla, Nazem Michel Wasfi. "Absorptive Capacity, Foreign Capital, and the Economic Development of Egypt: 1960-1972." The University of Connecticut, 1978.

Examines the efficiency of foreign capital in the economic development of Egypt, considering the performance of Egypt's economy and problems of servicing the growing debt. Asserts that foreign capital's inefficient utilization--caused by lack of adequate infrastructure, economic and political instability, inexperienced managers and planners, and limited availability of sound projects--has led to problems in the post-1972 era.

605. Abisourour, Ahmed. "An Econometric Model of the Moroccan Economy." The University of Connecticut, 1978.

Offers a 43-equation econometric model of the Moroccan economy. Studies the evolution of the economy 1960-1974 as underdeveloped, dualistic, and with the government playing a major role as both consumer and producer. Finds econometric research nonexistent, and economic forecasting "based on the naive concept that the economic evolution of the country is more likely to be the

196 Administration and Development

same next year as it is this year." Generates dynamic multipliers for the years 1975-1985 as a guide to policymakers for the next decade.

606. Abohobiel, Abdulfattah Abdulsalam. "An Economic Model for the Libyan Economy, 1962-1977." Indiana University, 1983.

Constructs an econometric model that reflects the structure of the Libyan economy, to be used for policy analysis.

607. Adham, Mazen Abdussalam. "The Role of Money and Banking in the Libyan Development Process." University of Colorado at Boulder, 1979.

Constructs a simple econometric model to detect the real money supply in Libya. Finds that monetary expansion originated in massive government spending and public holding of currency rather than demand deposits. Compares credit and interest rate policies before and after nationalizations of banks; finds monetary expansion proceeding in the context of economic development, minimizing inflation. Also discusses interest rates and forms of external investment.

608. Al Muakkaf, Ahmed Amer. "Public Housing Policy in Libya." Indiana University, 1976.

Examines the effectiveness of Libya's public policy to provide better housing and facilities for low-income groups in Tripoli. Surveys low-income families receiving government housing from 1969-1974 to determine the degree of popular satisfaction. Finds that current public housing policy is effective in meeting the needs of the majority, which is satisfied and considers its standard of living raised.

609. Al-Ebraheem, Yousef Hamad. "The Optimal Rate of Oil Production and Economic Development: The Case of Kuwait." Claremont Graduate School, 1984.

Utilizes optimal control technique to establish a national economic planning model through which Kuwait's oil extraction policy is determined with relation to the structure of the economy.

610. Al-Eyd, Kadhim Ali. "Oil Revenues, Absorptive Capacity, and Prospects for Accelerated Growth: A Case Study of Iraq." The George Washington University, 1978.

    Discusses the impact of the oil sector on the economy, development planning, and factors that limit absorptive capacity. Extrapolates estimated absorptive capacity and compares it with actual domestic capital formation following the rise in oil prices. Recommends that non-oil developing countries press for better terms of trade (rather than foreign aid).

611. Al-Falah, Noura M. "Obstacles to Development in the Third World: The Case of Egypt." New York University, 1976.

    Uses the dependency model to explain the persistence of backwardness in this area of the Third World. Examines the social structure of Egypt before the occupation (1805-1882) and during 1882-1952. Contends that data support the hypothesis derived from the dependency model: (1) Every colony has experienced change in its social structure as its national economy integrates with the world market, (2) The stronger the link to the metropolis, the greater the degree of dependence, and (3) The greater the dependency, the higher the degree of underdevelopment.

612. Al-Gabbani, Mohammed Abdelaziz. "Community Structure, Residential Satisfaction and Preferences in a Rapidly Changing Urban Environment: The Case of Riyadh, Saudi Arabia." University of Michigan, 1984.

    Studies the rapid rate of urban growth and spacial expansion in the city of Riyadh.

Evaluates the new residential environment based on a household survey of residents. Identifies preferences for type of dwelling, neighborhood, and location.

613. Al-Hasso, Nazar Tawfik. "Administrative Politics in the Middle East: The Case of Monarchical Iraq, 1920-1958." The University of Texas at Austin, 1976.

Describes politics as a "struggle among elite members for personal power," manifested in an overlapping network of "mutually reinforcing formal and informal dimensions" such as government positions, wealth, kinship, group membership, and British influence. Details competition among elite cliques culminating in British military intervention in 1949, patterns of political violence, and the later burgeoning of a professional middle class. "Policies backed by the traditional politics of personalism and cliquishness could not cope with the increasing demands of new social forces"; thus, the system crumbled in 1958.

614. Al-Hudaithy, Abdullah Soliman. "An Analysis of the Role of the Agricultural Bank and Extension Services on the Changing Pattern of Agriculture in Al-Qassim Region of Saudi Arabia." University of Northern Colorado, 1983.

Examines the role of the Agricultural Bank and Extension Services in changing patterns of agriculture in Al-Qassim Region. Presents eleven statistical hypotheses dealing with type of crops, livestock, farm size, production, transportation, and marketing.

615. Al-Husain, Zaid Abdullmohsein. "Development Planning: A Realistic Approach for Saudi Arabia." Ed.D. dissertation. University of Northern Colorado, 1981.

Investigates development planning theory and practice in Saudi Arabia, with emphasis on the

Dissertations/Development 199

second five-year development plan. Finds that seven of seventeen development planners participating in development plans lacked basic knowledge of development and basic skills, methods, and techniques of planning; and most planners were specialized in unrelated fields. Concludes that difficulties and deficiencies inherent in current Saudi planning hinder achievement of its real purposes.

616. Al-Ibrahim, Abdulla Ali. "Regional and Urban Development in Saudi Arabia." University of Colorado at Boulder, 1982.

Indicates that special distribution of population and economic activities in national economies has serious impact on economic efficiency. Points out that existing national development plans in Saudi Arabia have not adopted explicit, coherent spacial policies to deal with the country's urban and regional imbalances. Argues for an appropriate special development strategy for Saudi Arabia to integrate rural areas into the national economy.

617. Al-Jarallah, Ahmed J. "Impact of Industrialization on the Small-Sized Town of Jubail, Saudi Arabia." D.B.A. dissertation. University of Northern Colorado, 1983.

Investigates the impact of placing a government-sponsored industrial complex in Jubail, which multiplied the town's population from 8,000 to 81,000 between 1973 and 1983. Reports data gathered through field observation and a 1983 questionnaire administered to 281 households. Describes increases in employment, population and business as well as changes in ethnic composition, educational level, and standard of living.

618. Al-Khalil, Mowaffaq Ali. "Oil and Economic Development in OPEC Countries, with Case Studies about Iraq and Algeria." The Florida State University, 1984.

Examines the impact of the increase in oil prices in 1973 and thereafter on economic development in the Organization of Petroleum Exporting Countries, particularly in Iraq and Algeria, judging performance according to various specially developed criteria. Concludes that the increased expenditures led to an expansion in welfare programs, an increase in per capita income, and more equal access to educational and health services. However, policies led to increase in inflation, rural-urban migration, a decline in agricultural production, and low productivity and inefficiency, particularly in the industrial sector.

619. Al-Qudsi, Sulayman Shaban. "Growth and Distribution in Kuwait: A Quantitative Approach." University of California, Davis, 1979.

Deals with growth and distribution patterns in an oil-dominated economy based on "exportation of financial capital and importation of human capital." Shows that sixty-three percent of economy's growth is traced to its capital stock; labor's contribution is just more than seventeen percent, while technical progress accounts for the residual. Cites the existence of discriminative laws designed to mitigate foreign labor's edge over domestic labor. Shows that government has been active in reducing inequality and increasing social welfare.

620. Al-Qunaibet, Mohammad Hamad. "An Economic Analysis of the Municipal Demand for Water in Kuwait." Oregon State University, 1984.

Seeks to establish a plausible demand function to consider the minimum amount of water necessary for daily needs, called the domestic base-line water use level. Uses six models to estimate demand: "Stone-Geary Utility function," linear, semi-log, exponential, price-exponencial, and double-log forms. Bases data on monthly time series (1973-81). Reports results and comparisons with other countries.

Dissertations/Development 201

621. Alawad, Said Abdelrahman. "Development, Planning and Optimal Control: A Case Study of the Kuwaiti Economy." Southern Methodist University, 1982.

Applies the optimal control theory to the problem of planning and development. Constructs a dynamic simultaneous equations model to represent the economy, embodying some unique features distinguishing the it. Presents analysis of optimal control, asserting that "results obtained seemed encouraging" where possible policy recommendations on government spending and oil pricing strategies were considered.

622. Aldoasary, Fahad Saad. "Impact of the Oil Sector on the Development of the Non-Oil Economy of Saudi Arabia." The American University, 1983.

Analyzes the pattern of growth and the character of structural transformation of the non-oil economy during 1963-1980, with particular focus on the domestic manufacturing sector.

623. Ali, Taleb Ahmad Mohammad. "Economic Integration as a Strategy for Economic Development: Prospects for Five Arab Gulf States." University of Colorado at Boulder, 1980.

Finds "ample theoretical and practical justification" for economic cooperation among five homogeneous countries: Bahrain, Kuwait, Oman, Qatar, and the UAE. Urges this "Gulf region" to "force economic development by promoting industrial development to the point where a unified ...industrial system can be established." Suggests creating a Gulf Industrial Council to administer the scheme, and a Gulf Industrial Development Bank to undertake technical and financial matters.

624. Alkayed, Nail A. Hafez. "The Relationship Between Foreign Aid and Development: The Jordanian Experience." University of Southern California, 1981.

202 Administration and Development

Describes Jordan's dependence on foreign aid, affected by international and interregional political developments, making Jordan's financial future uncertain. Recommends adopting economic policies to more effectively use aid resources, basing planning projects on feasibility studies, encouraging economic cooperation with Arab and other friendly countries, and emphasizing rural development.

625. Alnowaiser, Mohamed Abdullah. "The Role of Traditional and Modern Residential Rural Settlements of the Quality of Environmental Experience: A Case Study of Unyzeh and New Alkabra in Saudi Arabia." University of Southern California, 1983.

Evaluates the influence of rural traditional and modern settlements on the quality of environmental experience: behavior, activities, perceptions, and preferences. Compares environmental experience of traditional Unyzeh and modern Alkabra by interviewing subjects age 23 to 105 (both sexes).

626. Alohaly, Mansoor Nasser. "The Spatial Impact of Government Funding in Saudi Arabia: A Study in Rapid Economic Growth with Special Reference to the Myrdal Development Model." The University of Oklahoma, 1977.

Analyzes the developmental process during 1964-73. Utilizes an empirical diagnoses of regional inequalities in their spatial and temporal dimensions based on an Index of Regional Inequality. Finds the Myrdal model generally inapplicable to Saudi Arabia. Suggests that the modernization throughout an underdeveloped region can be achieved rapidly given sufficiently large applications of capital under central direction.

627. Amamou, Habib. "Imperfect Knowledge, Risk and Efficiency: Wheat Production in Northern Tunisia." University of Minnesota, 1983.

Studies farmers' efficiency in growing wheat in Northern Tunisia and assesses how risk attitudes and risk perceptions affect varietal choice and resource allocation decisions. Surveys 158 during the 1980-81 crop year and estimates their preferences and choices.

628. Ameri, Anan. "Socio-economic Development in Jordan (1950-1980): An Application of Dependency Theory." Wayne State University, 1981.

Examines some of the basic assumptions of dependency theory and offers an alternative framework to "enhance our understanding of the phenomenon of underdevelopment." Uses Jordan as a case study, investigating (1) reasons for donors to subsidize an underdeveloped system, and (2) what socio-economic structures would emerge from such a capital transfer.

629. Ammarin, Faris Adib. "An Assessment of Water Pollution Issues Under Conditions of Development: The Jordan Zerka River Case." University of Southern California, 1984.

Explores issues related to pollution problems of the Zerka River. Offers decision-makers choices and alternative doctrinal and organizational approaches in developing future policies.

630. Anani, Jawad Ahmed. "A Comparison Between the Effects of Fiscal and Monetary Actions on Economic Activity-Case of Jordan." University of Georgia, 1975.

Assesses the dominances of two factors--fiscal action and monetary action--to economic activity in two periods divided by the June 1967 War. Applies the St. Louis model by regressing quarter-to-quarter changes in GNP to such changes in money supply and government expenditures and revenues; simplicity of the model "prevents the researcher from adopting specific policy recommendations."

631. Arabiyat, Suleiman Mufleh. "Interindustry Analysis as an Aid in Planning for Economic Development in Underdeveloped Areas: Application to the Jordanian Economy." Mississippi State University, 1975.

Constructs an input-output model of Jordan's economy, projecting the output of twenty-nine processing sectors. Studies food manufacturing, wood and cork, leather, petroleum refining, and tobacco manufacturing; pinpoints need for detailed data on public administration, finance, imports, and indirect taxes. Indicates "total economic impact of an increase in final demand for the output of Jordan's economy could be increased if greater interaction between local sectors were maintained."

632. Asad, Mohammed Ahmed. "The Possibility of Change in Bedouin Society: A Study of Current Developments in Saudi Arabia." Claremont Graduate School, 1981.

Makes clear the distinctions among Bedouins, villagers, and townspeople. Describes the decline of Bedouin life over the past thirty years as government programs ease the process of resettlement.

633. Atram, Mohammed A. "Availability of Periodicals in Major Saudi Arabian Libraries: A Descriptive Study of Factors Contributing to Availability Within the Framework of National Librarianship." University of California, Los Angeles, 1984.

Determines the availability of periodicals in fifteen major Saudi libraries against a list of 4,450 titles. Finds overall weakness varying with the development of library (academic libraries being richer than public libraries). Finds English titles on modern science issued in the West more numerous than Arabic titles, as well as humanities and social services titles. Argues for integrating improved collections into an organized national system with objectives defined by a comprehensive national library policy.

634. Auerbach, Stephen D. "Occupational Options and Adaptive Strategies in a Tunisian Town: The Effect of the Tunisian Government's ideology of Modernization." University of Illinois at Urbana-Champaign, 1975.

Documents the effects of the Tunisian government's commitment to an ideology of modernization on the occupational choices and strategies of young men in Ksar-Hellal, a town in the Sahel region. Shows that the government has succeeded, through educational programs and the use of mass media, in convincing young people that industrial occupations are better than hand crafts. Concludes that nonmonetary ideological and social factors are the motivating forces behind decisions by young men to seek jobs in the modern sector of the economy because they could earn more money in one of several traditional occupations.

635. al-Rawaf, Othman Yasin. "The Concept of the Five Crises in Political Development--Relevance to the Kingdom of Saudi Arabia." Duke University, 1980.

Applies the model of the five crises of political development formulated by the Social Science Research Council: identity, distribution, participation, penetration, and legitimacy. Examines developments relating to each "crisis," including the impact of Islam, modernization, impact of oil wealth on income and wealth distribution, taxation, demands for political participation, the effectiveness of "Desert Democracy" (the open Majlis policy), the country's administrative problems, etc. Asks, what are the chances any of the developmental crises may produce destabilizing forces, threatening the socio-political order? Identifies penetration, manifested in administrative problems, lack of effective system of local administration, and inequalities of allocation to government services, facilities, and funds; effects on the socio-political order "may become rather serious."

636. Babiker, Musa Mohamed. "Multi-sectoral and Multiple Objective Models for Economic Development Planning-Case of Sudan." Kansas State University, 1980.

Approaches the ineffectiveness of the planning process in the Sudan by: modeling the economy, combining planning and implementation, and using multiple objective decision making (MODM) models. Develops a heuristic methodology to obtain an updated input-output table from the annual national income accounting data for Sudan, consisting of reconstruction, updating, validating, and an exogenous modification of the technical coefficients of the table. Uses a set of real data of Sudan (the six-year plan 1977/78-1982/83). Compares two specific MODM (STEM and MMSG). Attempts to introduce a dynamic interactive MODM with an implied feedback. Concludes that the models proved to be valid and meaningful for planning and research.

637. Badr, Abdel-Moneim Mohammed. "Rural Development and Rural Income: The Cases of Egypt and Kenya and a New Rural Development Plan for Egypt." The Pennsylvania State University, 1978.

Profiles rural development activities and achievements over the last quarter century in Kenya and Egypt, analyzing successes and failures. Finds evidence that both countries have achieved most of their rural economic development goals, with Kenya slightly more successful. Recommends a new rural development plan in Egypt to bring about changes in rural population and institutions and to establish a ministry for rural development.

Dissertations/Development

638. Ballool, Mukhtar Mohammad. "Economic Analysis of the Long-Term Planning Investment Strategies for the Oil Surplus Funds in Saudi Arabia: An Optimal Control Approach." University of Houston, 1981.

Demonstrates a planning technique focusing on the determination of the optimal expenditure of oil revenue surpluses to ensure that the economy will maintain its overall economic position in the post-oil era. Advances a two-stage planning model that (1) explains the basic structure and characteristics of the economy and (2) uses an algorithm method and runs from 1971 to the year 2000, when "the oil revenue in Saudi Arabia will have sufficiently dwindled that the resource will then be regarded as exhausted."

639. Bani-Hani, Mohammad Sulieman Nahar. "Economic Integration in the Arab World: Application of some Economic Concepts." University of California, Riverside, 1979.

Develops a workable scheme of integration to suit prevailing conditions in the Arab world. Dismisses European free trade style as unsuitable, leading to unequal distribution of costs and benefits among countries. Urges, instead, a gradual and regulated scheme that would liberalize trade but also harmonize national development plans and create a joint investment development program. Applies a regional development policy and n-persons non-zero-sum cooperative game theory.

640. Basabrain, Abdulla Abdulrahman Ahmad. "Modernization of Agriculture: An Analysis of Incentives, Disincentives, and the Economical, Educational Factors Influencing the Adoption of Agricultural Innovations in Saudi Arabia." University of Massachusetts, 1983.

Investigates the adoption of improved agricultural technology through dependent and

208 Administration and Development

independent variables. The former consist of a composite score given three indicators (improved seeds, fertilizer, insecticide); the latter include seven socio-economic factors.

641. Baz, Ahmed Abdullah Saad. "Political Elite and Political Development in Kuwait." The George Washington University, 1981.

Examines the role of the political elite in political participation and institutionization from 1921-1981. Describes four groups: the Al-Sabah royal family, the merchant community, the bedouin tribes, and the "emergent elite." Details the evolution of political reforms. Covers political pressure by the merchant community, independence from Britain in 1961, parliamentary rule (1961-1976), and the suspension of four key articles of the constitution by Amir Sabah Al-Sabah in August 1976.

642. Ben Amor, Amanallah M. "The Role of Financial Intermediaries in the Economic Development of Tunisia." New York University, Graduate School of Business Administration, 1974.

Attempts to measure the extent to which the financial sector has been passive or active in development matters over a ten-year period. Reports that the financial sector succeeded in raising the effective level of savings, and the ratio of foreign funds to the G.D.P. Concludes that, despite tremendous growth, the financial sector "relies essentially on the demand side for its services and awaits development in the non-financial sector."

643. Boals, Kathryn. "Modernization and Intervention: Yemen as a Theoretical Case Study." Princeton University, 1970.

Examines and criticizes contemporary concepts of intervention in political science, international law and organization, foreign policy decision-making, and "advice to princes." Discusses the concept of intervention in each of these areas and the application to the internal war in Yemen that began in 1962. Concludes with a reformulation of international law from the perspective of modernization and a discussion of intervention as a strategy for modernization.

644. Boutata, Mohammed. "Education and Socio-Economic Development: The Case-Study of Morocco in the Post-Colonial Period (1956-1980)." University of Colorado at Boulder, 1983.

Examines the relation of education to economic growth, employment, and inequality. Concludes that quantitative growth of schooling, taking place in the context of an inefficient and unequal education system, had no appreciable impact on economic growth. Points out that educational policies failed to deal with the shortage of skilled workers. Profound changes are necessary to meet the needs of development.

645. Braun, Frank Hans. "The Role of the Intelligentsia in Modernization: The Case of Morocco." The University of Texas at Austin, 1971.

Suggests that socio-political transformation in the developing countries has occurred largely under the impact of counter-elites on traditional politics. Observes that the case of Morocco indicates that, contrary to the often-made assumption, transformation is not the direct result of modernization policies of Westernized elites, but the dialectical response to the particular conditions created by the contradiction between Western modernization concepts and traditional politics. The political style of professional-bureaucratic intelligentsia, shaped by Western values, has primarily implied technocratic reform from above, while its politics have been committed to traditional forms of direct bargaining (clan and family politics).

210 Administration and Development

646. Carapico, Sheila Helen. "The Political Economy of Self-Help: Development Cooperatives in the Yemen Arab Republic." State University of New York at Binghamton, 1984.

Describes how local and regional associations have helped extend roads, primary education, utilities, and other services to small towns and rural areas in the Yemen Arab Republic. Analyzes the emergence of "self-help" and its contribution to socio-economic change using documentary and interview materials.

647. Cooper, Mark Neal. "The Transformation of Egypt: State and State Capitalism in Crisis, 1967-1977." Yale University, 1979.

A historical study attempting to integrate concepts of class and interest with concepts of power and authority to explain the process of societal transformation. Argues that the political economy of Egyptian Arab socialism was inherently unstable and had begun to disintegrate before the 1967 war. Finds the failure of the ensuing course of liberalism to take root a prime cause of the October 1973 war, inflation, and foreign debt. Cites frustration of the opposition, driven underground, and power concentrated in the hands of the president. Offers new analytic frameworks for conceptualizing political liberalism and analyzing Egyptian foreign policy.

648. Daghistani, Abdulaziz Ismail. "Economic Development in Saudi Arabia: Problems and Prospects." University of Houston, 1979.

States that Saudi Arabia's first two economic development plans (1970-1980) tried ambitiously to achieve too much in too little time. Recommends a strategy for producing only the oil needed to maintain current development plans, recognizing possible international political and economic effects. States that public administration and organization need reform, and that conservative religious groups often oppose changes. Uses a descriptive and statistical approach to examine whether there is consistency between economic development planning and potential economic resources, sustainable economic growth after oil depletion, and an economic model applicable to the unique structure of the Saudi economy.

649. Demongeot, Patrick D. "Agricultural Development Policy Analysis and Planning in Morocco." University of Pittsburgh, 1975.

Investigates agricultural development policy and explores ways to improve policy-making. Examines the PPB approach, arguing that analytical shortcomings of planning might be remedied through selective application of PPB concepts if analysis is used by policy-makers. Discusses the 1973-77 plan formulation process and the administrative/political environment for policy analysis in the Ministry of Agriculture. Concludes that failure to resolve conflict between short-term political goals and long-term economic and social objectives has thwarted formulation of an agricultural development and agrarian reform strategy.

650. Deuson, Robert Roger. "The Lower Moulouya Irrigation Project: An Assessment of its Socio-Economic Impact on the Northeast of Morocco." University of Minnesota, 1983.

Attempts to reappraise the economic viability of the Lower Moulouya irrigation project and determine the structure of the economy created by the project's inception. Achieves the first objective by carrying out an ex-post financial benefit-cost analysis; the second by building an input-output model of the Moulouya economy.

651. Duella, Abdunasser Ibrahim. "An Econometric Model of Iraq (1960-1976)." University of Cincinnati, 1983.

Develops a general-purpose macro-model for studying the workings of the Iraqi economy in

212 Administration and Development

quantitative terms, to be used for economic forecasting as well as multiplier analysis.

652. de Mabior, John Garang. "Identifying, Selecting, and Implementing Rural Development Strategies for Socio-economic Development in the Jonglei Projects Area, Southern Region, Sudan." Iowa State University, 1981.

Hypothesizes that the first fundamental issue of socio-economic development in Sudan's Jonglei Development Project Area is identification and selection of an appropriate rural development strategy consistent with citizens' aspirations and national goals. Establishment of requisite agrarian structure and institutions is second. Specifies steps necessary for a rural development strategy in the JPA that goes beyond "misery management."

653. Eccel, Arthur Chris. "Rapidly Increasing Societal Scale and Secularization: A Century of Higher Muslim Education and the Professions in Egypt." The University of Chicago, 1978.

Uses a historical approach to study a non-Western religion and society; documents linkages between religious and secular social institutions, economic foundations, or culture. Seeks to determine the degree to which increasing societal complexity is a causal variable underlying significant disruption in religious, social, and cultural institutions. Includes case study, an ecological-confrontation model, and generation of hypotheses. Concludes that rapid increase in societal scale is directly responsible for secularization and disruption of religious life.

654. Eckstein, Zvi. "Rational Expectations Modeling of Agricultural Supply: The Egyptian Case." University of Minnesota, 1981.

Suggests a framework for investigating the impact of product prices on agricultural production and land allocation. Uses time series observations and a dynamic linear rational expectations model. Shows that cotton land allocations fluctuate in response to shocks in price; interprets fluctuations as optimal response of farmers because of deterioration in land productivity.

655. El Tayeb, Hassan Abbasher. "A Critical Appraisal of the Management of River Basin Development Systems with Particular Reference to the Gezira Scheme in the Sudan." The George Washington University, 1977.

Explores the nature of institutional problems in river basin projects and suggests viable and effective institutional arrangements. Argues for a systems approach as a way of thinking about the institutional problems of projects such as Gezira, where effectiveness is attributed largely to the development of useful institutional arrangements.

656. El Younsi, Bechir. "Financial Intermediation and Economic Growth: The Tunisian Case." Northwestern University, 1974.

Hypothesizes that the financial system cannot be held responsible for the slow growth of the economy, but "it nonetheless failed to act" to prevent it. Traces the development of the financial sector, analyzes real sources and uses of funds, uncovers imbalances in the banking system, and investigates the role of financial institutions in the savings process. Points out the inadequate level of the interest rate, resulting in low savings rate and reliance on self-finance and foreign capital.

657. El-Fakhery, Mahmoud Said. "A Simulation Model of an Oil-Based Economy: The Case of the Socialist People's Libyan Arab Jamahiriya." University of Colorado at Boulder, 1978.

Develops a simulation model to describe the basic characteristics of the Libyan economy and

214   Administration and Development

study its dynamic properties and stability. Covers 1962 to 1974 based on annual data. Asserts that the model "can be simulated in many directions in accordance with alternative assumptions concerning the behavior of exogenous variables."

658. El-Fathaly, Omar Ibrahim. "The Prospects of Public Political Participation in Libyan Local Government." The Florida State University, 1975.

Examines data from samples of the public, appointed modernizing leaders, potential traditional leaders, and popularly elected committee members. Finds that the public supported full participation but recognized its "shortcomings" and preferred limited participation. Reports that popular committee members, "though more committed to public participation," were less able to mobilize the public than traditional leaders.

659. El-Haddad, Yahya Fayez. "Social Change and the Process of Modernization. Jordan: A Case of a Developing Country." University of Missouri-Columbia, 1974.

Reexamines the current developmental approach to studying newly developing countries and proposes a theoretical frame of reference that states temporal, social-structural, behavioral, and cultural development phenomena. Studies the interaction of class structure and the political system in Jordan with emphasis on the new professional middle class.

660. El-Hammali, Abdullah Amir. "Modernization Trends in Libya." University of Pittsburgh, 1974.

Examines four dimensions of modernization--aspirations and expectations, consumption patterns, attitudes toward women's emancipation, and attitudes toward the modern family--based on a random-sample survey of 300 men. Reveals that mass media exposure is the most consistent predictor of aspirations and expectations in rural and transitional communities, while education prevails in the urban context. Shows that education and mass media exposure are the best predictors of women's emancipation across all three communities.

661. El-Hawat, Ali El-Hadi. "Social Change and Patterns of Development: The Case of Libya." Washington University, 1974.

Studies the process of social change via a 1972 field study and review of literature, documents, and primary sources. Finds that Libya is experiencing specialization and differentiation within traditional groups and organizations conjunctive with the development of new groups and organizations.

662. El-Hurani, Mohamed Haitham Mahmoud. "Economic Analysis of the Development of the Wheat Subsector of Jordan." Iowa State University, 1975.

Focuses on dryland wheat production to investigate low yield and identify obstacles to "improved inputs adoption." Bases findings on comprehensive surveys of farmers, agribusiness suppliers, wheat merchants, millers, bakers, and government policymakers. Reports that farmers are aware of the importance of improved inputs but do not adopt them because of unavailability of agribusiness services in rural areas, low economic return from wheat production, financial incapacity, and problems of small land ownership.

663. El-Kassim, Badie M.M. "Rural Development Project: A Model for Educational Innovation in Iraq." Ed.D. dissertation. Rutgers University, The State University of New Jersey (New Brunswick), 1980.

Analyzes the "Pilot Experimental Project in an Integrated Approach to Education for Rural Development" based on review of literature, field

216 Administration and Development

study, interviews, questionnaire, and analysis of data according to a seven-stage model. Finds that the project has been continually evaluated by UNESCO experts, that all programs have not yet reached diffusion stage, and that "most people are willing to use innovative technology...if it does not conflict with their deep cultural values." Suggests an Inter-ministerial Advisory Committee to coordinate a "broad spectrum of innovations."

664. El-Sharif, Younis Hassan. "An Empirical Investigation of Libyan Professional Accounting Services." University of Missouri-Columbia, 1978.

Analyzes the condition of professional accounting services in Libya, utilizing library research, personal interviews, and statistical tests. Offers recommendations for meeting the growing demand for new public and business accounting services.

665. El-Sheikh, Salah Ismail. "An Econometric Model of Egypt." Queen's University at Kingston (Canada), 1980.

Designs an econometric policy model dealing with the interaction of financial sector, balance of payments, producing sectors, and prices. Draws on development theory, considers peculiarities of the Egyptian economy, and integrates "the appropriate policy instruments, targets, and constraints." Offers the model as a "sound quantitative framework for Egypt's macro and sectoral policy design."

666. El-Zoobi, Ahmad Mouhamad. "Agricultural Extension and Rural Development in Syria, 1955-1968." The Ohio State University, 1971.

Investigates the relationship between agricultural extension educational programs and agricultural development; formulates guidelines for rapid agricultural development in Syria.

Concludes that innovation of the agricultural cooperative movement has been the result of extension work; agricultural extension educational programs had special significance for the process of economic and social change; and agrarian reform in Syria proved to be an effective institutional vehicle for the agricultural extension program.

667. Elfiki, Fakhry A. "Foreign Economic Assistance and the Egyptian Economy." Clark University, 1984.

Tests the impact of foreign economic assistance on domestic savings and other parameters of the Egyptian economy. Uses a single equation regression analysis with domestic savings as the dependent variable. Finds foreign economic assistance had a positive impact on domestic savings during 1951-1966, but a very slight negative impact during 1974-1980. Consequently, what matters is not the volume of foreign economic assistance, but the way in which it is used.

668. Elgari, Mohamed Ali. "The Pattern of Economic Development in Saudi Arabia as a Product of its Social Structure." University of California, Riverside, 1983.

Hypothesizes that the pattern of economic development in Saudi Arabia was a product of its social structure, dominated by the merchants of the region of Al-Hijaz. Investigates the period between 1925 and 1975, finding that merchants who controlled the bureaucracy did not seek to improve industrial and agricultural sectors, which would have contradicted the interests of the importers. Argues that during the 1970s new and different developmental policies were pursued, reducing the influence of the Hijazi merchants.

669. Elhuni, Mustafa Salhen. "Economic Growth Constraints: The Case of Libya and other North African Countries." Oklahoma State University, 1978.

218 Administration and Development

Studies financial and nonfinancial constraints using linear regression, programming techniques, and statistical inferences. Identifies saving as Libya's main financial constraint, manpower and administrative institutions the top nonfinancial constraints, findings similar to other North African countries. Emphasizes need to develop regional economic cooperation to meet the developmental objectives.

670. Elremisy, Rifaat Ali. "Comprehensive Planning in Egypt and the Role of the Public Sector." The American University, 1976.

Provides historical and comparative study of development efforts. Sees the public sector, which shouldered abandoned private sector projects, as "an engine of economic growth...and a means of promoting equitable income distribution." Analyzes planning strategies, finding failures to meet targets. Discusses "massive public investments"; wage, rent, and profit controls; and nationalizations. Sees foreign capital as a significant factor in Egypt's development.

671. Elsabbagh, Zoheir Naim. "An Analysis of the Impact of the Political Changes on Labor Unions in Egypt." North Texas State University, 1977.

Deals with the development of labor unions, legislation, political changes, and evaluation of socialist laws and their impact on economic development. Concludes that labor unions had a minimal role within the industrial relations system, especially in formulating socialist union law; socialist laws had restrained the economic development process; and the wage structure was a disincentive to produce.

672. Fadlalla, Fadlalla Ali. "Sudan: A Quest for a Model: A Critique of the Capitalist, Communist, Nasserite, and Conglomerate Models." D.P.A. dissertation. University of Southern California, 1978.

Dissertations/Development 219

Assumes that the administrative, economic, political, and social theories inherent in the above models have little analytical relevance for understanding the realities of the Sudan. Asserts that only through open "research confrontation" will the political system be reformed and the ambiguities removed. Enumerates deficiencies of each model, then offers an alternative based on the inter-tribal, inter-communal social system in which members have developed somewhat stable relations to achieve goals and objectives.

673. Gafsi, Salem. "Green Revolution: The Tunisian Experience." The University of Minnesota, 1975.

Determines economic and institutional forces underlying the adoption of high-yielding bread and durum wheat varieties by North Tunisian growers to aid formulation of a policy to encourage development and diffusion of new farm practices. Indicates a need for institutional reform to provide the farmer with market incentives to produce, technical information, seeds, and other inputs.

674. Ghuloum, Mohammad Haider. "A Model of the Monetary Sector of Kuwait." Claremont Graduate School, 1984.

Studies factors influencing monetary development in Kuwait from 1973-1982. Concludes that government domestic expenditures and domestic credit expansion are the major forces influencing monetary growth.

675. Haider, Mohammed Isaq. "The Impact of Egyptian Agricultural Policies on Farm Income and Resource Use." Colorado State University, 1982.

Assesses the impact of Egypt's agricultural policies on cropping patterns, resource requirements (particularly water), and farm income. Suggests shifting from a governmentally planned and administered farming system to a free market.

676. Hammad, Khalil Nayef. "Foreign Aid and Economic Development: The Case of Jordan." Southern Illinois University at Carbondale, 1981.

Investigates the role of foreign aid in economic development in developing countries through a case study of Jordan. Presents statistical results that show aid as a significant explanatory variable in both government investment and consumption functions.

677. Harik, Bassam Elias. "Economic Integration in Less Developed Countries: Prospects for Six Arab Countries." Wayne State University, 1978.

Explores the possibilities of economic integration among Iraq, Jordan, Kuwait, Lebanon, Saudi Arabia, and Syria. Emphasizes industrial or project cooperation. Focuses on estimating market size for various basic commodities to determine whether project cooperation would be beneficial. Shows that petro-based, light industries would exhibit sizable economics of scale in the regional market.

678. Hassan, Yousif Suddik. "Economic Analysis of Agrarian Reform in Iraq: Productivity, Income Distribution, and Employment." Michigan State University, 1975.

Evaluates Iraq's agrarian reform program in terms of increasing agricultural production, income distribution, and creation of employment opportunities. Finds that increase in agricultural and food production did not keep pace with the increase in demand; provided opportunities through redistribution of land to 312 thousand farm families; and increased the number of labor force workers employed in the agricultural sector by 50 percent.

679. Hassanain, Mahjoob Ahmed. "An Economic Review of the Saudi Arabian Planning Framework." University of Pittsburgh, 1971.

Constructs an "appropriate framework of the systems of national balances" to serve as an aggregate framework for testing the consistency of development targets and resource availabilities for Saudi Arabia. Examines projected growth rates in terms of availabilities and uses of resources. Concludes that planners must learn to increase productivity and diversify the economy's sectors without affecting the growth of the petroleum sector.

680. Hay, Michael J. "An Economic Analysis of Rural-Urban Migration in Tunisia." University of Minnesota, 1974.

Compares migrants and nonmigrants and evaluates the effects of a number of factors hypothesized to be determinants of the probability of migration based on a human capital migration model. Analyzes such variables in the probability function as age, schooling, occupational skills, urban job contacts, marital status, and rural income.

681. Hayek, Peggy Francoise. "An Investigation of the Role of Oil in the Economic Development of Egypt." Columbia University, 1979.

Examines development and prospects of the oil industry and its impact on critical dimensions of the economy. Analyzes public investment, foreign investment, and human resource development from the standpoint of how they affect (or are affected by) the development of the oil sector. Uses methodology based on contribution/burden concept adapted from cost/benefit. Derives data from eighty-three interviews conducted over nine months with executives of U.S. and Egyptian companies as well as Egyptian planning and banking officials.

682. Heiba, Farouk Ibrahim. "A Progressive Collaborative Pre-planning Methodology: A Systems Approach Applied to the Discovery of New Functions and Roles for the Future of Cairo in

222   Administration and Development

Relation to the Overall Development of Egypt." University of Pennsylvania, 1978.

Aims to apply interactive systems planning to the common complex problematic situations in less developed countries, focusing on problems of capital cities. Attempts to develop a pre-planning methodology that systematically identifies core problems, introduces feasible solutions, and allows field feedback and modifications; and to facilitate the development thinking of Egyptian planners and policy-makers in dealing more effectively with the continuous critical problems of the country and its capital.

683. Hoffman, Michael Louis. "Urban Planning and the Underdevelopment of a Third World City: Meknes, Morocco, 1912-1956." University of Wisconsin, Madison, 1984.

Examines the role of urban planning and policy in the underdevelopment of Third World cities. Establishes a conceptual framework, considering issues in a historic setting with reference to Meknes during the French Protectorate. Finds planning to have limited autonomy; improvements in planning practice could be made, particularly in the analysis of economic and institutional environments of planning, and by the choice of economically and culturally appropriate models and standards for plans.

684. Hujeij, Marwan M. "The Role of Agriculture in Tunisian Economic Development." University of Miami, 1979.

Describes Tunisia as predominantly agricultural with more than half the population earning a living from agriculture. Finds disagreement on a modernization program during a 1977 visit, with opponents fearing elimination of jobs and shift from labor-intensive to capital-intensive agriculture. Recommends mechanization for the cereal sector.

685. Hummadi, Ismail Aubaid. "Economic Growth and Structural Changes in the Iraqi Economy with Emphasis on Agriculture, 1953-1975." University of Colorado at Boulder, 1978.

Investigates empirically the nature of Iraq's economic growth, structural change in composition of employment, pattern of income distribution, role of the agricultural sector, etc. Relies on official data, devises a socio-economic index to measure the urban-rural gap, and constructs a planning model to assess the impact of potential structural changes on the economy. Finds that Iraq has the ingredients for stable growth from diversified sources.

686. Jones, Marie Thourson. "Public Influence on Government Policy: Family Planning and Manpower Development in Tunisia." Princeton University, 1979.

Studies the government's relationship with its citizens by examining the evolution of social policy. Finds that "pursuit of development can push a government to try to limit citizens' autonomy." Concludes that despite Tunisia's international reputation for energetic reform—and its relative absence of deep social cleavages—the political leadership has combined with "imperatives of socio-economic development to reinforce control, paternalism, distaste for public dissent," and limited political participation.

687. Kader, Ahmad Abdul. "The Role of Oil Export Sector in the Economic Development of Iraq." West Virginia University, 1974.

Examines the impact of oil export (90 percent of total export and 30 percent of GNP) on the growth and economic development of Iraq, 1973-1969. Uses descriptive and statistical methods; concludes that direct contribution of oil export was minimal. Oil revenue has a much stronger impact on total consumption than total investment.

224 Administration and Development

Indicates that the allocation pattern of oil revenue has led to a rapid increase in aggregate demand and its components without a corresponding increase in aggregate supply.

688. Kalkas, Barbara Ellen. "Aborted Economic and Social Development in Egypt: New Leaders in an Old System." Northwestern University, 1979.

Collects biographies of one hundred and thirty-five Egyptian capitalists and histories of 534 corporations. Discusses economic development in Egypt from the industrial and commercial renaissance of the 1920s to the failed modernization efforts of the 1930s.

689. Kara, Mustapha. "Problems of Development Financing in Algeria." University of Pittsburgh, 1978.

Analyzes monetary and financial flows, savings and investment balance, and different aspects of development financing (1967-77) in Algeria's rapidly industrializing economy. Examines structure and implementation of policies relating to taxation, deficit financing, and foreign borrowing. Proposes more efficient monetary and budgetary management of the economy.

690. Kattan, Jack Nicola. "Financial Institutions, Money, and Prices in Jordan, 1950-74." University of Georgia, 1976.

Examines the evolution of the financial system of Jordan and its consequences for monetary stability and economic growth. Reports that the Jordan Currency Board (1950-64), operating under rigid rules, produced "remarkable monetary stability" and a favorable growth rate. Sees the establishment of the Central Bank (1964-1974) as a turning point, outcome of the unpopularity of the connection with Great Britain and the government's decision to adopt central planning. The bank "paved the way for greater government manipulation of the financial system" and resulted in the worst inflation since 1946. Concludes that government economic policies have occasioned inflation and the "poorer performance of the economy."

691. Kattan, Robert Anton Said. "The Impact of Government Expenditures in the Transformation Process of a Traditional Economy: A Case Study of Saudi Arabia." The George Washington University, 1982.

Utilizes Hirshman's perception of development as a record of "how one thing leads to another" and his generalized formulation of the concept of "linkages." Investigates whether fiscal linkages induced by government oil revenues and expenditures had a positive impact on private sector domestic capital formation during the period of development planning (1970-1980).

692. Khalaf, Rima. "The Distribution of the Trade Effects of the Arab Common Market." Portland State University, 1984.

Assesses the level of implementation and benefits derived by members of the Arab Common Market. Argues that removal of tariffs between states did not ensure free flow of trade because of other instituted barriers of licensing and foreign exchange allocation. Analyzes the impact of state trading in Syria and Iraq on the Market and finds it significant in a positive or negative way depending on political relations between states.

693. Khatib, Abdullah Hamid. "The Jordanian Legislature in Political Development Perspective." D.P.A. dissertation. State University of New York at Albany, 1975.

Examines the Jordan Legislature from its creation in 1921 to its dissolution in 1974. Asserts that "the unconstitutional practices of the executive in rigging and managing elections and its continuous dissolution of the Chamber of

Deputies" did not preclude the National Assembly from playing a significant role. Chronicles achievements of the legislature, such as formalization of unity between Jordan's two banks, Transjordanization of the administration, management of conflict, linking constituents with bureaucracy, and defending individual liberties.

694. Khatrawi, Mohamed Ibn Faraj. "A Diversification Strategy for the Saudi Arabian Economy." Georgetown University, 1976.

Explores the possibility of using the output typical growth patterns in guiding diversification efforts 1974-1984. Analyzes 1960s patterns and appraises efforts implicit in the first Five Year Development Plan. Selects Chenery's industrial typical growth patterns to guide diversification efforts under three assumptions about the growth rate in non-oil and real GDP. Indicates "a great potential" to realize the level of real sectoral value added per capita suggested by the typical growth patterns over the coming decades.

695. Kjellstrom, Sven Bertil. "The Impact of Tourism on Economic Development in Morocco." The University of Michigan, 1974.

Estimates net gains of tourism, finding the public sector and unskilled labor the main beneficiaries. Reports that tourism sustains 3.6 percent of the labor force. Concludes that if the public sector divested itself of unprofitable hotels, gains would be substantially increased.

696. Krichene, Noureddine. "Growth and Employment in Tunisian Manufacturing." University of California, Los Angeles, 1980.

Defines growth in capital per worker as the major source of productivity gains in small and private manufacturing, with technical change proving important in public and large manufacturing. Concludes that a new investment policy "failed to induce a labor-using technical change in small and private manufacturing and to enlarge their factor substitution capacity."

697. Kuko, Mustafa Hamza. "An Evaluation and Analysis of the Effects of Regional Economic Development on Internal Migration in the Sudan." University of California, Riverside, 1984.

    Examines the effects of the regional economic development after independence (1956) and the chances of reducing out-migration and creating jobs outside Khartoum-Gezira--where 75 percent of development projects existed. Cites difficulties in transport, poor management, and inefficiency as problems preventing success and needing solutions.

698. Labban, Muntasir M. "A Development Planning Model for an Underdeveloped Economy with Special Reference to Lebanon." State University of New York at Binghamton, 1972.

    Attempts to analyze distinct features of the Lebanese economy, its special structure and consequences, and the role government can play. Applies various planning models to the Lebanese experience in development; investigates the problem of a "dualistic economy with highly developed service sector existing side-by-side with backward agriculture and industry." Advocates the encouragement of medium-to-large firms to accumulate more savings for investment and increase the tax-base.

699. Larbi, Ezzeddine. "Foreign Capital Inflow and Optimal External Indebtedness for the Tunisian Economy: The Application of Control Theory to Policy Problems." University of California, Los Angeles, 1976.

    Optimizes a quadratic cost function over a ten-year planning period (1972-81) to determine optimal paths for growth, investment, deficits in the current balance of payment, debt service

228 Administration and Development

payments, and foreign debt. Represents
constraints in seventy-nine equations. Shows that
"it is feasible for the Tunisian economy to grow
at a 'reasonable' rate...without massive inflows
of foreign capital and with a reduction in its
external debt." Asserts that increased export
capacity and import substitution permit "the
alleviation of problems with foreign debt." Finds
self-sustained growth not achievable by the end of
the planning period.

700. Laouisset, Djamel-Eddine. "The Growth of the
     Algerian Iron and Steel Industry." University
     of Miami, 1983.

   Argues that the development of basic industry
   such as steel creates the necessary conditions for
   national development, contrary to the opinion of
   economists who advise against it. Points out
   benefits of capital formation, savings in foreign
   exchange, employment, and skill formation that
   accrue from steel industry, as the Algerian
   example illustrates.

701. Lutfi, Sultan Najib. "The Impact of the 1967 War
     on the Economy of Jordan." The George
     Washington University, 1979.

   Surveys current literature on the classical
   theory of international trade; discusses Jordan's
   economic environment. Investigates the macro-
   economic impact of the 1967 war on the refugees,
   military cost, balance of trade, budget. Examines
   the impact of the war on the rate of return of
   factors of production, namely interest rates,
   rent, wages. Considers whether the East Bank of
   Jordan is better off or worse without the West
   Bank. Includes twenty-five tables of economic
   indicators.

702. Martan, Said S. "Domestic Development and the
     Management of Oil Revenues in the Economy of
     Saudi Arabia." The University of Nebraska-
     Lincoln, 1980.

Describes the management of oil revenues 1974-78, analyzes the country's expenditures and economic achievements, and develops a strategy for managing Saudi Arabia'a foreign investments. Finds that investment of surplus revenues has led to $10 billion in losses (for 1978). Finds improvements in construction, transportation, and communications undermined by waste, overbidding, and corruption. Concludes that high levels of oil production at low prices serves neither Saudi Arabia's interest nor the world's.

703. Miesse, Thomas William. "Investment and Economic Development in Egypt: A Study of Local Entrepreneurs and Business Patterns During the Open Door Policy." Wayne State University, 1984.

Argues that the Open Door Policy developed to deal with Egypt's economic maladies promoted private business, foreign corporations, and government to the detriment of economic development; new business has added little to the overall productive capacity of the country, deepened its dependency, made economic improvements more difficult, and not benefitted the majority of Egyptians.

704. Mirghani, Mohamed Ali. "The Role of Accounting in the Economic Development of Developing Countries: The Case of the Sudan." D.B.A. dissertation. Indiana University, Graduate School of Business, 1979.

Analyzes the role of the accounting function in Sudan's economic development process. Includes results of a survey of perceived accounting information needs based on structured personal interviews. Recommends improvements in the role of accounting in planning, programming, budgeting, and financing the economic development process.

705. Mitri, Bassam Najib. "The Dependence Features of the Lebanese Economy." University of Arizona, 1971.

230 Administration and Development

Analyzes the dependence of the economy on foreign trade and foreign capital as sources of instability. Indicates that Lebanon's dependence on the foreign sector has created problems of income distribution and employment. Recommends diversification of services, facilitating trade relations with the Arab countries, and creating an increase in employment and improvement in income distribution by increasing the share of income from industry and agriculture.

706. Mohammad Said, Ibrahim Abdul-Hadi. "A Plan for Improving Industrial Productivity in Iraq." Ed.D. dissertation. The University of Tennessee, 1981.

Analyzes the major causes of productivity problems in Iraq and ways to deal with it. Focuses on motivational factors, organizational leadership, and participants' involvement.

707. Moliver, Donald Matthew. "Oil and Money in Saudi Arabia." Virginia Polytechnic Institute and State University, 1978.

Tests the Saudi Arabian case against H.R. Heller's "global theory of inflation." Establishes that excessive expansion of Saudi Arabian money supply during 1969-1977 was a major determinant of kingdom's twenty-percent inflation. Rejects, however, Heller's hypothesis that growth of a country's international revenues is original cause of country's inflation. Explains that central monetary authority, commercial banks, and oil industry are all owned by the kingdom. Therefore, changes in the monetary base occur not from deposited foreign assets, but because of government net domestic expenditures.

708. Mousa, Osama Mohammed Zaki Abdalla. "The Impact of Monetary Policy on the Economic Growth of the Arab Republic of Egypt During 1961-1973." University of Illinois at Urbana-Champaign, 1976.

Formulates and tests several propositions and hypotheses on a macro-economic level using the reduced form approach. Presents equations, stating as the main objection "to establish, on the basis of a statistical test, the relationship between change in money supply, government expenditures and receipts, and economic performance." Urges policy-makers to take advantage of monetary actions' swift impact on economic activity.

709. Moustafa, Salem Mohamed. "An Econometric Model of the Libyan Economy, 1962-1975." Southern Methodist University, 1979.

Develops a general purpose macro-model consisting of 45 equations. Simulates for the period 1965-75; "forecasts" for 1976, predicting that year's upturn and a growth rate of 24 percent. (Actual growth rate was 21 percent.)

710. Muasher, Rajai Saleh. "Marketing in a Developing Economy: A Study of the Distribution of Jordan's Imports and Exports." University of Illinois at Urbana-Champaign, 1970.

Analyzes the marketing of Jordan's major imports and exports in three major parts: a theoretical construct developed by utilizing findings of marketing and economic development; an analysis of Jordan's socio-economic characteristics; and an analysis of Jordan's marketing institutions.

711. Mullen, Thomas William. "Elites, Continuity and Change in the Baathist Regimes of Syria and Iraq." University of Maryland, 1982.

Inspects social bases and recruitment policies of the two countries to show to what degree Ba'athist regimes have fulfilled their original goals. Traces career paths of prominent members of the two Ba'athist elites to indicate the social and political bases of the regimes. Establishes

232   Administration and Development

that both regimes rely on ascriptive, sectarian, primordial, and regional criteria to fill top positions.

712. Nabli, Mustapha Kamel. "An Econometric Model for Tunisia: The Use of a Growth and Development Model for Policy Simulation and Evaluation." University of California, Los Angeles, 1974.

Constructs a large econometric model of Tunisia emphasizing supply, capital accumulation, and savings. Focuses on the period 1960-1971 to assess dynamic historical simulations. Evaluates the effects of different policies of investment allocation using simulated techniques. Offers the model as "a very useful tool" for the study of growth and development in Tunisia.

713. Nasser, Saleh Ahmed. "The Importance of Community Development in the Development Program of the Southwest Region of Saudi Arabia." Michigan State University, 1976.

Selects the Southwest Region for study because of its isolation; despite having almost one-third of the population, it "still is confronted with a significant backlog of unmet social needs, education services, and health care delivery systems." States the need for community development, particularly the need for trained personnel to implement programs.

714. Nedelcovych, Mima Sava. "Determinants of Political Participation: A Survey Analysis of Moroccan University Students." The Florida State University, 1980.

Finds, from a survey-questionnaire of 402 university students in Rabat, a large majority who are highly interested in the political system, have a low opinion of it, and "display attitudinal and behavioral preferences that are not congruent with the quasi-democratic institutions of the present regime." Finds that students most likely to become active are those in opposition. Concludes that the regime has lost touch with university students, casting doubt on its "future viability."

715. Nygaard, David Fergus. "Risk and Allocative Errors Due to Imperfect Information: The Impact on Wheat Technology in Tunisia." University of Minnesota, 1979.

Creates a model to permit the estimation of the "risk preferences" of agricultural producers; empirically tests it on 125 durum wheat producers in northern Tunisia during the 1976-77 growing season. Finds that 73 percent of farmers are "risk averse," which keeps them from using "economically optimum levels of modern inputs," leading to losses such as 16,000 tons of wheat from underutilization of phosphate fertilizer. Asserts that influencing farmers' perceptions will "increase the rate of adoption" of technology.

716. Odhiambo, Mark Ollunga. "Production Risk and Decision Making: Testing Alternative Econometric Models with Evidence from Egyptian Cotton Production." University of California, Davis, 1983.

Develops and applies theoretical and empirical methods for evaluating alternative stochastic production models and assessing the degree to which incorporating production risk in decision models helps explain farmers' behavior.

717. Omair, Saleh Abdulaziz. "A Study of the Association between Absorptive Capacity and Development Strategy in Saudi Arabia." Texas Tech University, 1976.

Identifies major aspects of a strategy by which to pursue economic development in an efficient manner taking absorptive capacity constraints into account. Discusses unusual aspects of current development problems. Assumes that Saudi Arabia

234 Administration and Development

seeks to become a modern society; shows that it faces a complex set of cultural, social, and institutional relationships impeding optimal utilization of existing resources as well as development of new ones. Suggests policy measures to relieve specific absorptive capacity constraints, thereby increasing the aggregate absorptive capacity.

718. Omer, Ali Abdel-Hafeez. "Industrial Development; A Case Study of the Sudan 1956-1975: Plans and Goals, Policy Measures and Outcomes." University of Pittsburgh, 1979.

Focuses on Sudan as a case study for industrial development policy. Discusses incentive policy measures, structural changes, and relationship between public and private industrial sector. Measures effective rate of protecting import-substituting industries. Examines the problem of financing industrial development. Includes conclusions and policy recommendations.

719. Parks, Terrance Clinton. "The Impact of the Petroleum Industry on the Economic Development of Libya." University of Illinois at Urbana-Champaign, 1974.

Discusses the impact of the oil industry on the economy, including its "little direct impact" in industrialization and labor training, the rise of government spending programs, the decline of agriculture, rural-urban migration, problems of capital absorption, severe manpower shortages, and obstacles to economic development. Reviews the archaic land tenure system and traditional attitudes toward women.

720. Pfeifer, Karen Ann. "Agrarian Reform and the Development of Capitalist Agriculture in Algeria." The American University, 1981.

Investigates methods and institutional changes accompanying agrarian reform, both on macro and

Dissertations/Development

micro levels, for twenty communities representing all agricultural regions. Finds the number of poor peasants and workers who benefitted from the reform was small in proportion to the eligible population. Asserts that some capitalist tenures benefitted from the reform, and that even large-scale tenures were generally left intact.

721. Putman, Diana Briton. "A Cultural Interpretation of Development: Developers, Values, and Agricultural Change in Somali Context." Bryn Mawr College, 1984.

Assumes that barriers to planned cultural change are a result of the culture of the developers as well as the "beneficiary community." Argues for simultaneous treatment of change agents and recipients when examining the political and economic environment in which development bureaucracies must operate.

722. Rhazaoui, Ahmed. "Private Foreign Investments and Development in Morocco." New York University, 1976.

Reviews dependency theory with its variants against the more empirical approaches of conventional schools as explanations for the impact of private foreign investments in Morocco (multinationals). Uses information from questionnaires, interviews, and documents from companies and their affiliates. Emphasizes direct investments in manufacturing companies. Measures impact on the Moroccan economy, including degree of integration, national income effects, balance of payments, technological, and labor effects. Finds an overall negative impact of American investments, although their relatively low volume reduces somewhat the significance of these results.

723. Richards, Alan Rutherford. "Accumulation, Distribution and Technical Change in Egyptian Agriculture, 1800-1940." The University of Wisconsin-Madison, 1975.

236   Administration and Development

Studies the consequences of Egypt's integration into the world market for distribution of land ownership and formation of social classes. Also examines the impact of technical change and the diffusion of new agricultural techniques. Covers large-scale cotton production, transformation of the irrigation system, rise of private property rights, peasant land loss, and--after 1880--decline in cotton yields, decline of the landless class, and adoption of agricultural innovations. Argues that "the way in which the economy was integrated into the capitalist world economy" produced agricultural underdevelopment.

724. Sadowski, Yahya Michael. "Political Power and Economic Organization in Syria: The Course of State Intervention." University of California, Los Angeles, 1984.

Analyzes the pattern of state intervention in the Syrian economy during the years between independence (1946) and unification with Egypt (1958). Concludes that despite political differences between various parties and factions, "Syrians generally concurred on a strategy of state capitalism," because it proved an effective response to the obstacles that had to surmount in the development process. "Politically active Syrians, whatever their particular philosophy or class affiliation, have shown an enduring commitment to the fundamentals of this strategy."

725. Sagi, Eli. "An Econometric Study of Some Issues in the Economic Development of Egypt: Agricultural Supply, Industrial Growth, and the Burden of Defense Expenditures." University of Pennsylvania, 1980.

Studies Egypt's basic problem of imbalance between demographic and economic growth. Focuses on the stagnation of agriculture, slow development of industry, and economic implications of involvement in "the Middle Eastern military confrontation." Takes the multiproduct production function approach in testing an agricultural model. Also develops a growth model to evaluate the industrial sector. Combines these two sectors with others into a macro-econometric model. Includes retrospective simulations and forecasts.

726. Said, Abdulrahman H. "Saudi Arabia: The Transition from a Tribal Society to a Nation-State." University of Missouri-Columbia, 1979.

Deals with the traditional social system of the Bedouin component of the population and the manner in which it has been affected by ideological and material changes. Draws from the historical record since the emergence of the Unitarian Movement in 1745. Focuses on processes and forces that acted as catalysts for the transition to nation-statehood, including the role of ARAMCO, the Hejazi elite, the bureaucracy, and the national political leadership (king). Enumerates Bedouins' response to larger society's socioeconomic structure. Finds "essential incompatibility between the Bedouins' social system and the nation-state" most evident in the bureaucracy's plans for Bedouin settlement.

727. Saivetz, Carol Richman. "Socialism and Egypt and Algeria, 1960-1973: The Soviet Assessment." Columbia University, 1979.

Asserts that Soviet studies of development problems in Third World countries represent "major strides in analytical development literature." Focuses on Soviet interest in Egypt and Algeria as (in the '60s) "states on the road to noncapitalist development." Finds that Soviets have moved beyond "prescriptive listings of development problems to analyze the sources of political instability, including the political ramifications of specific economic policies, leadership problems, and even regime institutionalization."

728. Samater, Ahmed Ismail. Self Reliance in Theory and Practice: A Critique of Somali Praxis, 1969-1980." University of Denver, 1984.

238 Administration and Development

Examines the concept of self-reliance for developing a national strategy that disengages development from existing economic political, and military patterns. Concludes that neglect of economic growth, militarism, and "the absence of any degree of participatory politics" created a "massive exodus of skilled cadres, and, most of all, atavistic nationalism" that got Somalia efforts of development "marooned and deranged."

729. Samhan, Muhammad Hussein. "The Role of the State in the Economic Development of Egypt." The American University, 1982.

Examines two major questions: (1) What are the determinants of the state's economic policies? and (2) What are the effects of these policies on capital accumulation?

730. Senani, Ahmed H. "Underdeveloped in Capital-Rich Economy." Iowa State University, 1983.

Argues that traditional sociological theories of development and social change are not appropriate in understanding and explaining processes of change in underdeveloped countries. Suggests as an alternative the dependency theory, which recognizes the specific historical process that characterizes these countries. Indicates that capital-rich Saudi Arabia may pose a challenge to dependency perspective because of that country's uniqueness; however, Saudi Arabia reflects the same syndrome of underdevelopment as other dependent nations.

731. Smith, Shelby L. "Nation-building in Tunisia: The Impact of Education and Socialization." Louisiana State University in New Orleans, 1973.

Attempts to determine the role of education and socialization on the interaction between the forces of modernization and traditionalism in Tunisia. Analyzes data accumulated during 1972; suggests that religious, cultural, and political

forces converged into an ideology not covered by
the concepts of a Western-oriented field of
comparative politics. Concludes that the
community orientation, as opposed to the
individualism of the West, creates a sense of
belonging and identity with a Moslem community,
which, when desacralized, forms a nationalist
sentiment defined as "desacralized Islamic
nationalism."

732. Stevens, Candice Ann. "The Effects and Evolution
of Economic Policy in Egypt and Syria: 1960-
1970." The American University, 1978.

Analyzes Egyptian and Syrian economic policies
and performance to determine degree of achievement
of economic goals. Focuses on agricultural, industrial, and social sectors. Discusses Arab
scialist philosophy. States that vast improvements were made in social sectors, but goals for
economic productivity and diversification were
unmet. Cites large defense expenditures and rapid
population growth as constraints on development.

733. Stino, Laila El-Sayed El-Masry. "A Visual
Preference Study of Urban Outdoor Spaces in
Egypt." University of Michigan, 1983.

Studies large, newly planned communities that
have been developed at a very fast pace around
Cairo with little consideration to the characteristics of natural environment or perferences of
potential residents. Attempts to determine
people's visual perferences, as well as their
experiences of urban outdoor spaces, through the
use of a photo-questionnaire.

734. Suraisry, Jobarah Eid. "Development of a
Dualistic Economy: A Case Study of Saudi
Arabia." University of Colorado at Boulder,
1979.

Attributes dualism of the Saudi economy to
Western technology and development of the oil

240 Administration and Development

sector, which separated it from the indigenous elements. Constructs a model taking dualistic elements into account and incorporating public and private sectors.

735. Sutcliffe, Claud R. "Change in the Jordan Valley: The Impact and Implications of the East Ghor Canal Project 1961-1966." Princeton University, 1970.

Analyzes the economic, social, psychological, and political impacts of the East Ghor Canal on farmers taking part in the USAID-financed project. Tests hypotheses about the relationships between aspects of modernization and their political consequences. Surveys 278 farmers, 101 project farmers, and 177 nonproject farmers; includes anthropological research; and develops a model of the relationship between the project and processes of change in the Jordan Valley between 1961-1966. Applies this to policy goals, alternatives, and recommendations.

736. Taher, Abdullah Mahmoud. "External Borrowing and Economic Growth in Jordan During the Period 1955-1975." University of Illinois at Urbana-Champaign, 1979.

Observes that Jordan, as do many less developed countries, finances much of its economic development by external borrowing (twenty-five percent of GNP). Presents empirical tests showing the effects of net borrowing on economic variables and the economic structure. Uses econometric and mathematical approaches in the analyses. Concludes that borrowing positively affects total consumption, total investment, imports and exports (with effect on imports greater), and inflation. Recommends use of borrowing to achieve objectives of economic development.

737. Tahtinen, Dale R. "The Role of the Single Party in the Modernization Process of Five Middle Eastern States." University of Maryland, 1974.

Tests three hypotheses: (1) To bring about large-scale modernization in the social, economic, and administrative areas, extensive modernization must first occur in the political realm; (2) A pragmatic single-party system with a strong grassroots organization is more effective in achieving overall modernization than an ideologically oriented, one-party system; and (3) A grassroots mass mobilization single-party system is more effective in achieving modernization than an elitist one-party system. Finds "preliminary support" for validity of hypotheses based on evidence from Turkey, Egypt, Tunisia, Algeria, and Syria.

738. Tetreault, Mary Ann Reed. "The Organization of Arab Petroleum Countries: Foundation for Arab Community or Petroleum Cartel?" Rice University, 1979.

Describes a new corporate form for economic development undertaken by OAPEC: joint venture companies owned by (but independent from) member governments. Names drydock and ship repair facility most successful such venture. Finds OAPEC a community-building organization, not a cartel.

739. Tongun, Lako Loponi. "The Political Economy of National Planning in the Sudan: Determinants of Choices and Priorities." University of California, Davis, 1983.

Examines failure of development plans to achieve declared objectives; explores the resulting crisis of development. Focuses on three problems: the process of implementation of the plan; internal constraints on planning (dominant groups have largely determined objectives and performance of the plan); and external factors, which--allied with domestic interests--have distorted priorities and promoted plans that are not equity-oriented.

740. Waltz, Susan Eileen. "Value Conflict and Alienation: The Case of Rural Tunisia." University of Denver, 1980.

242 Administration and Development

Asks, What happens to individuals in the wake of intense social change? Designs a model to explain the incidence of social alienation. Gathers data via a survey administered to 395 randomly selected peasants in 12 very small Tunisian villages. Indicates alienation least frequent in villages when perceived value conflict is minimal. Finds political participation and a sense of efficacy mitigating against alienation, with the former a stronger antidote than the latter.

741. Whiting, Steven Hilton. "Essays on the Structure of the Egyptian Financial System, 1961-1981." University of Michigan, 1983.

Discusses the development and magnitude of Egypt's informal financial sector, examines the role of the household sector, and looks at government policies.

742. Yahya, Hussein A. "Human Capital Migration from Labor-rich Arab States to Oil-rich Arab States and the Consequences for the Jordanian Economy." Oklahoma State University, 1980.

Uses single equation regression models to study labor migration determinants and a macro-economic model to study consequences of emigration for the Jordanian economy. Finds that oil revenues and destination income have a strong "pull" effect on labor migration. Concludes that workers' remittances have a significant favorable effect on national income but mild effect on Jordan's balance of payments. Indicates a structural shift in the Jordanian economy since the 1967 War.

743. Younis, Abdul Razeq Mustafa. "Components of a Proposed Resource Sharing and Information Network for Academic and Special Libraries in Jordan." University of Pittsburgh, 1983.

Assesses the feasibility of establishing an information network among libraries in Jordan to improve service and efficiency. Extrapolates from data based on analysis of literature, questionnaires, interviews, and site visits. Finds cooperation among libraries limited and informal. Suggests cooperative acquisitions, processing, interlending, storage, and delivery.

744. Zabarah, Mohammed Ahmad. "Traditionalism vs. Modernity--Internal Conflicts and External Penetrations: A Case Study of Yemen." Howard University, 1976.

Uses Yemen as a case study. Examines effects of internal conflicts and external penetrations on its transformation from a traditionalist to a relatively modernist society. Evaluates the isolationist period, the era of economic and political transition, and the civil war and revolutionary period. Evaluates the problem of national reconciliation and rational integration. Asserts that national integration is a natural extension of the Yemen historical experience.

745. Zeineldin, Aly Mohamed. "The Future of the Egyptian Economy as a Choice Among Alternative Scenarios: An Input-Output Strategy." New York University, 1979.

Compares the Egyptian economy of 1970-71 to a projected economy in 1980, 1990, and 2000. Constructs an input-output model to display interrelationships possibly evolving in future decades. Divides the economy into twenty-one sectors: agriculture, manufacturing, utilities, construction, transportation, communication, import-export, etc. Develops three scenarios based on differing assumptions concerning population growth and income targets.

746. Zeitoun, Mohamed Ahmed. "Egyptian Development and Trade Policies, 1947-1965." Indiana University, 1976.

Examines the "growing controversy in the economic literature" over the role of foreign trade in the economic development of developing countries. Asserts that countries can benefit from the trade-sector contribution if they take into consideration the principle of comparative advantage when designing development policies. Finds such policies equate industrialization-at-all-costs with development. Examines Egypt's development plans 1960-1965, revealing weaknesses such as unrealistic targets.

indexes

Author Index

A-Shami, Hashim, 602
Abalkhail, Sulaiman, 427
Abbadi, Suleiman, 603
Abbondante, Paul J., 380
Abdalla, Elhadi, 428
Abdalla, Nazem, 604
Abdalla, Ismail-Sabri, 283
Abdeen, Adnan, 429
Abdel Khader, Soha, 76
Abdel-Fadil, Mahmoud, 144, 284
Abdel-Jaber, Tayseer, 77
Abdel-Khalek, Gouda, 145
Abdelghany, Abdelghany, 521
Abdelhamid, Nimer, 522
Abdelmagid, Mohamed, 523
Abdelrahiem, Zahir, 430
Abdelrhman, Mohamed, 431
Abdo-Khalil, Zeinab M., 432
Abdun-Nur, Nabil, 298
Abegaz, Berhanu, 524
Abisourour, Ahmed, 605
Abohobiel, Abdulfattah, 606
Abou-Helwa, Ahmad, 525
Abtan, A.J.H., 1
Abu El-Soud, Ahmed, 2
Abu Ras, Abdullah, 526
Abu-Laban, Baha, 78
Abu-Laban, Sharon, 78
Abu-Lughod, Janet L., 3, 146
Aburdene, Odeh, 285
Abusin, Ahmed I., 433
Abussuud, Alawi, 434
Achilli, Michele, 286

Adams, Martin E., 287
Adham, Nazen A., 607
Ahmad, Eqbal, 147
Ahmed, Elamin, 435
Ahmed, Hashim M., 527
Ahmed, Rafia H., 436
Ahsan, Syed Aziz-al, 148
Ajami, Riad, 4
Akkad, Adnan, 528
Al Moulla, Eisa A., 529
Al Muakkaf, Ahmed, 608
Al-Abdalwahed, Ahmad M., 530
Al-Abdul-Razzak, F., 288
Al-Abdulkader, Ali A., 531
Al-Alloush, Khaled M., 532
Al-Araji, Asim, 5, 6
Al-Arrayed, Thuraya E., 437
Al-Awaji, Ibrahim M., 438
Al-Ayoubi, Sudiq, 53
Al-Baadi, Hamad M., 533
Al-Dabbagh, Taher H., 439
Al-Easa, J.S., 233
Al-Ebraheem, Yousef H., 609
Al-Eyd, Kadhim A., 610
Al-Falah, Fouad A.S., 440
Al-Falah, Noura M., 611
Al-Farsy, Fouad, 149
Al-Gabbani, Mohammed A., 612
Al-Ghamdi, Abdullah A., 441
Al-Ghamdi, Mohammed S., 534
Al-Hareky, Saad M., 535
Al-Hashil, Ismail L., 536
Al-Hasso, Nazar T., 613

Al-Hegelan, Abdelrahman, 7, 442
Al-Hudaithy, Abdullah S., 614
Al-Humaidi, Bader, 289
Al-Husain, Zaid A., 615
Al-Ibrahim, Abdul R., 537
Al-Ibrahim, Abdulla A., 616
Al-Jallal, Abdulaziz A., 538
Al-Jarallah, Ahmed J., 617
Al-Jenabi, Muhamed N.J., 539
Al-Jibouri, Sadia J.J., 443
Al-Jumaily, Fathia H., 540
Al-Kandari, Jasem Y., 541
Al-Khaldi, Abdullah M., 444
Al-Khalil, Mowaffaq A., 618
Al-Kubaisy, Amer K., 8, 445
Al-Kufaishi, Hassan A.R., 542
Al-Kuwari, Ali K., 290
Al-Mazroa, Suliman A., 446
Al-Mehawes, Mohammed A., 543
Al-Mizjaji, Ahmad D., 447
Al-Moammar, Abdallah A., 544
Al-Musallam, Bassama K., 545
Al-Neaim, Hamad A., 448
Al-Nifay, Abdullah M., 449
Al-Nima, Sameer K., 546
Al-Nimir, S., 9
Al-Obaid, Abdullah S., 547
Al-Okush, Fawzi A.A., 450
Al-Omar, Jasem E., 451
Al-Otaiba, Mana S., 291
al-Rahim, Salah M.A.K., 558
al-Rawaf, Othman Y., 635
Al-Qudsi, Sulayman S., 619
Al-Qunaibet, Mohammad H., 620
Al-Sabah, S.M., 292
Al-Sabban, Aidros A.S., 452
Al-Sabban, Mariem A., 548
Al-Sadhan, Abdulrahman M., 10
Al-Shaibi, Hameed A.M., 453
Al-Shami, Ibrahim A., 549
Al-Shirawi, Yousuf, 150
Al-Shuaib, Shuaib A., 454
Al-Tall, Ahmad Y., 81
Al-Tarrah, Ali A., 550
Al-Tawail, Mohammed A., 455
Al-Tell, Tarik, 125
Al-Teraifi, Al-Agab, 11, 12, 456
Al-Thubaity, Awad M., 457
Alassam, M., 13
Alawad, Said A., 621
Aldoasary, Fahad S., 622
Alessa, Shamlan Y., 79
Alexander, Lyle, 314
Alexander, Sidney S., 174
Alexander, Yonah, 367
Alghofaily, Ibrahim F., 551
Alhumaid, Abdulrhman I., 458
Ali, Abbas J., 459
Ali, Amal E., 460
Ali, Taleb A.M., 623
Aliboni, Roberto, 293, 294
Alkayed, Nail A., 624
Allman, James, 80
Almana, Aisha M., 552
Almaney, Adnan, 14
Alnasrawi, Abbas, 295, 296, 297
Alnimir, Saud M., 461
Alnowaiser, Mohamed A., 625
Alohaly, Mansoor N., 626
Alrayes, Tarik M., 462
Altuhaih, Salem, 15
Aly, Abd al-Monein S., 151
Aly, Hamdi F., 298
Amamou, Habib, 627
Aman, Mohammed, 152
Amer, Abdulgader A., 463
Ameri, Anan, 628
Ameziane, Ahmed, 553
Amin, Galal A., 153
Amin, Samir, 154, 299
Ammarin, Faris A., 629

Author Index

Amry, Mohammed A.Y., 464
Amuzegar, Jahangir, 155
Anani, Jawad A., 630
Anderson, R.R., 156
Andriamananjara, Rajoana, 554
Anthony, John Duke, 157
Antoun, Richard, 158, 159
Aperjis, Dimitri, 300
Arabiyat, Suleiman M., 631
Arkoun, Muhammad, 160
Arntsen, Andrea, 555
As'ad, Ibrahim A., 465
Asad, Mohammed A., 632
Ashford, Douglas E., 161
Askar, Ali G., 556
Askar, Samir A., 466
Askari, H.G., 94
Askari, Hossein, 16, 301
Assad, Soraya W.E., 557
Atieh, Sulayman H., 467
Atram, Mohammed A., 633
Atta, Jacob K., 332
Auerbach, Stephen D., 634
Awad, Mohammad H., 162
Ayoubi, Zaki M., 468
Ayubi, Nazih N.M., 17, 18, 82
Babiker, Musa M., 636
Badawi, Abobakr A., 469
Badawi, Ibrahim M., 470
Badi, Yousef M., 471
Badr, Abdel-Moneim M., 637
Badran, Sanaa M., 472
Badri, Kashif, 83
Baffoun, Alya, 84
Bagader, Abubaker A., 559
Bahroun, Sadok, 19
Bahry, Louay, 85
Ballool, Mukhtar M., 638
Bani-Hani, Mohammed, 639
Barakat, Halim, 163
Barbour, K.M., 302
Barnett, Tony, 303
Basabrain, Abdulla A., 640
Bashaireh, Ahmed S., 473
Bashir, Iskandar, 20

Bassetti, Piero, 304
Batatu, Hanna, 164, 165
Baz, Ahmed Abdullah S., 641
Beblawi, Hazem, 305
Bechtold, Peter K., 166, 167
Beeson, Diane, 117
Behbehani, Kazem, 87
Belarabi, Aicha, 86
Ben Amor, Amanallah M., 642
Berque, Jacques, 168
Bill, James A, 169
Binsaleh, Abdullah M., 474
Birks, J.S., 88, 89, 90, 91, 92, 127, 129, 133
Blake, G.H., 21
Boag, Ian, 306
Boals, Kathryn, 643
Bolay, Friedrich, 44
Boutata, Mohammed, 644
Bowen-Jones, H., 27, 307
Bowie, Leland, 170
Bracher, Astrid, 308
Braun, Frank Hans, 645
Brooks, Hugh C., 372
Bruton, Henry J., 309
Buera, A., 22, 23
Buera, Abubadr M., 475
Busniena, Saddeg M., 476

Canjar, Riec Eileen I., 477
Cantori, Louis J., 171
Carami, Mohamed S.G., 560
Carapico, Sheila H., 646
Carr, David W., 310
Casadio, Gian P., 311
Causey, Margaret Cameron, 24
Chackerian, Richard, 25, 30, 31
Chaib, Andre E., 312
Chapman, Richard A., 26
Chatelus, Michel, 313
Choucri, Nazli, 93
Churchill, Charles W., 228
Clarke, John I., 27
Clawson, Marion, 314

Clegg, Ian, 28
Clements, Frank A., 172
Cleron, John Paul, 315
Cole, Donald P., 173
Cooper, Charles Al, 174
Cooper, Mark N., 175, 647
Coulson, Noel J., 176
Costello, V.F., 29
Crane, Robert D., 316
Croze, Harvey, 32
Cummings, John Thomas, 16, 94, 301
Cunningham, Robert B., 177

Daghestani, Fakhruddin, 32, 178
Daghistani, A.I., 648
Deeb, Marius, 179, 317
Deeb, Mary Jane, 179
Dekmejian, R. Hrair, 180
de Mabior, John Garang, 652
Demir, Soliman, 318
Demongeot, Patrick D., 649
Deuson, Robert R., 650
Devlin, John F., 181
Diab, Lutfy N., 234
Dickinson, James M., 319
Donaldson, William, 320
Donini, Giovanni, 321
Duella, Abdunasser I., 651
Dughri, Abdurrazzagh M., 561
Duguid, Stephen, 95
Durra, Abdel Bari, 478

Eccel, Arthur C., 653
Eckstein, Zvi, 654
Edens, David G., 322, 323
Eickelman, Dale F., 182
El Tayeb, Hassan, 655
El Younsi, Bechir, 656
El-Amin, Ahmed E., 562
El-Azhary, M.S., 324
El-Bushra, El-Sayed, 183
El-Fakhery, Mahmoud S., 657
El-Faki, Salah El Din H., 479

El-Fathaly, Omar I., 30, 31, 184, 658
El-Ghannam, Taher A.M., 563
El-Haddad, Yahya F., 659
El-Hammali, Abdullah A., 660
El-Hawat, Ali E., 661
El-Helw, Mahmoud, 325
El-Hindi, Adnan H., 480
El-Huni, Ali M., 564
El-Hurani, Mohamed H.M., 662
El-Kassim, Badie M.M., 663
El-Khaldi, Ghanem, 326
El-Khoraz, M. Nabil, 112
El-Kuwaize, Abdulla, 327
El-Mallakh, Dorothea H., 333, 334
El-Mallakh, Ragaei, 328, 329, 330, 331, 332, 333, 334, 335,
El-Rashidi, Galal, 185
El-Rawi, Mohamed F., 481
El-Sanabary, Nagat, 117
El-Sharif, Younis H., 664
El-Sheikh, Salah I., 665
El-Shinnawi, Abdel A., 406
El-Tom, M.E.A., 96
El-Zoobi, Ahmad M., 666
Elbadri, Sadat A., 565
Eldahry, Ahmed K., 482
Elfiki, Fakhry A., 667
Elgari, Mohamed A., 668
Elhuni, Mustafa S., 669
Eljazz, Awad A.M., 483
Elmehrik, Yusef, 32
Elremisy, Rifaat A., 670
Elsabbagh, Zoheir N., 671
Elsayed, Mohamed S.E., 566
Entelis, John P., 97
Erb, Richard D., 186
Esposito, John L., 187

Fadaak, Tarek Ali, 484
Fadlalla, Fadlalla Ali, 672
Fahim, Hussein M., 336
Faksh, Mahmud A., 98

Author Index

Farah, Tawfic E., 188, 189
Farley, Rawle, 337
Fenelon, K.G., 190
Findlay, Allan M., 99
Fleming, Quentin W., 191
Fouad, Mahmoudi H., 338

Gafsi, Salem, 673
Galal, Khamis A., 567
Garrison, Jean L., 192
Gerner, Deborah J., 339
Ghantus, Elias T., 340
Ghattas, Emile, 341
Ghosheh, Zaki R., 33, 34, 485
Ghuloum, Mohammad H., 674
Girgis, Maurice, 87
Glick, Leslie Alan, 342
Glove, Michael, 16
Glueck, W.F., 22, 23
Golimo, Frank Ralph, 193
Gray, Albert L. Jr., 343
Guariso, Giorgio, 72
Gubser, Peter, 35, 194
Guecioueur, Adda, 344
Gulick, John, 195
Gummed, Amer Ali, 568

Haddad, Hassan S., 196
Haddadeen, Muhiba, 36
Hafiz, Talal K., 345
Hahn, Lorna, 197
Haider, Mohammad I., 675
Hakiki, Fatiha, 102
Hale, Peter B., 346
Hallwood, Paul, 347
Halta, Salim S., 486
Hameed, K.A., 348
Hammad, Khalil N., 676
Hammam, Mona, 103
Hammour, Mirghani A., 487
Hanna, Nagy K., 488
Hansen, Bert, 104
Harik, Bassam E., 677
Harik, Iliya, 159, 171, 349
Harrim, Hussein M., 489
Haseeb, Khair El-Din, 350

Hashim, J.M., 351
Hassan, Abdel-Salam H., 569
Hassan, Yousif S., 768
Hassanain, Mahjoob A., 679
Hay, Michael J., 105, 680
Hayek, Peggy F., 681
Hazelton, Jared E., 352
Heiba, Farouk I., 682
Helms, Christine Moss, 198
Helmy, Eglal I.M., 570
Hermassi, Elbaki, 199
Hershlag, Z.Y., 353
Hill, Allan G., 106
Hinnebusch, Raymond A., 107, 200, 201, 202
Hoffman, Michael L., 683
Howeedy, Mostafa A., 490
Howell, John, 287
Hudson, James, 354
Hudson, Michael C., 203, 204
Hujeij, Marwan M., 684
Humaidan, Saleh H., 355
Hummadi, Ismail A., 685
Hyde, Georgie D.M., 108

Ibrahim, Barbara L., 571
Ibrahim, Ibrahim, 206
Ibrahim, Saad E., 37, 207
Ikram, Khalid, 356
Islami, A.R.S., 208
Ismael, Jacqueline S., 357, 209, 210
Issa, Mahmoud S.A., 572
Issawi, Charles, 358
Istasi, Cecile W., 491

Jadallah, Salih M., 492
Jalal, Ferhan, 359
Jallad, Saud S., 573
Jarawan, Eva Muawwad, 493
Jawad, Shawki, 38
Johnson, Katherine M., 39
Johnson, Mead, 45
Jones, M.T., 109
Jones, Marie T., 686
Joseph, Suad, 211

Jreisat, Jamil, 40, 41, 42, 43
Jureidini, Paul A., 212

Kader, Ahmad A., 687
Kadhim, M., 335
Kalkas, Barbara, 360, 688
Kapoor, Ashok, 361
Kara, Mustapha, 689
Kattan, Jack Nicola, 690
Kattan, Robert A.S., 691
Kavoussi, Rostam M., 362
Kay, Shirley, 213
Kazimi, M.S., 363
Kedourie, Elie, 214
Keely, Charles B., 110
Keilany, Ziad, 215, 368
Kelidar, Abbas, 216
Kelley, Allen C., 111, 112
Kerr, Malcolm H., 217
Kettani, M. Ali, 113
Khader, Bichara, 218
Khalaf, Rima, 692
Khaldi, Mohamed, 286, 364
Khalfallah, Ramadan A., 574
Khalifa, Ali M., 494
Khalifa, Atef M., 112
Khalifa, Mohammed Ali, 219
Khangi, Abdelrahman A., 577
Khashoggi, Hani Y., 495
Khatib, Abdullah H., 693
Khatrawi, Mohamed I., 694
Kheir, Abubaker M.M., 496
Khouja, M.W., 365
Khouri, Rami G., 366
Khoury, Enver M., 220
Khoury, Nabeel A., 221, 222
Khuri, Fuad I., 46, 223
Khuthaila, Hend M., 575
Kilmarx, Robert A., 367
Kirwan, Frank, 114
Kisnawi, Mahmoud M., 576
Kjellstrom, Sven B., 695
Knauerhase, Ramon, 369
Konig, Klaus, 44
Koontz, Harold, 45
Kordi, Khalil A.K., 497

Krichene, Noureddine, 696
Kubursi, Atif, 370
Kukhun, Amin Bader Ali, 578
Kuko, Mustafa Hamza, 697

Labban, Muntasir M., 698
Lackner, Helen, 371
Landsberg, Hans, 314
Laouisset, Djamel-Eddine, 700
Lapham, Robert J., 115
Larbi, Ezzeddine, 699
Lawless, R.I., 21
Lawson, Fred H., 224
Lees, Francis A., 372
Leila, Ali, 47
Lethbridge, Christopher, 373
Levy, Victor, 225
Liebesny, Herbert J., 226
Long, David E., 48, 401
Looney, Robert E., 227
Lotfy, Nasr, 406
Loustaunau, C.A., 346
Lutfi, Sultan Najib, 701
Lutfiyya, Abdulla M., 228

Mabro, Robert, 374
Madi, Mohammed A., 498
Mahmoud, Fatima Babiker, 229
Mahmoud, Mahgoub E., 579
Makdisi, Samir A., 350, 375, 376, 377
Makhamreh, Muhsen A., 580
Makhoue, J.I., 363
Makli, Adnan H., 581
Mansfield, Peter, 230
Mansour, Taha A., 582
Martan, Said S., 702
Marouf, Nawal, 49
Marr, Phebe Ann, 50
Martin, Philip L., 124
Marzouk, M.S., 87
Mason, John P., 231, 232
Matejka, Jacqulin C., 499
Mazur, Michael P., 378

Author Index

McCarthy, Justin A., 116
McLaurin, R.D., 212
Mdaghri, Druss Alaoui, 51
Meleis, Afaf I., 117
Melikian, Levon H., 233, 234
Micaud, Ellen C., 52
Michail, W.M., 379
Miesse, Thomas W., 703
Milyani, Hisham M., 500
Mirghani, Mohamed A., 704
Misallati, Abdalla S., 501
Mitri, Bassam Najib, 705
Mohammadsaid, Ibrahim A., 706
Mohammed, Adam Azzain, 502
Mohammed, Hassan Y., 503
Mohammed, Shamil K., 504
Moliver, Donald, 380, 707
Moneef, Abdullah A., 505
Moore, Clement Henry, 118
Morsy, Mohamed A., 583
Mourad, Ahmed A.F., 53
Mousa, Osama M.Z.A., 708
Moustafa, Salem M., 709
Muasher, Rajai S., 710
Mullen, Thomas W., 711
Muna, Farid A., 54
Murshid, Talal A., 506
Musa, Omar el-Hag, 235
Mussa, Safi Imam, 584

Nabli, Mustapha K., 712
Nabti, Farid George, 585
Nagi, Mostafa H., 119
Nakhleh, Emile A., 120, 236, 237
Nakib, Khalil, 55
Nama, Ahmad Mohammed, 586
Nasser, Saleh Ahmed, 713
Naur, Maja, 238
Nedelcovych, Mima S., 714
Nellis, John R., 381
Niblock, Tim, 239, 240, 241
Nijim, B.K., 196
Norris, M.W., 56
Nugent, Jeffrey B., 57, 242

Nusair, Naim Ogleh, 507
Nygaard, David F., 715

Odeh, A.F., 382
Odhiambo, Mark O., 716
Oesterdiekhoff, Peter, 383
Omair, Saleh A., 717
Omer, Ali A., 718
Omran, Abdel-Rahim, 121
Osman, Mohamed, 587
Osman, Osama A., 58
Othman, Osama A., 59

Palmer, Monte, 7, 9, 47, 55, 184, 243
Park, Thomas K., 508
Parks, Terrance C., 719
Pasha, Hafiz A., 509
Penson, John B. Jr., 384
Peterson, J.E., 60, 245
Pfeifer, Karen Ann, 720
Pillai, Vel, 385
Plascov, Avi, 246
Platt, C.J., 386
Polk, William R., 247
Poulson, Barry W., 387
Pounds, Bonnie, 388
Presley, John R., 389
Putman, Diana Briton, 721

Qasem, Subhi, 178
Quandt, William, 248
Qubeisi, Hafeth A., 122

Rabhi, Mohammed, 61
Radwan, Samir, 104, 374
Rahman, Fazlur, 249
Rassam, Amal, 123
Redjeb, Mohamed S., 588
Reid, Donald M., 250
Rhazaoui, Ahmed, 722
Richards, Alan, 124, 390, 391, 723
Roberts, M. Hugh P., 62, 251
Rodinson, Maxime, 252
Ronall, J.O., 392

Roy, Delwin A., 63, 64
Rugh, William, 253

Sabie, Ahmed, 589
Sadek, S.E.M., 65
Sadik, Ali Tawfik, 393
Sadik, Muhammad T., 66, 67, 254
Sadler, P.G., 365
Sadowski, Yahya M., 724
Sagi, Eli, 725
Said, Abdulrahman H., 726
Said, Edward W., 255
Saivetz, Carol R., 727
Saket, Bassam K., 110, 125, 178
Sakr, Naomi, 256
Salama, Galal Ahmed, 590
Salem, Elie Adib, 68, 257
Salih, Siddiq A., 510
Samater, Ahmed I., 728
Samhan, Muhammad H., 729
Samman, Nizar H., 511
Sanger, Richard Hl, 258
Sanyal, Bikas C., 126
Sardar, Ziauddin, 259
Savory, Roger M., 260
Sayigh, Yusif A., 394, 395, 396
Schemeil, Yves, 313
Schliephake, Konrad, 397
Searby, Daniel M., 398
Seibert, R.F., 156
Senani, Ahmed H., 730
Serageldin, Ismail, 127, 128, 129
Seymour, Ian, 399
Shadukhi, Suliman M., 512
Shahatit, Kamel Farhan, 591
Sharif, Walid, 400
Sharma, Rabinder Kumar, 592
Shaw, John A., 401
Shaw, Paul R., 130, 131
Sherbiny, Naiem A., 132
Sid Ahmed, A.K., 402
Siegel, Gilbert B., 69
Simmons, Andre, 403

Simmons, John L., 261, 404, 405
Sinclair, Clive A., 88, 89, 90, 91, 92, 129, 133
Sinclair, Stuart W., 347
Skinner, M., 94
Skold, Melvin D., 406
Smith, Tony, 407
Smith, Shelby L., 731
Snavely, William P., 67, 254, 323
Socknat, James, 92, 127, 129
Springborg, Robert, 408
Stephens, Robert, 409
Stevens, Candice Ann, 732
Stino, Laila El-Sayed, 733
Stone, Russell A., 261
Stookey, Robert W., 262
Stuart, Madeleine F., 593
Suleiman, Michael W., 263
Suliman, Ali Ahmed, 410
Suraisry, Jobarah Eid, 734
Sutcliffe, Claud R., 264, 735
Swanson, Jon C., 134, 135
Szyliowicz, Joseph S., 70, 265

Taha, Abdel-Rahman E., 594
Taher, Abdullah M., 736
Tahtinen, Dale R., 737
Talafha, Hussain A., 595
Talahite, Claude, 102
Tawati, Ahmed M., 513
Taylor, Alan R., 266
Tetreault, Mary Ann, 411, 738
Thomas, T.H., 242
Tibi, Bassam, 267, 268
Tignor, Robert, 145
Tikriti, Mwafaq Haded, 514
Toboli, Abulkasem O., 596
Tongun, Lako L., 739
Townsend, John, 412
Trebous, Madeleine, 136
Tuma, Elias, 137, 269, 413

Author Index

Turki, Hedi, 515
Turner, Bryan S., 270
Tutwiler, Richard, 271

UNESCO, 138

Van Fleet, David, 15
Vandewalle, Dirk, 272
Vatikiotis, P.J., 414
Voll, Sarah P., 415

Wagner, J.G., 156
Wahba, M.M., 71
Wai, Dunstan M., 274
Wallace, Myles, 387
Waltz, Susan E., 273, 740
Ward, Richard J., 139
Ware, John Alex, 597
Waterbury, John, 275, 276, 416
Weinbaum, Marvin G., 277
Weiss, Dieter, 417
Wenner, Manfred, 151
Wilkinson, J.C., 418
Wilson, Rodney J.A., 419, 420, 421
Witty, Cathie J., 278
Whiting, Steven H., 741
Wittington, Dale, 72
Wohimuth, Karl, 383
Wohlers-Scharf, Traute, 422
Wolfe, Ronald G., 279
Wright, Peter, 73
Wynn, R.F., 423

Yacoub, Suheil A., 516
Yahya, Hussein A., 742
Yahya, Mahmud M., 517
Yassin, El Sayed, 217
Young, Arthur N., 242
Young, Jerome E., 518
Younis, Abdul Razeq M., 743

Zabarah, Mohammed A., 744
Zaghal, Ali S., 140
Zahlan, A.B., 74, 141, 142, 280
Zahlan, Rosemarie Said, 425
Zahra, Shaker, 75
Zahrani, Saeed A., 598
Zain, Mohamed Gaffar, 143
Zalatimo, Farouk R., 599
Zalatimo, Yasira N., 600
Zarouq, Hassabelrasoul, 519
Zarroug, Khalid H., 601
Zarrugh, Omar Salem, 520
Zartman, William, 281
Zeineldin, Aly M., 745
Zeitoun, Mohamed A., 746
Ziadeh, Farhat J., 282
Ziwar-Daftari, May, 426
Zreigat, Sami, 125

Country Index

Algeria, 24, 28, 97, 102,
115, 136, 138, 141, 199,
281, 296, 353, 381, 397,
407, 477, 689, 700, 720
Arab world, 4, 5, 14, 16,
21, 27, 29, 30, 32, 33,
34, 37, 40, 41, 42, 43,
46, 54, 57, 61, 62, 63,
64, 65, 66, 70, 73, 74,
77, 78, 88, 89, 93, 94,
99, 101, 106, 113, 114,
115, 121, 122, 123, 124,
127, 128, 129, 130, 131,
132, 137, 138, 139, 141,
142, 147, 148, 150, 152,
153, 154, 155, 156, 157,
158, 159, 167, 168, 169,
171, 174, 176, 185, 187,
188, 189, 191, 195, 196,
199, 203, 204, 205, 206,
207, 213, 214, 217, 218,
221, 226, 228, 230, 234,
241, 243, 245, 246, 247,
249, 251, 252, 254, 255,
256, 259, 260, 266, 267,
268, 269, 270, 282, 283,
286, 289, 290, 293, 294,
295, 296, 299, 300, 301,
304, 305, 306, 308, 311,
313, 314, 318, 319, 321,
322, 324, 325, 326, 335,
338, 339, 340, 344, 346,
347, 348, 350, 351, 352,
353, 358, 361, 363, 364,
367, 370, 373, 382, 386,
387, 393, 394, 395, 396,
399, 402, 403, 408, 409,
411, 413, 414, 419, 421,
422, 451, 499, 532, 603,
639, 677, 692, 730, 737,
738

Bahrain, 67, 120, 157, 186,
191, 223, 236, 237, 241,
242, 245, 254, 290, 307,
400, 437, 623

Egypt, 2, 17, 18, 43, 45,
47, 57, 71, 72, 75, 82,
88, 91, 98, 100, 103,
104, 107, 108, 111, 112,
114, 116, 118, 119, 126,
138, 141, 144, 145, 151,
155, 170, 171, 175, 180,
192, 205, 207, 217, 224,
225, 226, 250, 263, 275,
277, 281, 282, 284, 302,
309, 317, 319, 336, 340,
343, 349, 353, 356, 360,
374, 386, 390, 391, 406,
415, 416, 417, 420, 432,
466, 469, 470, 472, 481,
482, 521, 525, 549, 563,
566, 567, 569, 570, 571,
572, 583, 587, 590, 602,
603, 604, 611, 637, 647,
653, 654, 665, 667, 670,
671, 675, 681, 682, 688,

703, 708, 716, 723, 725,
727, 729, 732, 733, 737,
741, 745, 746

Gulf states, 67, 90, 120,
150, 157, 176, 186, 237,
242, 246, 256, 279, 280,
282, 291, 305, 307, 324,
327, 370, 400, 412, 425,
426, 623

Iraq, 1, 6, 8, 38, 42, 50,
57, 132, 138, 155, 165,
171, 186, 210, 216, 240,
241, 246, 282, 296, 297,
319, 353, 359, 403, 443,
445, 453, 459, 504, 514,
516, 536, 539, 540, 542,
546, 558, 581, 589, 610,
613, 618, 651, 663, 677,
678, 685, 687, 706

Jordan, 36, 41, 42, 43, 57,
81, 88, 110, 125, 114,
140, 158, 171, 177, 178,
194, 212, 222, 264, 282,
353, 366, 378, 379, 385,
450, 467, 468, 473, 478,
480, 485, 486, 489, 507,
522, 578, 580, 582, 591,
593, 595, 597, 603, 624,
628, 629, 630, 631, 659,
662, 676, 677, 690, 693,
701, 710, 735, 736, 742,
743

Kuwait, 15, 49, 79, 87, 94,
117, 132, 186, 188, 191,
209, 241, 288, 289, 290,
292, 296, 305, 307, 318,
332, 339, 357, 365, 392,
396, 398, 400, 403, 409,
427, 440, 454, 462, 541,
545, 550, 556, 599, 603,
609, 619, 620, 621, 623,
641, 674, 677

Lebanon, 20, 35, 42, 43,
55, 68, 155, 163, 171,
211, 220, 234, 257, 278,
282, 298, 312, 341, 354,
375, 376, 493, 677, 698,
705

Libya, 22, 23, 31, 132,
138, 179, 184, 193, 231,
232, 238, 258, 281, 282,
296, 337, 386, 403, 463,
471, 475, 476, 501, 520,
561, 564, 565, 568, 574,
596, 606, 607, 608, 657,
658, 660, 661, 664, 669,
709, 719

Morocco, 3, 39, 51, 86,
115, 138, 146, 199, 276,
281, 353, 508, 553, 554,
592, 605, 644, 645, 649,
650, 683, 695, 714, 722

North Africa, 84, 160, 281

Oman, 60, 172, 182, 191,
241, 245, 320, 330, 400,
418, 623

Qatar, 67, 94, 120, 157,
186, 191, 229, 233, 237,
241, 245, 254, 290, 296,
307, 339, 400, 403, 537,
586, 623

Saudi Arabia, 7, 9, 10, 25,
26, 36, 41, 48, 58, 59,
85, 92, 94, 95, 132, 133,
138, 149, 155, 173, 186,
191, 198, 205, 207, 208,
226, 227, 239, 241, 242,
246, 248, 253, 265, 282,
285, 296, 315, 316, 321,
323, 333, 334, 339, 342,
345, 355, 362, 369, 371,
380, 386, 388, 389, 396,
400, 401, 403, 434, 438,

Country Index 259

439, 441, 442, 444, 446,
447, 448, 449, 452, 455,
457, 458, 461, 464, 465,
474, 484, 492, 495, 497,
498, 500, 505, 506, 509,
511, 512, 513, 526, 528,
529, 530, 531, 533, 534,
535, 538, 543, 544, 547,
548, 551, 552, 557, 559,
560, 575, 576, 584, 585,
598, 600, 603, 612, 614,
615, 616, 617, 622, 625,
626, 632, 633, 635, 638,
640, 648, 668, 677, 679,
691, 694, 702, 707, 713,
717, 726, 734
Somalia, 517, 721, 728
Sudan, 11, 12, 13, 56, 69,
83, 88, 96, 138, 162,
166, 183, 229, 235, 274,
287, 303, 340, 348, 372,
383, 386, 410, 423, 428,
430, 431, 433, 435, 436,
456, 460, 479, 483, 487,
488, 491, 496, 502, 503,
510, 519, 523, 524, 562,
577, 579, 594, 601, 636,
652, 655, 672, 697, 704,
718, 739
Syria, 42, 43, 53, 57, 88,
155, 164, 171, 181, 200,
201, 202, 205, 215, 282,
310, 319, 353, 368, 377,
384, 429, 666, 677, 711,
724, 737

Tunisia, 19, 52, 80, 105,
109, 115, 138, 161, 171,
197, 199, 261, 272, 273,
281, 353, 381, 397, 404,
405, 515, 555, 588, 627,
634, 642, 656, 673, 680,
684, 686, 696, 699, 712,
715, 731, 737, 740

United Arab Emirates, 67,
94, 132, 157, 186, 190,
191, 219, 241, 245, 246,
254, 256, 285, 290, 291,
296, 307, 318, 328, 331,
339, 400, 403, 490, 494,
527, 623

Yemen, North, 44, 88, 92,
134, 135, 171, 191, 244,
271, 321, 573, 643, 646,
744
Yemen, South, 88, 143, 191,
262, 744

Ref Z 7165 .A67 J73 1986
Jreisat, Jamil E.
Administration and
 development in the Arab

MAR 18 1987